OTHER HELPFUL BOOKS
BY HARRY SHEFTER

SIX MINUTES A DAY TO
PERFECT SPELLING (W50·35¢*)

Good spellers ~~are~~ ... ok will teach
you how ... y, accurately
and perr ... ne. Let this
tested m ... forever.

SHORT CUTS
EFFECTIVE ENG ... (W51·35¢*)

Thousands of classroom and television students have
used this method of learning effective English without
mastering a lot of complicated grammatical rules. It's
fast and easy. It will work for you. And it has a separate
section of questions from typical city, state and federal
civil service examinations to help you test yourself.

FASTER READING SELF-TAUGHT (W500·50¢**)

This simple five-step plan will enable you to read up to
100% faster and at the same time understand more of
what you read. It can be your key not only to more knowledge and culture but also to higher pay and a better job.

Get these famous books wherever paper-bound books are sold. If
you wish to order them by mail, send retail price, plus 5¢ per book
to cover postage and handling, to: Mail Service Department,
Washington Square Press, Inc., 1 W. 39th St., New York 18, N.Y.

---

*Price will be increased to 45¢ at the time of the next printing.
**Price will be increased to 60¢ at the time of the next printing.

Other books by Harry Shefter

Faster Reading Self-Taught
Short Cuts to Effective English
Six Minutes a Day to Perfect Spelling

Published by Washington Square Press, Inc.,
in WASHINGTON SQUARE PRESS

Shefter's Guide to

BETTER
COMPOSITIONS

HARRY SHEFTER

WASHINGTON SQUARE PRESS, INC. • NEW YORK

SHEFTER'S GUIDE TO BETTER COMPOSITIONS

1960

With the exception of the selections in Chapter 9, all material quoted is from *Reader's Digest*, to whom the author is most grateful. An acknowledgment of the original source will be found at the foot of the page on which the material appears. Starred selections in Chapter 9 appeared originally in *The New York Times*, through whose kind permission they are reprinted.

L

Published by
Washington Square Press, Inc.: Executive Offices, 630 Fifth Avenue; University Press Division, 32 Washington Place, New York, N.Y.

WASHINGTON SQUARE PRESS editions are distributed in the U.S. by Affiliated Publishers, Inc., 630 Fifth Avenue, New York 20, N.Y.

Where Do We Begin?

We begin with the understanding that both of us are experienced. I have taught more than 10,000 high school students through the years and have marked well over 100,000 compositions. You have been attending school somewhere between eight and eleven years and have already written hundreds of compositions of one kind or another in your various subject classes. Therefore, we can take certain things for granted.

You are not a beginner. You probably have some very good writing habits, which you should retain. Also you must have some rather serious composition weaknesses; otherwise you would not be seeking the help you expect to get from this book. The best approach, then, will be to build up your strong points, eliminate the weak ones, and add a few techniques that will make it easier for you to improve.

You know what a composition is. Teachers have told you time and again that whenever you write—a letter, a book report, an informal essay, an answer to a question on an examination—you are *composing* and that the rules are essentially the same for all the forms: a forceful beginning, a sensible and interesting middle, and a logical ending.

You don't have to be sold. By now you are completely convinced that it will be to your advantage to write well.

You've heard the story a thousand times and have had clear evidence of its truth even more often. You know that the good writers among your friends get better marks not only in English but in the social studies, foreign languages, the sciences—in fact, in any subject that requires the ability to express oneself. You know, too, if you are planning to go to college, that some day you will have to send along a sort of biography of yourself together with your application. You don't have to be told how important first impressions are. Nor does anyone have to tell you how much your chances of doing well on entrance and scholarship examinations depend upon your ability to write. On the other hand, if you are planning to go directly into a job or a business after graduation, you surely remember how often your counselors or representatives from industry have mentioned the many writing demands that are placed upon a person who seeks advancement or achieves a position of responsibility. Moreover, there is no need to remind you of the social obligations every adult must assume and the letters, notes, or, sometimes, prepared speeches that are part of everyday living. Yes, it has been quite obvious to you for a long time that when you put yourself down on paper you are exposing yourself to the judgment of other people in a more penetrating way than you do by your dress, speaking habits, or general personality traits.

You don't expect miracles. You've learned that some of your classmates seem to have been born with a gift for drawing or singing or playing an instrument. Others can take any topic assigned and in fifteen or twenty minutes dash off a piece of writing that more than 99% of the students couldn't approach even if they worked on it for a week. Gifted writers can be given guidance or direction by a good teacher, but native talent cannot be taught! You know that even among the students who average as high as 95% in English it is very unlikely that more than one in a thousand will ever be good enough to enter the professional writing field. That's why you don't expect me to make a poet, novelist, or dramatist out of you. Your main desire is to learn how to write a decent composition, one that is the best you are basically capable of writing.

You don't want a lot of talk. During my early years, like all young teachers, I used to talk too much. I would drone on endlessly about the meaning of communication, the writer's obligation to let the reader look into the mind and heart of the author, the interrelationships that exist among speaking, writing, reading, and listening. These are all very important concepts, to be sure. But for all my impassioned talk, I wasn't telling my students how the job is done. This taught me a valuable lesson.

You want to know how. You want to know *how* to handle a topic, assigned or voluntary, and say something interesting and appropriate about it. You want to know *how* you can start working without the annoying "staring at the ceiling" routine so many students go through. If the teacher returns your composition—and it looks as if a chicken had stepped out of a bottle of red ink and had walked all over your paper—you want to know *how* to "make your introduction more interesting," *how* to "improve the transition between paragraphs," *how* to "avoid dullness and repetition," *how* to "eliminate sentence structure and usage errors," and *how* to "stay on the subject."

All right, there won't be any lectures on the language arts, communication via mass media, or integrated thinking. One day you may want to investigate thoroughly these aspects of the philosophy of composition. But for our purposes we're going to be completely practical. One thing at a time. We will examine student compositions and analyze why one is worth a higher mark than the other. We will establish definite standards of good writing. Then we will go into the mechanics of starting, continuing, and finishing a composition that will meet these standards. The aim in the succeeding chapters will be to show you *how* to select better, to plan better, to write better, to revise better—much better than you have been doing up to now. If you mean business, if you are serious about your desire to improve, if you make an honest effort to master the few basic principles involved, you will be pleased and perhaps amazed at the progress you make.

It's going to mean work, but more than that it's going to mean concentration and practice. No skill is acquired by just reading or thinking about it. A recent tennis champion, in a magazine article, stated that for many years he practiced six hours a day to prepare for the occasional hour and a half it took him to win a match in tournament competition. That's what you'll have to discipline yourself to do—work on your weaknesses on a regular basis until you have eliminated every one of them!

It won't take you six hours a day. You may not have to spend that much time even in a month. However, just reading these pages will do you no good at all unless you *apply* the techniques you have learned *every time you write*. This is the last and most significant thing we can both take for granted.

Table of Contents

To
my first audience—
Grandma Shefter

How Do You Rate As a Writer?

When you go to see a doctor, the first thing he does is ask you to describe what is bothering you. He needs this information so that he can begin his diagnosis. I said *begin* because, after you get through talking, the competent medical man conducts his own examination. He must probe beyond the surface evidence. It wouldn't do to treat a stomach disorder if further study proved that the real trouble was something entirely different. For instance, emotional upset can produce aches and discomfort. Thus, after your doctor pokes around a bit, he may conclude that there is nothing physically wrong with you at all. What you left out of your story may turn out to be more important than what you put in.

Now, you and I know that your teacher cannot possibly give as much individual attention to your writing weaknesses as a doctor does to his patient's illnesses. As many as 35 students must be handled in the time it takes to give two people medical checkups. Obviously, a complete job is too much to expect from any teacher in the classroom alone. In most schools below the college level, individual conferences just can't be fitted into the heavy programs. In the average composition unit, there is barely enough time to assign a topic, collect the papers, criticize and mark them, return them, and go over a few with the group. As a result, your hidden writing faults may never be remedied unless you do something about them yourself.

At this stage of your school career you've had papers returned often enough for you to know by heart what your

surface weaknesses are. They have doubtless long since fallen
into a pattern that keeps repeating itself. But, as was suggested above, your being able to rattle off your list of usual
errors is only the beginning of the diagnosis. Like the doctor,
we want to get to the bottom of your total problem, what you
leave out of a composition as well as what you put in. We
will do that by letting you examine what other students have
done and compare your efforts with theirs.

You will profit in another way from this procedure. It will
enable you to consider your writing weaknesses from a practical angle, too. How much are they costing you in marks? It
is not uncommon for a student to be aware of his shortcom-
ings and still not accept the justice of a particular grade,
thus depriving himself of the incentive to improve. A few
words about teacher ratings, therefore, seem to be in order at
this point.

Here are some typical comments you hear whenever you
get together with your friends to discuss the eternal mystery
of marks:

"You know what he does. He throws the papers up in the
air. Those that stick to the ceiling, pass. The rest fail."

"It's simple. Miss Ferguson weighs each report. One pound
—A, half a pound—B, my two ounces—F."

"What do you expect? If I were a blond, and pretty, I'd
get a 90."

You don't really believe what you hear, but behind it all
is an honest puzzlement. And from time to time, usually in
self-defense, disturbing questions come to your mind. Why
don't all teachers mark the same way? Why did my composition get a 7, and George's a 7½? What did he do for the
half point? On that exam question, I got 23 out of 30. Why
not 24 or 22?

As we go along here you will find the answers to your
questions. You are entitled to know how writing standards
are translated into grades. It is the most concrete way of im-

pressing upon you how much weight is given the various parts of a composition.

Don't misunderstand. A mark is certainly not your ultimate objective, although it may well seem that way while you are attending school. In general, you want to write better, now and for good. That's the main idea. But an explanation of why you did not get an extra point or two not only will put your mistakes into proper focus but will provide a clearer picture of what is missing from your work. For example, it can help you understand why a paper with no technical errors may be rated *fair* rather than *good* or *excellent*.

As a rule, the system operates like this. For students in the early years in high school, teachers give more credit to *form* (sentence structure, paragraph unity, organization, grammatical correctness, etc.) than they do to *content* (ideas, language variety, interest, ingenuity, etc.). The ratio usually is 60% for form and 40% for content.

A high school freshman who writes a very interesting piece full of all kinds of careless errors may be disappointed when he gets an F or a 60%. The material sounded so good to him! Because it did to the teacher, too, she gave the composition 35 out of 40 for the content and less than half of 60 for the form, hence the failing mark.

In the upper grades the percentages are often reversed. A senior who hands in a flawless paper, but one which shows no originality or animation, may get only a 70% or C—a full 60 for form and only 10 for content. Had the composition contained at least one or two interesting sentences, it might have received 5 more points. This explains a 75 as against a 70.

It works the same way with examination answers. If 30 credits have been assigned to the question, the teacher first arrives at the percentage mark as outlined above, and then converts it into points. Thus a 70% will equal 21 (70% of 30), an 85% will be either 25 or 26 (85% of 30), depending upon whether the marker thinks the answer is worth maximum or minimum credits within the range.

We come now to another of your queries. Why don't all teachers mark alike? It's true that occasionally one instructor may give 60% to a paper that another may value at 90%. Rest assured, however, that this situation does not arise as often as popular legend would have you believe. In my experience, competent teachers almost invariably reach similar judgments about the quality of a student's work, differing no more than a few percentage points at most. The best proof that marks are based upon universally accepted standards can be found in a review of the over-all record of any student. If he has been getting 70's, and makes no honest effort to improve, he will continue to receive 70's no matter who his teachers are.

So much for marking systems. Before we get to our complete diagnosis, I want to say something about the samples of writing we are going to use throughout the book to make points clear. Most will be taken from papers actually produced by high school students. There is not much logic in showing you the work of professionals, except as occasional proof that certain techniques are used by all good writers. Nothing is more frustrating than to be asked to duplicate something that can be achieved by very few among us, or which we have no desire to attempt even if we could. If you can learn to do as well as some people who are no older or more experienced than you are, you will be doing better than most.

Now let's get to the samples. They have been taken from a recent state examination in English that was administered to about 75,000 high school seniors. The papers were marked in committee, and at least two teachers had a hand in the final grading of any one composition. Usually there were a first reading and marking, a second by someone else as a check, and a third or fourth review, if necessary. You can assume, then, that the grades are as close to being standard for any school in the country as it is possible to get them.

You have two objectives in studying the models and the comments made on them. One is to analyze why one composition was rated higher than another. The other is to determine how much your weaknesses are costing you and what you can do to upgrade your own work.

"Shadows" is the subject or topic of each of the compositions selected for this diagnosis. Although there were fourteen other titles available to the students, I am sure you will agree that the differences in quality will stand out more sharply if you can see how well each one performed while facing the same problems. Read every sample through as a whole first. Then go back over it as you study the comments. You may be disappointed in some of the models and wonder how they got as much credit as they did. Remember what we said about marks. Teachers try to be objective and fair. If they looked for perfection, very few students would pass.

The numbers to the right of the paragraphs will be used as a means of referring to individual paragraphs when they are discussed in the "Comments" that follow each selection.

I. EXCELLENT COMPOSITIONS

(*Ratings: A or 90–100%*)
(*Credits: 27–29 out of 30*)

Sample #1

The child is in bed, awake, frightened by the howling wind and the shadows dancing on his walls. His toy animals seem enormous as they are magnified on the ceiling by the dim light outside the room. His clothes, laid carelessly on a chair, also throw off peculiar shadows. He sees witches and goblins, dragons and giants. The child is afraid of what he sees. I would not be afraid. 1

The young woman hurries along, alone in the dark. The only light is a dim street lamp. The buildings all around her seem huge and horrible, their shadows fill her with fear. Even her own slim shadow frightens her. She imagines terrible things and begins to run. The only sound is the noise of her heels tapping on the sidewalk. She is afraid of what she sees and of what she doesn't see. I would not be afraid. 2

The soldier waits anxiously at the door. Through the

window shades he can see the figures of a man and a
woman, with their heads bent as if they were whispering.
It is difficult to determine to whom the shadows belong.   3
He prays that his sweetheart has not found someone new
during his long absence. He hesitates before ringing the
bell. He fears what he sees. I would not be afraid.

I would not fear the shadows on the walls. They would
be my friends. I would watch them dance and dance   4
with them. O, what beautiful shadows I would see.

I would not fear walking in the dark and seeing the
shadows of tall buildings. The buildings protect me and   5
keep me warm. They would be friendly shadows.

I would not fear seeing the shadows of two people
through a window. They are my friends waiting for me.   6
They would be happy shadows.

I would not fear shadows. I pray for them instead. I
would love to see a shadow, any shadow, big or small,   7
for just a moment. I am blind.

Comments on Sample #1

√ **Form:** Strictly speaking, there is no formal opening paragraph, but writers often start *in medias res,* in the midst of
things, if they wish to develop a special effect, and it is clear
that such is the purpose here the first time you read "I
would not be afraid." The absence of a regular beginning
paragraph under the circumstances is perfectly legitimate.
Certainly interest is created and the contents of the rest of the
composition are indicated.

Paragraphs 2 and 3 logically develop the main idea. Each
is a tight unit, with a very good topic sentence, internal unity,
and a provocative closing.

In Paragraphs 4, 5, and 6, the author re-emphasizes her
splendid organization by briefly half-summarizing and half-
projecting her attitude with its note of mystery.

The main idea is skilfully brought back into focus in
Paragraph 7 as the conclusion is reached.

With the exception of one questionable point, the material
is technically excellent. The comma at "horrible, their shadows" (Paragraph 2) should be a semicolon or a period. This

may not have been a mistake since a writer of this caliber may have used the comma deliberately for some reason not clear to me. Punctuation and usage are above reproach.

√ *Content:* The writer has intelligently narrowed the scope of the rather vague topic down to a few sharply etched pictures and has given her imagination full sway. There is fine originality displayed at the very beginning, and the reader is immediately intrigued by what seems to be an odd emotional twist.

The body of the composition continues to build up toward a climax in mature and colorful fashion. The deliberate repetition of "shadows, fear, afraid," rather than detracting from interest as it often does, adds to the heightened effect, much like a background of beating drums. The language is superior throughout. "Enormous, magnified, peculiar, dragons, goblins, dim, huge, tapping, anxiously, whispering, warm, friendly" are relatively simple words but ones that make the difference between dullness and interest or color. The bright, sensitive personality of the writer shines through the words, and we marvel at her inventiveness. Perhaps the one weakness is found in Paragraph 3. In the first two the author is talking about experiences that she has lived through, whereas, judging from the somewhat formal description of the lover, it would seem that this scene had not stemmed from personal emotional episodes.

Paragraph 7, of course, is a gem. It effectively solves the puzzle introduced early and leaves nothing else to say.

The sentences are varied in length and expertly formed. The paragraphs show good use of comparison, contrast, and detail in their development. You can understand why this composition received 29.

Sample #2

If there is one thing in my early childhood that caused me endless suffering and unrelinquished fear, it was the threat of seeing unidentified shadows in the middle of ¹ the night. About 8:00 P.M. was the middle of the night for me during those tender years.

The most frightening shadow that haunted me in those days was the one I was sure belonged to a little green man who hid under the bed every night. I was positive this tiny ogre was going to stick his hand out ² and grab my foot while I was sleeping, thereby carrying me to the depths of Hades. Fortunately, he never accomplished this feat.

A most horrible experience which usually occurred every night was when I awoke from a nightmare to find my entire room a mass of winding shadows. For two or three hours I would not move an inch, fearing I would give away my presence to these demons who would not hesitate to pounce upon me and chop me up into little ³ pieces, which they might preserve in cans. But I finally built up enough courage to flick on the light, which revealed the monstrous shadows to be nothing more than my old friends, Mr. Chair, Mr. Sofa, and Mr. Lamp. What a relief!

The last of the shadows was the one which confronted me after every story book reading my mother gave me on Monday and Thursday. I would fall asleep happily, not realizing the horrible dream about to make itself known to me. Waking up (I didn't actually wake up; ⁴ this was part of the dream), I saw to my complete horror shadows creeping across the living room window in the forms of Humpty Dumpty, Mother Goose, and the Big Bad Wolf. Gads, what a scare!

So, as you can see, shadows played a prominent part in my growing up. Although I was afraid when I first had these hallucinations, I can now laughingly joke about ⁵ them in my nightly conversations with the green ogre, the shadowy demons, and Humpty Dumpty. Actually, there not bad fellows at all!

Comments on Sample #2

√ *Form:* Here we have the regular type of introduction that promptly establishes the main idea to be discussed in the body, supplies the background from which the thoughts will emanate, and sets the general tone.

Paragraphs 2, 3, and 4 present neat little pictures of the writer's experiences. Here, too, each is a well-developed unit, with its topic sentence, a few related sentences, and an interesting closing.

The conclusion (Paragraph 5) ties everything together and leaves the reader with something to chuckle about as well. Organization throughout is very good.

There are more technical errors in this one than in Sample #1. In Paragraph 1, "there is" should read "there was"; in Paragraph 3, "which" and "was" should be eliminated from the first sentence, and the last one should read "But I would finally build up . . ."; in Paragraph 4, the tense of "saw" should be "would see" (third sentence); and at the very end, "there" should be "they're," of course.

√ *Content:* The introduction, although relatively standard, nonetheless gets to the heart of the main idea with a minimum of words and succeeds in giving the reader a glimpse of the writer's sense of humor.

The middle paragraphs give just enough examples, described with wit and detail, to indicate exactly how the author felt when he was a youngster. Language use is generally superior, even if wiser choices could have been made for "unrelinquished" (Paragraph 1) and "accomplished this feat" (Paragraph 2). The writer's personality comes through readily, particularly by virtue of his charming personalization of objects and his obvious hints that he is not to be taken seriously.

The ending brings the composition nicely to an appropriate conclusion. The novel note suggested in the final sentence enhances the writer's efforts to keep the material on a light level.

The sentences are varied and formed with technical maturity. The paragraphs show a facility for vivid description and graceful phrasing. This piece of work received a 27.

The lower rating was dictated by the more frequent errors in construction and the relative absence of ingenuity. In general, however, this was a first rate composition.

II. GOOD COMPOSITIONS

(Ratings: B or 80–89%)
(Credits: 24–26 out of 30)

Sample #3

The shadows of the past constantly haunt me. As I lie awake at night, my deeds reappear and mock me. Like Scrooge who viewed his past cruelties and mistakes, I can relive the past. How frustrating it is, to watch but not to be able to act.

The poet once stated, "Saddest are the words, 'It might have been!'" How true this line is. My life might have been completely different if I had had the knowledge and experience I now possess. I realize now there were far wiser solutions for my problems than the ones I chose. More important, though, is the time I wasted. If only I had spent this time studying and pursuing various fields of learning, I might have been more successful in my later endeavors. But "Youth is wasted on youth."

Then there are the people I took advantage of, and thus hurt. Why was I so selfish? The words I could have spoken which might have comforted others haunt me. More annoying are the words I never should have spoken. Why was I so rash? But these lamentations are senseless and can not remedy past blunders.

The shadows are not all dark and unpleasant. There are happy memories too. How nice it is to remember these past joys. But as Keats wrote, "Melodies heard are sweet, but those unheard, far sweeter." I know there are greater joys to be experienced in the future.

Both the good and the bad aspects of my past are now a part of me. The good to provide a pleasant respite; and the bad to prevent my duplicating former mistakes. I must live in the present and look forward to the future. This is the only mature and realistic attitude I can take. The shadows of the past are not forgotten, but are incorporated in that broad classification—"experience!"

Comments on Sample #3

✔ *Form:* Paragraph 1 does its job of creating interest and suggesting the direction of the composition.

In the middle paragraphs, it is clear that the writer attempted to organize her thoughts into three aspects of her main idea, and the final paragraph does attempt to summarize and predict.

With the exception of one sentence fragment, "The good to provide . . ." (Paragraph 5), technical errors are kept to a minimum.

✔ *Content:* This is a good example of a composition that is written with structural skill and correctness, but fails chiefly because of the content to merit an excellent rating. Paragraph 1, although it performs its proper task, is marred by needless repetition, both of the "haunting" concept and the word "past." You will recall how deliberate repetition in Sample #1 was very effective, but here no special effect is being attempted.

Paragraphs 2, 3, and 4 have the same defects: generalities and hints but no *specific* details that would have made the ideas much more meaningful. Not once is an actual incident described to support the questions raised by the writer.

The conclusion seems to be somewhat contradictory. Both indifference to and concern about the past are simultaneously expressed, although the writer does succeed in stressing the need for profiting from experience.

There is good variation in sentence structure, but the paragraphs are underdeveloped, largely because of the absence of supporting examples. One should not use quotation marks unless the statement ascribed to an author has been accurately duplicated. Moreover, excessive use of this device can be as disturbing as needless repetition.

All that has been said so far amounts to quite a bit of adverse criticism. And yet the composition was rated *good* for valid reasons. Positive factors are the correctness of expression, the good organization, the attempt to introduce novelty through the quotations, and the sincerity of the mood. Thus the official mark of 26 out of 30 is reasonable. You can see how just a few more sentences of the right kind in the right places might have turned this paper into a superior piece of work.

Sample #4

He awoke that morning with the sun shining through his windows, casting a shadow behind him. He washed and dressed and then entered the bustling streets of the [1] city. The sun cast shadows all around, tall buildings, high towers, large flag poles, small, insignificant people all had shadows.

The door in his office cast a shadow on the floor. Trees in the park, outside his office window, cast shadows on the building, and the birds in flight left a momentary shadow on the beds of grass. Nurses with baby carriages cast pleasant shadows, dogs on leashes cast imposing and striking shadows. Trucks and big-finned Cadillacs cast their ominous shadows upon the streets of the city. He left his office for the day, casting a hazy shadow brought on by the twilight. The dim lights of the swank restaurant left his lean shadow on the wall. His grand [2] bouquet complete, he entered the street, to meet her. Their shadows were hazy for it grew dark as they entered the club. The shadow of the couple drinking and dancing was warm and meaningful. As they left, their dim shadow entered his big limousine. The shadow moved quickly as the lights from the lampposts followed them. The shadows grew passionate. The evening was coming to an end, and one could almost sense the coming of the morning's shadows with the rising sun.

But for him, there were no longer any shadows. They had all cleared up, and neither the strongest ray of light from the sun nor the brightest light could cast a shadow upon him. Death had come. She closed the apartment [3] door and tossed the knife into her pocketbook. Her shadow was a very morbid one, one which would tear at her conscience, and follow her the rest of her life.

Comment on Sample #4

√ *Form:* The introduction is sharp, incisive, and effective. There are, however, serious paragraph weaknesses in the body of the composition. Paragraph 2 should have been broken up into at least four units: the office scene, the departure for the date, the activities in the club, and the limousine episode. The conclusion is technically satisfactory.

Semicolons should have been used in the last sentence of Paragraph 1, and a period should have been placed between "pleasant shadows" and "dogs on leashes" (Paragraph 2). In the same paragraph, a comma is needed after "Their shadows were hazy . . ."

√ *Content:* The writer took a very interesting approach to the topic. He shows flashes of brilliance in phrasing and language usage. Good examples of the latter are "bustling streets," "momentary shadow on the beds of grass," "big-finned Cadillacs," and "lean shadow on the wall." The word "cast" is used too often.

The body of the composition is developed vividly and with splendid detail. The writer displays a maturity and intensity that are commendable.

Unfortunately, the whole idea is weakened at the end. The insertion of a melodramatic note without any basis disrupts the mood and seems to indicate that the writer used this device because he could think of no better way to finish than to copy a routine television script.

Because of the inadequacies in organization, paragraph structure, and logical development, this composition falls short of an excellent rating, regrettably so because the potential for superior writing is there. The 26 out of 30 is about right as the mark.

III. AVERAGE COMPOSITIONS

(Ratings: C or 70–79%)
(Credits: 21–23 out of 30)

Sample #5

Shadows can bring on different feelings at different times. For example, if you have ever walked down a lonely road or street late at night, and sudenly you have seen a shadow coming from an ally, you may become a little nervous and approach the ally with caution. What a relief it is when you get by the ally and see that the shadow is one of a pole or something like that. Another type shadow is when your lying in bed, looking up at the ceiling, and watching the shadows of the cars passing your window. This is a good way for you to fall asleep, at least its a change from counting sheep.   1

Then also there is a good use for shadows. This use is that of telling time. For many years that was one of the chief methods of telling time. Then, also, how many times have you seen a good western in which the indians are holding hostages, and the chief rides up to the fort, sticks his lance in the ground and says "When the shadow of the lance is three quarters around, from where it now is, the hostages will die, unless you return my son to me." This leads to a big comotion at the fort, and wouldn't you know it, some cowboy rescues the hostages before the shadow gets half way around the lance.   2

Then there is the time children start playing with their shadows, by seeing how long they can make them, or how short, or even if they can beat their shadows to the door of their home.   3

This is how shadows bring on different feelings and emotions to different people at different times. This also gives a few uses the shadow play's in life.   4

Comment on Sample #5

✔ **Form:** This composition is rather poorly organized. The introduction becomes confused with the body in Paragraph 1, in Paragraph 2 the content starts off in one direction and winds up in another, Paragraph 3 is underdeveloped, and the conclusion is a bald statement of what has presumably preceded. There is a tendency toward overlong sentences, which inevitably leads toward run-on errors, an example of which is the last sentence in Paragraph 1.

There are numerous spelling errors: "sudenly, ally, its, your, indians, comotion, play's." However, punctuation is generally good and many difficult words are spelled correctly, so we can attribute most of the technical mistakes to carelessness.

✔ *Content:* The beginning and ending paragraphs show no originality and are poorly defined. Paragraphs 2 and 3 lack unity and emphasis.

On the favorable side are the student's efforts to introduce wit and emotional tone in the material; his imaginative language use in phrases like "a change from counting sheep, holding hostages, lance in the ground, beat their shadows to the door"; and his use of a pattern in developing his ideas, even if it doesn't quite come off. With a strong determination to observe the mechanics of composition more carefully, the writer could produce quite acceptable work. This is so true of the average student and explains why the rating was 21 out of 30, or just a little better than the minimum passing mark. Notice how close this paper is to either outright failure or above average success.

Sample #6

One night I was awakened with a start. There on the wall behind my bed was a climbing object. At first I thought it was a five headed monster, but that was impossible. Or was it? What could it be, I thought, my heart in my mouth, as I began sinking silently under the covers. Suddenly I raised my eyes toward the cieling and I saw it. A large chandelier was swinging lazily from it's braket and casting it's monsterous shadow across my bed. "Oh what a relief," I exclaimed, as I fell calmly back into the arms of slumber.

This is a very common experience. Others tell of similar ones, such as hearing fire engines on a dark moonless night and looking up to find that the curtins and blankets make shadows on the wall that are very similar to black smoke. Another similar experience would be coming home on a cold cloudy night and imagining that you see the shadows of someone following you. These are all common occurances. They have happened to almost anybody at some time or other. [2]

Shadows are only the playing of lights on objects in a dark place. They may be harmless in themselves, but they are very frightening. They can also be used in constructive ways. One way they are used to amuse children is by a person, working his fingers behind a screen or in front of a flashlight, so that the people watching think that there are animals or other objects. Along with these uses are pantemime or making pictures by standing behind a screen with a light shining on it. The result of this is called a silluette. Even if they do have some constructive uses when seeing a figure in dark, gloomy, terrifying surroundings we just want to run and get away from it, whatever it is. [3]

Comments on Sample #6

✓ *Form:* Once again we have a composition marred by poor organization. In this instance, a promising beginning deteriorates into a loosely developed body paragraph and a closing that should more properly have been worked into a few middle paragraphs. Only the last sentence suggests what the writer had in mind about her conclusion. Although the sentences are complete and varied, they are often awkwardly constructed, the worst example of which is in Paragraph 3: "One way they are used to amuse children . . ."

Spelling is poor: "cieling, it's, monsterous, curtins, occurances, braket, pantemime, silluette." Incidentally, some schools that maintain very high standards would have failed Samples #5 and #6 on spelling alone, regardless of how promising the material was. Perhaps the only reason these compositions were given passing grades was that they were typical of the average. If you stop to think about it, the average student's spelling is shockingly bad, isn't it?

✔ *Content:* We could repeat here what we said about Sample #5. The paragraphs are undefined, lack unity, and are improperly developed. However, there is an occasional good phrase and, despite the spelling, the writer shows fair language power, especially in the better than average vocabulary use. On a comparative basis, then, we cannot quarrel with the average mark this paper received.

IV. BORDERLINE COMPOSITIONS

> *(Rating: D or 65%)*
> *(Credits: 20 out of 30)*

In each of the next two categories, only one sample will be offered. As you observed in the average ones, the unsatisfactory aspects begin to repeat themselves as the quality goes down. Accordingly, what is true of Samples #7 and #8 is true of a thousand other papers that fall into the same classification. The borderline type is usually given the lowest passing grade because the writer shows some good qualities and leaves some hope for improving himself to the point where his work will be at least average. The failing grade indicates a need for a complete overhauling of the writer's understanding and employment of basic principles. Comments will be brief since many of the failings will be easily recognizable because of what has already been said about the previous samples.

Sample #7

Shadows are funny things they can be the most frightening thing in the world at one minute, and something for a child to play with the next. 1

Did you ever see a boy or girl play with there shadows? Then try to catch there heads with there feet or race there shadows down the block. I've seen them stand a play with there shadows for hours. 2

Sometimes shadows can be very frightening. Did you ever wake up in the middle of the night and see some weird looking shadows around the room. They are just shadows of the things in the room but you get scared 3 anyway. Everybody is frigtened by a weird shadow at one time or another.

Shadows are sometimes so frightening that people use them for things other than amusement. I heard of a man who used the setup of the furniture in a room in his home, and the way the light of the moon hit the wall, to create a perfect murder. The person he was ⁴ trying to murder had a bad heart. If he was awakened in the middle of the night by weird noises and there is the shadow, he would very likely have a heart attack.

Shadows are weird things. All they are is the reflextion of light on a wall or floor, etc. But they create many different moods, the excitement of children when playing with there shadows, the horror of somebody waking up ⁵ and seeing frightening shadows on the wall, the amusement you get when the next morning you realize it was only the arm chair.

Shadows have different effects on different people at different times. Have you seen any real good shad- ⁶ ows lately?

Comments on Sample #7

You can see that there is a fair grasp of what organization means and a certain ease with the language. It is these two factors that leave hope for the writer, plus the fact that many of his bad spelling and sentence errors are the products of gross carelessness, as can be observed in his spelling "frighten" correctly at one time and incorrectly at another on the same paper. Many teachers would be inclined to fail this paper. When it gets down to a point or two making the difference, it would not be inconsistent if the mark went either way.

V. FAILING COMPOSITION

(Rating: F or below 60%)
(Points: 18 or less out of 30)

Sample #8

Gee Mom!" here it's Sunday afternoon already and I have to read fifty pages of Ethan Frome for Monday." "I guess I will lay in bed and read Mother. "But Martin ¹

every time you do that you fall asleep." my Mother.
Said. Not this time Mother.

Oh this book is so dull and I rather think abouts lasts
nights date to the movies with Marsha. But I am get- 2
ting so tired, I think I will close my eyes.

"Good night," Marsha, . I will call you during the
week. It's very dark tonight, I better hurry home after 3
that double feature I am very tired.

Who's who just came out of the alley that I passed.
He looks very large from the reflection of the street light.
I better walk a little faster, just in case. Now he is also
walking a little faster to, I better start running, but he is 4
also running. What shall I do? Shall I keep walking or
stop, Yes that is what I shall do stop. But now he is
putting his hand around my neck.

No! No! Stop Please stop, You are killing me. Wake
up, Martin, wake up, called my mother. Where am I, I
called, in your own bed my mother answered. And no
man killed me last night. Of course not I drove both 5
you and Marsha to the movies and drove you home myself. Do you mean I was dreaming all this up. That
right, Martin, you fell asleep reading Ethan Frome.

Comment on Sample #8

There are over 50 technical errors in this composition, so
the less said about them, the better. The dream sequence is
the eternal novelty to students who will not use their imagination to be original, and the writer's use of this age-old device
shows what little thinking he did before beginning his composition. About the only redeeming feature is the presence of
some concept of organization and paragraph structure. But
the incredible carelessness is what makes teachers' hair turn
gray. No one can help this young man until he makes up his
mind that he must rid himself of his complete indifference to
the most elementary principles of correctness of expression.
The rating of 16 out of 30 was more than generous.

You have completed the analysis of eight compositions
written with varying degrees of skill. Probably one of them
reminded you strongly of the kind of writing you generally

produce. It is also likely that the comments on the samples helped you establish more firmly in your mind the importance of what the writers failed to do, *what they left out,* as well as *what they put in.* It should not be too difficult for you to determine your own rating as a writer at this moment. I am not referring to the grades you have been getting. That kind of evaluation of your skill has been done for you quite legitimately by your teachers, as was suggested before. I am referring to your "plus and minus" rating—the techniques you should continue to use because they are good, the ones you should learn how to use because they will help you improve your compositions, and the ones you should eliminate because they interfere with your progress.

What Is Good Writing?

Electronic sorting devices are commonplace these days. They do equally well grading peas, tabulating election returns, or checking the quality of manufactured goods. It would be a wonderful thing if we had such a machine for evaluating compositions. Not only would it make English teachers forever grateful, but it would be very useful to us right now. We could toss into it the models presented in the previous chapter and arrange the sorting process so that out would come all the desirable features.

However, we don't have a composition machine yet. Therefore, we'll have to do the next best thing to help us take an inventory of the skills you already possess and the ones you have yet to acquire. We will convert the good qualities of the model compositions into a questionnaire which will serve two purposes. The questions will give you a summary of superior writing practices. Your answers will offer you a challenge to set up goals in your self-improvement program.

Take the best one of the last few compositions returned to you recently by your teacher. Go through it step by step as you consult the questionnaire that follows. Insert a check in the "Yes" or "No" column, letting your answer be determined by what you actually did when you wrote your paper. Be completely honest with yourself. A "Yes" should mean that you use the recommended technique *almost always*, not occasionally nor accidentally. What we are trying to do here is get a survey of your writing habits—what you put into a composition as well as what you leave out.

Question	Yes	No
1. Do you take care to *select* a topic, when you have a choice, or to *treat* it, when you don't, on the basis of your own interests and experiences?		
2. Do you limit the ground you want to cover (scope) to what can be properly discussed in the number of words required?		
3. Do you try to be original in your approach?		
4. Before you write, do you in some way prepare what you are going to say in the beginning, middle, and end?		
5. Is your opening paragraph as exciting and unusual as you can make it?		
6. Is each middle paragraph a thoroughly developed unit, complete in itself as well as a contribution to the main idea?		
7. Do you avoid generalities and repetition by using details, examples, or references to support your statements?		
8. Do you maintain continuity? Do the sentences and paragraphs tie in with the ones that come before as well as the ones that follow?		
9. Do you make a conscious effort to use words that are vivid and effective, that reveal your personality and imagination?		
10. Does your last paragraph leave the reader with the feeling that you have brought your		

Question	Yes	No
composition to a logical and interesting conclusion?		
11. Do you check your work for mechanical errors before you hand it in?		
12. Do you constantly seek self-improvement in correctness of expression? For example, if you have a spelling or sentence structure problem, have you made a really sustained effort to get rid of your bad habits in these fields?		

Your answers to the questionnaire have completed your self-diagnosis. Now you know where you stand insofar as what needs to be done about your desire to improve. The *No's* indicate those areas in which your greatest weaknesses lie, and they point a finger at the skills you must try to master.

If a summary card had come out of our imaginary composition machine, it would have read thus:

LEARN TO
—work with an appropriate topic
—narrow its scope to fit the length required
—look for an original approach
—prepare your material in outline form
—construct good beginning, middle, and ending paragraphs
—use language effectively
—use language correctly
—revise until the result is your best effort

This is the least that any high school graduate should be able to do. If you are planning to attend college, you will be interested in a statement found in a pamphlet entitled "Advanced Placement Program in English," prepared under the direction of the Division of Secondary Education of the

New York State Education Department. The recommendations are the result of consultation with the College Entrance Examination Board, teachers who have taught advanced English courses, and college instructors. Here's what they say:

"It is expected that college-level courses in composition teach the student to write well about something important. Certain specifics identify the level of writing which distinguishes the good college-level student from other good high school students:

* The college-level student will not merely reproduce standard patterns of organization (introduction, body and conclusion) and of paragraph development, such as may be found listed in any textbook in rhetoric, but will have developed such flexibility as to be able to adapt these patterns effectively to different kinds of writing assignment.
* The college-level student should have developed subtlety of thought, for example in recognizing implications in context, and in employing synonyms and comparisons with awareness of connotation and appropriateness of tone.
* He should be able to demonstrate his ability to sustain a certain complexity of thought and give it unity of expression, distinguishing between major themes and their subdivisions, and ordering his paper with a sense of purpose and progress.
* That the student's syntax and logic should be beyond reproach goes without saying."

" . . . no student should be continued . . . who has not already sufficiently mastered the mechanics and conventions of writing to be able to devote his whole attention to his thought and the effectiveness with which he can express it. And this thought should be of such strength and individual quality as to make his writing worthy of the attention of an adult reader—one who will hold him rigorously to account as an adult. The student must be required to examine his ideas, to say what he means precisely and to mean what he says."

"He must be discouraged from mere *pro-forma* writing. The merely correct will probably not satisfy the requirements. . . . The writing must have imagination in the sense that it is concerned with the perception of essential relationships and meanings; it must have integrity in the sense that it faces the problems proposed squarely and without equivocation."

What it all boils down to is that once you have left high school you are expected to be able to express yourself with maturity, intelligence, and originality. This stresses all the more the importance of your learning the basic principles of form and content in writing. Whether you go to college or not, there will be no escape from these standards. Every time you write you will be revealing the extent to which you have succeeded in disciplining your mind and your pen so that what you write makes good sense and is worth reading. The person who never learns how to convey his thoughts on paper in an acceptable fashion goes through life with a tremendous handicap. So you see, there is more to writing high school compositions than just getting a mark in an English class.

Something else must be said before we get to the *how's* of writing. You already have and will again come across professionally written material that seems to ignore many of the basic principles we will soon discuss. And you may be inclined to think: "If they can do it, why can't I?" Moreover, you have just read an excerpt from a pamphlet that suggests that the college-level student must be capable of flexibility in his handling of traditional forms. Your reasonable question can be answered simply. No matter what ability is being developed, the fundamentals must be mastered first. The artist, sculptor, musician, athlete, or author must begin by becoming completely familiar with the theories and practices that experts agree lead to the foundation skills. Only then

can the truly creative person perfect a style of his own that
will be distinctive and accepted.

Applied to compositions, what has just been said means
this. Learn everything you can about topics, planning, para-
graphing, language use, and revision. Master the techniques
so well that you do the right things automatically, by force
of habit. Then make whatever adjustments in the basic
principles suit your style or the particular piece you want to
write. Indeed, variations are desirable if they represent
originality.

Sometimes you may want to eliminate an opening paragraph of the usual kind (as was done in Sample #1), or you
may decide that a single sentence will suffice for a paragraph
under certain conditions. That's all right—provided your reader can see, too, that your departure from the fundamentals
of writing is deliberate and effective. Be yourself on paper,
but don't use your individuality as an excuse to cover up bad
habits of spelling, punctuation, sentence structure, or some
other writing mechanic. We might as well be blunt about it.
If you start out getting consistently excellent ratings, your
teachers will allow you great freedom in your handling of
form and content. But don't try any tricks until it will be
clear to your critics that you have done it by choice rather
than through error.

Now let's proceed to the *How's* of writing!

How Can You Choose the Right Topic?

He was just a boy when his father died and his family moved back from California to Massachusetts, where eight generations of his forefathers had lived. When the boy grew older, he worked in the mills, tried college for a while, taught school, made shoes, edited a newspaper, and finally settled down as a farmer. After struggling with the earth for eleven years, he sold out even though he loved the soil, went to England with his family and tried his hand at something that had been bubbling within him for a long time. He began to write poetry— about stone walls, hired hands, snowy evenings in the country, and tall birches. Later Robert Frost returned home to find himself acclaimed as the poetic voice of New England.

A young man from Illinois enlisted as an ambulance driver in World War I. He went from there to live a life full of adventure and excitement, showing a remarkable physical toughness. In the middle '30's he became actively engaged in the Spanish Civil War. On his return to this country, he scorned the big cities and found peace in a small Cuban fishing village. The ambulance driver wrote **A Farewell to Arms,** the most famous American novel about the First World War, and his subsequent rough and tumble escapades found expression in the remarkable short story "The Killers." The pain, suffering, and heroism that characterized the bloody revolt in Spain were admirably depicted in **For Whom the Bell Tolls,** and from the seacoast retreat emerged **The Old Man**

and the Sea. Ernest Hemingway's books are his lasting autobiography.

An aspiring young writer sits sadly at his desk. His first play has just been rejected for the third time. The criticism is always the same: "wooden character, unlikely situations, absence of genuine emotion."

These three brief sketches tell the story that lies behind every successful piece of writing. Our distinguished poet and novelist used what interested them in their own experiences to provide them with material to write about. They had lived in the places they described, had met people similar to the characters created by their pens, had felt the emotions that inspired their verse or prose, had witnessed the action that later appeared in their works. They knew down to the last detail what they were writing about!

The young playwright may have had tremendous technical talent, perhaps the literary potential of a Frost or Hemingway. But he had been doomed to failure from the start. Our would-be dramatist's fatal mistake had been to invent people who had never been alive, set up situations that didn't ring true, inject feeling where none existed even in himself. No one can describe the majesty of the Grand Canyon adequately if he has never seen it, any more than he can talk about love if he has never been in love. What critics have often said to beginning writers applied very well in this case. He hadn't "lived enough, hadn't been to enough places, hadn't suffered enough." In short, he didn't know what he was writing about!

Now, we have agreed that all you want is to be able to write better high school compositions, not to get a poem published or produce the great American novel. Then why bring up the problems of professionals again? This is why. Whether you write a sentence, a paragraph, or a whole book —as a paid author or a student—you are faced with the same question all writers must answer before they can even begin: "What shall I write about?" Unless you have a ready source of material, you are in trouble right from the start. Call it what you will—topic or subject for a composition, or title of a book for publication—you can't do a good job if you can't get your writing engine started. It may be capable of the most powerful performance but it won't run without gas in the tank. The proper kind of material to write about is the only kind of fuel that will light the fire of your imagination. Without it your ideas sputter and stop dead. The first *how* we must discuss, then, is the right way to look for ideas and where you can find them easily.

Compositions are usually assigned in one of three ways: a single topic for the entire class, a list of topics from which one must be picked, and the dreaded "Write about anything at all." The poorest writers generally prefer to be given one topic and be done with it. It resolves their problem of choosing from many and relieves them of a certain responsibility. They can always blame a bad result on the assignment! Most students would rather be given a list because it limits them to some extent and still offers them a freedom of selection. It isn't odd that only a handful like to be left to their own devices, to pick a topic out of the air, so to speak. These are the students who have a desire to express themselves and have an inexhaustible supply of subjects because they have learned most of the things we will shortly talk about. They aren't bewildered when told they are on their own.

Naturally, you are expected to be able to handle any kind of assignment, and it is on this basis that the suggestions that follow are offered. Although they are listed separately, you are not to assume that each is to be used by itself as a device. A good topic can be developed only if you use at least three or four of the suggested procedures simultaneously as a means of calling up ideas. The main thing to remember is that no topic is impossible if you spend a little time thinking about it and attack it from a number of directions. Be like the hunter who uses a round of buckshot. At least one of the pellets will hit the target even if there are many misses. Here's how it's done.

1. *Use your own experiences.* Is there anything you know better than yourself and the things you've lived through? Is there anyone who can tell you better what interests you than you can yourself? The richest source of material for any topic is what happens to you from day to day. Take a tip from the professionals. They reach into their past for the moments and episodes that brought them pleasure, excitement, even pain— anything, so long as it is interesting to look back upon. Or they go out and gather material by *living it.*

That's the formula: interest plus experience. Write about things you know first hand, incidents that stimulate some emotion in you when you review them, events that were a change from the routine, or sometimes the routine itself can be made exciting to a reader.

Take advantage of human curiosity. We are all born with the desire to pry into the private lives of other people. Tell others about yourself, what happens at home, in school, on vacations—the little things, the ones the reader will be able to compare with his own experiences.

Suppose, for example, you found a topic like "The Trials of a Gardener" among a list of fifteen. At first glance, you might say, to yourself:

"What do I know about gardening? I wouldn't know a rose bush from poison ivy."

Instead, you should say, if you are at all interested:

"Now, let's see. What has happened to me that can be used here? Or what have I seen about gardening as practiced by somebody else?"

Here is the answer to these questions that one student was able to work out and express beautifully in a composition on a test, no less, when there was little time to think. Notice how the charm of the piece is enriched because you have been given the opportunity to look inside a stranger's apartment door.

The Trials of a Gardener

Some years ago, my sister decided to take up gardening as a hobby. Since we are city dwellers, her interests were confined to small, sturdy plants.

To begin with, she bought a small ivy plant which began to climb the bedroom wall in almost no time at all. The first smell of success obviously went to Joyce's head because within a week's time she expanded her gardening interests to include a snake plant, another ivy, a begonia in full bloom, and a small geranium. Needless to say, our room began to look like a greenhouse.

I never uttered a word of complaint during the beginning stages of my sister's hobby. In fact, I rather enjoyed the colorful changes in the room. But then, alas, tragedy struck. The geranium, which had been doing so nicely all along, began to wilt. Joyce decided that it was time to transplant. Besides, I think she got slightly bored doing nothing but water and pick dead leaves off her blooming vegetation, and transplanting sounded like fun. She bought two large window boxes and a ten pound bag of soil. I tried to explain to her that it would be very messy to do any transplanting in the apartment. It did no good. She was being very noble and gallant and said that she was only doing it to save the life of her poor geranium.

It took only one window box and five pounds of soil to transplant the geranium. This was apparently not what the poor thing needed because it died within two weeks. I suppose this misfortune was too much for Joyce because in a short time she stopped taking care of the other plants, too.

Now we have about five flower pots and one window box filled with dry soil, one empty window box, and five pounds of unused, fertile soil to clutter up our room. Do you know anyone who is interested in gardening?

It is possible in practically every instance to *personalize* a topic by using the approach suggested above. Let's look at a few more examples of how this can be done. Of course, I can't tell you what to select from your experiences since you are the only one who knows them. But if you observe what I would choose to write about for various assignments, you will be able to adapt many of the ideas to your own work.

FREE CHOICE

I could write about the time I went to retrieve a tennis ball in a pasture and was chased by a bull. There are lots of similar vacation experiences.

Then there was the time I tried to drive a 1925 Packard and discovered it had no brakes.

I'll never forget the time some friends and I took some girls out to a fancy restaurant and had to borrow money from our dates because the bill was unexpectedly high.

I still recall the time I tore a new pair of pants and wondered how I would explain the disaster to my father.

The bully of the block, when I was thirteen, never knew how frightened I was when he decided to test out that new kid from Connecticut.

Do you get the idea? The little things that may have lasted only an hour or so make very interesting reading. Make your title interesting, too. Ones that come to mind for the experiences described are these:

> The Tennis Playing Toreador
> Driving a Museum Piece
> Dutch Treat à la Carte
> Jack the Ripper Goes Home
> Facing the Music

LIST OF TOPICS

Here are 15 topics given on a state examination some years ago. Notice how, with a little thought, every one of them could have been personalized.

Socialized Medicine

If you are for it, tell how it could have helped you once when you (or some member of your family, or a relative, or friend) were sick.

If you are against it, stress what harm it could bring to you if you became sick and couldn't get the doctor you wanted, etc.

Abundance and Waste in America

You may have been on a trip and seen forests destroyed by fire, or watched a farmer dump milk and thought of the slum kids back in the cities, or have thought of the books, teachers, buildings, and grounds furnished in such quantities by the states and the failure of some students to take advantage of this generous educational offering.

The Dispute Over Comic Books

This one is easy. You've read them. What do you think about them, how do they affect you, and are they all good or bad? Did they ever cause you trouble?

Voyage to the Moon

How would you feel as a passenger in a space ship? What would you expect to find on landing? Did you ever try to build a rocket?

International Student Relations

At first glance you might think of other nations, iron curtains, politics, and international suspicions. But to *personalize* you must go beyond the literal meaning of the topic, and, believe me, your teachers will welcome an original approach. You don't have to write about the broad concepts, if you aren't interested. Look to your own experiences in gaining new friends when you moved, went to a new school, or spent a summer away from home. Out of these recollections can come ideas that will enable you to write about this subject without the need for probing into the more complicated questions that you would rather leave to the political analysts. The technique of "looking beyond the topic" was used expertly by the student who wrote this composition, on a topic very similar to the one above:

Winning Friends Abroad

The best way I know how to win friends abroad is to put into practice the age old system of corresponding with pen-pals overseas. I don't know exactly when, where, or how this idea came to be, but I must admit I have enjoyed it very much for many years now.

Deena, a beautiful, petite, and very saucy French girl was the first friend I made in this manner. We have "watched" each other mature from mere children of twelve to young ladies of seventeen. With the exchange of letters, souvenirs, pictures, and gifts, I feel I am as close to Deena as I am to my dearest friend here in school. I have learned a good deal about her country and try to answer all her questions, and then some, about my country and city. Imagine her surprise one day when I wrote her a whole letter in French (using what I had learned in the four years I studied the language). Several of her friends have written to me, anxious to learn all they could about our food (especially **hot dogs**), entertainment, and our school system. I enjoy writing to them and feel I am making new and interesting friends.

I have added a host of new boys and girls to my list of pen-pals over the years. They include an Israeli girl who will soon be drafted into the women's army; Dino, an extremely handsome singer in Italy; and a girl who lives in a real palace in Baden-Baden, Germany, a town noted for its sulphur baths. Of course, we are all anxious to see each other some day, but right now we must be content to wait for pictures, letters, and I—my recordings from Dino.

I believe this is the best thing a person can do to win lasting friendships abroad, and I fervently hope that more young people as well as adults will learn to use this method. Perhaps then we shall have a broader understanding of the customs and traditions of the societies in which these people live.

Freedom for All People

We are now at our sixth topic. Wouldn't it be interesting if you wrote about the constant fight for freedom every teenager puts up against his parents? That would personalize it with a vengeance, wouldn't it?

Farm Horsepower

Practically everybody has been to a farm or the country at least once. Why not describe the various machines the farmer uses, *as you saw them,* and compare them to the kind your history books tell you he used years ago?

The Chairman Learns Many Things

Have you ever been the head of a committee, or tried to persuade others to do something you wanted, or been in charge of an activity? What were your experiences?

Financing the School Newspaper

This, of course, is another easy one. You talk about *your own ideas* on how the money should be raised, or simply what you do to get the necessary funds to support school projects like a newspaper.

My Musical Education

Even if you have never taken a lesson, you can talk about your voice training in the music classes and what it did for you, or the desperate efforts your parents may have once made to get you to play an instrument.

Old Foods—New Methods

How do you like frozen foods, or ready-made pizza pies, or dehydrated milk? You would probably have fun telling us about some of your adventures with products bought in a supermarket.

Unwanted

Everybody feels rejected by family or friends at least once in a while. Tell about one such time.

Keeping Up With History Today

This is another topic that sounds rather technical at first. However, "look beyond it" and you may decide to talk about the trouble you have doing your history homework, or how you go about faking reports for the history class. Confession is good for the soul, you know, and may even get you a good mark on your composition—and you can swear your English teacher to secrecy. Incidentally, your history teacher knows about it anyway.

Accidents Are Not Accidental

There must have been hundreds of occasions when, with a little more caution, you could have avoided a bump or a bruise or even a broken bone. Tell about one such occasion.

Gadgets

Pick out any appliance in your home that amazes you by its operation. It's a gadget you can readily write about, I'm sure.

There you are. Fifteen topics—fifteen opportunities to *personalize* if you "look beyond the topic" or just look back into your own experiences and pick out one for your material source. It can be done, without too much trouble. You are not to assume that because I am a professional writer that it was easy for me. Just reach into your memory of the things you've done and seen and you will gradually discover that inexhaustible supply of topics I mentioned earlier.

SINGLE ASSIGNED TOPIC

Now you know what to do about this kind of assignment, too. Just "look beyond the topic" and *personalize*. You come back after the summer's vacation and you are asked to write about it. You hate the idea because you are still in mourning for the lost golden days of vacation leisure. Well, pick out one of the golden moments. Mind you, I didn't say "days." It's the small event, usually, that does the trick. Build it up as was suggested.

Or the entire class is asked to enter an essay contest. The topic assigned is a very appetizing one, like "Why Every Citizen Should Vote." You aren't old enough to vote yourself, but you are expected to write about it. Well, what does your family do about this question? What have you heard your father or mother say? Perhaps you want the voting age lowered. Why? Why do you think you would qualify right now? If you could vote, what would your attitude be toward the topic? Perhaps you have heard adults argue the question. What was your reaction to their statements? Possibly you feel like a rebel. Everything is fixed in advance anyway, you think. All right. Tell why you think so and why citizens should not vote until . . .

We have just covered the basic secret of how to select proper material to write about. It must come *out of you* and *be about you,* if at all possible—and you have seen how it can be done. There are several other techniques you can also use.

2. Don't ignore the commonplace. When you were told to concentrate on the little things in using your experiences for composition material, you perhaps took it for granted that the reference was to the unusual incident or sight. Undoubtedly the out-of-the-ordinary provides the greatest interest for the reader and you should certainly try to use such material whenever you can. However, you can often create a very entertaining topic out of the routine daily occurrences that you never give much attention. Some of our most successful comedians have made their reputations by building stories around the commonplace: taking care of the lawn, going to the store on errands, family differences of opinion, or bringing up baby. If you look for it, you will find much to be said about buying a pair of shoes, combing your hair, making or eating a favorite dish, walking in ankle-deep snow, delivering grocery bundles after school, or piling a load of hay on a wagon. An assigned topic like "The Value of Mathematics" need not be impossible even if you shudder when you think of algebra, geometry, and calculus. Why not write about how you manage to stretch your weekly allowance to cover dating as well as chocolate ice cream sodas? I recall a very interesting composition on this subject by a student who described how he had used mathematics to explain to his mother what the best buy was in canned goods, checking contents in ounces against size and price. Here's what another student did when confronted with the topic "Visit Your Dentist Regularly":

> Whenever I must see my dentist, I defer the thought of it, like an ostrich with his head in the sand, until the morning of the dreaded visit. In his outside office I sit and hear my heart hammer away. I know that once I am in the chair I shall weather it somehow, but there is always the possibility, the fear—what if I should not?
>
> I begin to imagine the endless process of digging and drilling, the stiffness of my jaw from keeping my mouth agape, and the possible horrible need to ask my tormentor to hold everything for a moment until I can pull myself together. Since my dentist is a busy man, I feel humiliated at showing such childish anxiety, and that makes my heart hammer away even harder.
>
> I begin to concentrate on the disturbing painting on the wall. I get lost for a bit in the meaningless abstraction. Why did the artist have to communicate something which was not so much a challenge as a dare? Only he could know what the powerful strokes represented. Why was one area dark and blank and the other white, paint-daubed and spotted?
>
> The anxiety seems to have disappeared for a moment. No. It is coming back. My dentist opens the door and waves me in. I sit down, stare out of the window at the moving clouds, at the buildings, at anything in order to forget the nagging fear. My mouth is open, my head is buzzing with the noisy drill, and I am fighting to control myself. My palms are wet, my face is damp, and I may have to ask the poor man to stop. No. He is finished. I

am finished. I smile weakly, say I'll see him next Tuesday, and I'm out.

What a bright, happy world it is. I'll be in time for my skating appointment, too. I'll be able to keep my mouth closed for one whole week.

3. Vary your approach. Try taking an unexpected point of view toward a commonly accepted belief or tradition. Occasionally, this technique can be very effective. For instance, one is supposed to revere one's relatives, but note the extraordinary humor, albeit somewhat savage, in the following student effort:

TV Nightmare

Uncle Hyram died as he had lived, out of spite. For just plain being mean, we always said he could best anyone in town; but by how much we didn't know until after he was dead. I guess if I am going to tell this, I might as well do it right and start with the television set.

For a long time Uncle Hyram had been sick, mostly just old, I think, until one cold January night he went to bed and never got out again. For all of that year, and the next, and the next, and about ten or fifteen more, Uncle Hyram lay in that bed screeching like an old woman with a cramp. That's just about all I remember of my growing up years.

About a year ago, after being on the 'phone all day, Uncle Hyram surprised us all by announcing that he had bought a television set for his room, and if we would pay a little more attention to a sick old man, he might just let us come in and watch it sometimes. Of course, the kids were all excited, but the rest of us just pursed our lips and waited for the hitch to show itself; it did, soon enough.

The following day some men brought the set in and installed it in Uncle Hyram's room. That night we took chairs in and sat around waiting for the old man to turn the set on. He lay back on the pillows looking like a wet canary that had just eaten the cat. The kids couldn't sit still; they chattered back and forth about all the big shows we would be able to see now, and so on. Finally,

Uncle Hyram began to jigger the remote control thing he had and the set came to life for the first time.

Bits and pieces of the network shows we wanted to see snapped on and off as he turned the channel numbers dizzily about. In our town we have a local station which shows the really old and really bad movies, riddled with feature length commercials. I don't know anybody who ever watched this program unless he was too drunk to know what he was looking at. But that's exactly where Uncle Hyram turned to.

"Just love these old movies," he said, as he leered at us with his beady, little eyes.

And that's the way it was, night after night, 'till we had Blerble Kleener and Keystone Cops running out of our ears. He just did it out of meanness. With all the shows we were dying to see, he watched the old movies and so did we. Finally one night when there was to be a big spectacular on, we had just about come through as much as we could.

For the first part of the evening and the first half of a tired, flickering romance, we all sat quietly. But when the time came for the big show, Pa just got up, went to the set, and disconnected that remote gadget of Uncle Hyram's. Then, as the old man tried to get up enough breath to start yelling, Pa switched to the channel that we wanted to watch and returned to his seat. I've never seen anybody as hopping mad as Hyram was as he bounced around in that big old bed of his. He screamed and he hollered, but it didn't do him any good; we just sat and watched the show.

I guess he must have come to realize that it wasn't doing any good, his bellowing, that is, because he stopped and just sort of lay there for a minute. He looked around at us, each one. Then he gave a little yelp and flopped back on the bed, dead. I reckon he was out to spoil that show for us, one way or another.

It was a doggone good show, from beginning to end.

Other ways of varying your approach can be listed:

a) Write your composition in letter form. The topic might be "Science Fair." Pretend you are visiting one and write a letter to a friend about it.

b) Tell a story to illustrate your ideas on a serious question. For a topic like "Unrest Among Soviet Satellites," why not pretend you are a Hungarian boy or girl and describe your experiences? Tell why you and your invented parents are unhappy.

c) Write an entire composition in dialogue form, like a play. You pick "Car Insurance for Minors." All right, set the scene. There are a judge, some lawyers, an injured adult, and a reckless young driver. Let them talk it out.

d) Use the diary technique. Topic: "Counting Calories." Go through a week's starvation schedule. Let each day be a paragraph and reveal your darkest diary secrets.

e) Use the present tense throughout, especially if it is an action piece you are composing. This heightens the movement and suspense.

4. Get the facts. Never attempt to write on a topic about which you are poorly informed. Your scanty knowledge will show through like an elbow out of a threadbare sleeve. If you are not permitted to personalize or you don't want to with a particular assignment, make sure you have the necessary facts before you plunge in. Go to the library and do some research, if there is time. Perhaps some book at home will do the trick. Certainly the writer of the following composition had his material well in mind before tackling his topic:

Alaska—Our 49th State

Alaska was purchased sight unseen in 1867 through the efforts of James Seward, our Secretary of State at the time. It was sold to us by Russia at the incredible bargain price of fifteen million dollars. Seward was ridiculed for what appeared to be a flamboyant disregard of the American purse. The purchase of Alaska was called "Seward's Folly" or "Seward's Icebox."

The Secretary of State was called upon to justify his action before an outraged Congress. He told them that the fifteen million dollars was a gift to Russia for her support of our policies abroad. He also hastily added that it kept another nation off the North American continent, in line with our policy of isolation. Little did he or Congress suspect, then, that in less than one hundred years Alaska was to become a state.

Our new state is twice the size of Texas, which was formerly our largest. It contains millions of acres of tall, straight trees, providing a nearly endless natural lumberyard for our future needs. There are still vast deposits of gold ore in spite of the Klondike rush. Alaska's mineral wealth alone is comparable to that of all the other states combined. The climate, although cooler than it is where we live, is not abnormally cold in many places. Its southern shores are warmed by the passing Japanese current.

The products of Alaska are many and varied. Fish ranks as its leading export. Most people make their living fishing or packing fish for shipment. Among the other products are sugar beets, furs, oleo and salmon extract.

Since Alaska will soon become a new state, it is a new frontier for the United States. The government gives anyone who cares to migrate 160 acres of land. Business is booming because of the stationing of troops near many large cities. Large markets have been opened for manufacturers. Alaska seems to be the new "land of opportunity." However, there are matters to consider before packing and heading north-northwest.

At least ten thousand dollars are necessary to insure a good beginning in this land. In the winter there are fewer than four hours of daylight each day for six months. Life is rugged and will be for a while, although many of the larger cities look already much like our own. So if you have an adventuresome nature and an eager foot, Alaska is for you!

You can appreciate why the writer chose this topic. He knew enough facts to support his ideas and make them sound convincing.

For some topics it is a good idea to act like a newspaper reporter. Suppose you are assigned something like "What Businessmen Expect of Beginners." Don't guess. Go to a businessman in the neighborhood and ask him. He'll be glad to talk to you. Or you might be asked to write about "Careers for the Handicapped." Visit a center where these people are trained and find out the kinds of jobs they become capable of accepting.

If the topic doesn't lend itself to personalizing, then do the next best thing. Build up your background so that you can use details to good advantage. But let me repeat. Never choose a topic that calls for information you do not possess at the time you do your writing.

5. Limit the scope. This is one of the most important cautions you must observe. It means simply that the ground you expect to cover with your topic must be no broader than is dictated by the number of words you have been asked to write. If the composition calls for 250-300 words, avoid handling your topic so that you would need 10,000 words to do it justice.

For example, you have been asked to write on "Television Troubles." Millions of lines could be written on this subject, but you are not expected to write them. At most, your teacher probably wants no more than four or five paragraphs. You must narrow down your area of discussion to a decent size. Should you write about television commercials? No, this is still too much to cover. How about one particular commercial you like very much or detest rather strongly? That's better. Now you can concentrate your fire. You won't be like the man who tries to use a cupful of paint to cover four walls and the ceiling.

Here is a good illustration of how a writer can limit the scope of a broad topic and produce a composition rich in detail:

Television Troubles

When you invite guests to your home for an evening of television, you have a chance to see televiewers at their best and at their worst. All you need to do is watch the people who are watching the screen.

At least one of the visitors may be the restless type. He periodically sprints from his chair to the set to adjust the controls. The fact that he has no set of his own seems to fill him with the desire to play with yours. First he experiments with the volume. The sound is a little too loud or too soft for him and, he is sure, for the other listeners as well. Having adjusted the dials so that every muted violin can be heard, he must leap forward whenever the blast of the commercial comes on. He becomes intoxicated with his power over the machine. He hunts for programs other than the ones you have selected. He keeps switching back from channel to channel. The result of his unfailing devotion to duty is a jumble for the eyes and an assault on the nervous systems of the viewers.

Then there is the professional critic. He talks about the bad casting, the poor direction, the implausible story, and the waste of time it is to watch at all. You feel tempted to wonder out loud why he came at all.

How different is the guest who accepts your invitation to see a certain program and does precisely that. He takes the good with the bad. He doesn't eat up all your fruit and candy. He even wipes his feet before he comes in. That one you ask again.

The problems presented by guests have given me an idea for a new business. I'm going into the printing field. I'll sell signs to homeowners with this motto: "Visitors should be seen but not heard after the set has been turned on by the host!"

The broad topic cut down to a few lively pictures became quite manageable for the average 300 word composition. Incidentally, limiting the scope gives you greater flexibility, too. Suppose you were told to write about "The Power of the Supreme Court." You know that you are not expected to go back to John Marshall and trace the development of judicial control over the past hundred and fifty years. If you have been asked to write 500 words, you may decide to use two cases to make your points clear. If the assignment is 250 words, one case will do; if only a paragraph has been requested, part of one case will be enough. Keeping your material within bounds, therefore, will help you adjust your target so that you will be able to aim with reasonable accuracy.

6. *Take a stand.* Whenever you must write about a controversial topic, don't sit on the fence. If you do, the result will generally be weak and unconvincing. Make up your mind and swing out hard, one way or the other. If you are for the idea, be 100% for it, but be sure to back up your statements with acceptable arguments. If you are against the idea, go all out to oppose it and fire away with all the factual weapons you have at your command. Never allow yourself to be found with both feet planted firmly in the air. Stay on solid ground, use statistics and references, and say *Yes* or *No* in a loud voice.

You will hear people say that nothing is all right or all wrong. That's true. But the convincing speaker or writer, having thought through the controversy, makes up his mind about which is the more desirable point of view. Then he lets you know his position. It is so much easier for him to influence your opinion if he has one of his own.

You have been told to write about "Political Indifference in the United States." You don't believe that people are indifferent. Fine. Say so, prove it, and don't give an inch. Additional research may help you change your mind later on, but at the time you write you should have a strong belief so that you can write with strength.

Here is what a young man wrote about nuclear weapons. He even personalized a bit! Does he leave any doubt about where he stands?

One Good Suggestion Toward International Understanding

In discussing international understanding, we must realize that even a beginning cannot be made until the parties involved are meeting on equal ground. This is hardly possible while major powers are struggling to produce bigger and better bombs and rockets. As one temporarily surpasses another in this race, it becomes increasingly harder to achieve this equal stand. What, then, is the key?

I think the answer is the prohibition of testing nuclear

devices for other than peaceful purposes. Hiroshima and
Nagasaki proved the capabilities of what are now small
bombs. The results were almost beyond the imagination.
So much property and so many lives were destroyed in
one devastating blow. With this horrible shadow constantly over them, how can nations be expected to come
together so long as any one of them has the means of
delivering even heavier blows?

Excuse my sounding like a movie title, but I want to
live. Life is short enough as is and for a reason as wasteful as war, I would hate to lose mine. I say let people
stop worrying about the future and they will soon find
avenues along which they can walk together. I couldn't
be very cordial to you if you carried a club behind your
back which you might use as soon as I disagreed with
you.

Only through the elimination of these deadly nuclear
weapons can we achieve the equal ground necessary to
obtain international understanding. Only through such
understanding can we achieve world peace. And only
through world peace can I hope to live out my three
score and ten.

Let's sum up. If you have a free choice of topic, I would
suggest that you *personalize* every time. It's the surest way to
be interesting. I want you to read one final sample. The writer
was a poor student who specialized in dullness and made
many technical errors. But he finally got the message about
how to select good material to write about. I'm sure you will
agree that his composition shows great promise because he
learned to look to himself for inspiration. Most of the errors
have been corrected because I want you to concentrate on
what personalizing did for him.

True Friendship

Throughout my life my pets have been a great help to
me and a wonderful pleasure. Animals have also been
some of my truest friends.

Wolf was the first friend I ever had. When I was three
years old my father came home one night with a large
box which contained a German police dog. Wolf seemed

to understand me better than my mother or father. We lived in the country so there was no one but the dog to look after me. As I grew older Wolf and I spent many happy days playing together. He even pulled my wagon when I played stagecoach. My mother never had to worry about my eating for Wolf wouldn't let me leave the table until I had eaten all that had been given to me. When I became seven we moved to Texas and the dog was left with some neighbors.

Triangle was a bay stud horse that was owned by the man in the next ranch. Everyday after school I would run to the fields where he would be eating. After a few months we became the best of friends and Triangle let me ride him. One day I saw my father talking to Mr. Aston, our neighbor and also the owner of my new friend. They called to me and I advanced with some fear. Mr. Aston had seen me ride Triangle and he was telling my father that I was mounting a stud horse that had never been broken. I was quite shocked but I didn't let the men know. My father died shortly after, and we had to move again. Triangle was left in Texas.

Since we now lived in a city and I don't think it is fair to coop up animals, I got myself a fish tank. There was no greater pleasure for me than to watch for hours the different types of fish on the other side of the glass. It was almost as if I had a window that looked into another world. As school became more important to me I had less time for my fish and so my mother took care of them.

It is a wonderful feeling to have a warm friend waiting for you when you get home. It matters little whether it is a dog, cat, or even a monkey. I hope everyone can have the pleasure from pets that I have had.

Not bad for a borderline student, is it?

Before *you* choose a topic:

Pick the one that allows you to personalize.

If you have no choice, try to personalize the one that has been assigned.

Don't ignore the commonplace.

Be well-informed about factual or controversial topics *before* you write.

Limit your scope in proportion to the number of words required.

Make up your mind about topics that can be argued, and then argue with all your skill.

EXERCISES

(There can be no "answers" here because many possibilities exist in each example. However, at the end of the chapter there will be suggested solutions. Compare your results with the ones listed to see whether you were on the right track.)

1. How would you *personalize* the following topics:

> Newspapers As Benefactors
> Is the Farmer a Profiteer?
> A Woman for President
> The Battle for Asia
> Mathematical Machines

2. Select 5 ordinary things you do every weekday morning before you leave the house. Phrase these routine activities into topics.

3. What would be an unusual approach in handling the following topics:

> Medical Research
> The Shrinking Dollar
> Are Horses Obsolete?
> The New Look in Houses
> A Great Composer

4. What would you do to get information about each of the following:

> A Nursing Career
> Is Professional Baseball Really a Game?
> The Romance of Words
> Dating on a Dime
> Scientists Work for the Police

5. What limited topics could be devised from the following very broad ones:

> Travel
> Deep Sea Fishing
> Modern Music
> Clothes Make the Man
> Keeping Livestock Happy

Suggestions for Handling the Questions

1. *Personalizing topics:*

Newspapers As Benefactors Tell how a newspaper helps you with your assignments, or gave you an idea from which you profited, or settled an argument for you, or (as an odd twist) made excellent wrapping paper for fish.

Is the Farmer a Profiteer? If you live on a farm, talk about your father's problems, or talk about what you have observed when you visited a farm or two.

A Woman for President If you are a girl, describe what you would do if you were elected. If you are a boy, explain how a woman president would make your life different.

The Battle for Asia Any topic of international scope can be reduced to the effect the outcomes of the disturbance could have upon you and your future.

Mathematical Machines Describe that genius in your math class who does things mentally that take you long hours with pad and pencil, or describe your experiences when you had the opportunity to observe an electrical calculating machine.

2. *Topics from the ordinary:*

> The Art of Brushing Teeth
> Catching Those Extra Few Winks
> Last Minute Cramming
> Eating on the Run
> What Shall I Wear?

3. Unusual approaches:

Medical Research Pretend you are a human guinea pig. Describe your heroic suffering in the cause of the advancement of medical knowledge. Pretend you are a doctor and make entries in a log of an experiment.

The Shrinking Dollar You are the dollar. Explain what has happened to you in the last twenty years. Or you have found a menu years old. Compare the prices then and now.

Are Horses Obsolete? You are a cowboy, peddler, jockey, etc. Answer it from the point of view of one of these people.

The New Look in Houses Prepare an advertisement for a newspaper describing a new house you are planning to build. Perhaps you are a scientist who has harnessed the energy of the sun. Take it from there and describe how you would save on fuel, electricity, etc.

A Great Composer You are listening to a great symphony. Describe what the music tells you about the life of the composer. Write a letter to your school newspaper complaining about the lack of recognition accorded your favorite popular songwriter.

4. Getting information:

A Nursing Career Visit a hospital. Ask a nurse about her job and the preparation for it.

Is Professional Baseball Really a Game? Call up the general office of a professional baseball club and ask for an appointment with one of the players. Tell why you want to talk to him. Your request will be granted, I'm sure.

The Romance of Words Go to the library. There are many fascinating books on the subject of word derivations and development.

Dating on a Dime Try it yourself first and then write about it, or ask one of your friends who has done it to tell you how.

Scientists Work for the Police There are books on the subject of crime detection through laboratory experiments, but the best way would be to visit a police laboratory.

5. Limited Topics:

Travel

How to Pack Bags Efficiently

A Canoe Trip

Eating on a Train, or Plane

Deep Sea Fishing

One Big Catch

The Proper Bait for Tuna

Conquering Seasickness

Modern Music

The Job of the Bass Violin

My Favorite Vocalist

What Is Swing Music?

Clothes Make the Man

Are Bermuda Shorts Here to Stay?

Dressing for an Interview

Saturday Night Dress

How Should You Prepare to Write?

Across the street several tree experts were cutting down a huge old oak that had been hit carelessly by the builder's bulldozer and had not recovered from the shock. The upper leafy fringes were sawed off first. As they fell, ropes caught them momentarily before they were lowered to the ground. Then the main branches were removed, section by section. That done, a power saw made short work of the massive trunk. Finally, a trench a foot or so deep was dug around the base, the heavy root formations were sliced away, and the last traces of the tree disappeared after soil had been shoveled back into the excavation. Everything proceeded neatly and quickly, step by step.

Here, in the efficient removal of a dead oak, was a striking example of how important it is to work with an orderly procedure and with a plan in order to bring about desired results. The men had had to make certain, *in advance,* that none of the falling pieces would injure them or the nearby house and shrubs. Experience had taught them that it made a difference whether they started in one place or another. Even had they been working in a field and been intending to drop a tree by sawing only its base, they would have had to plan the proper cutting angles so that it would fall without crashing down on their heads.

In a way, the workmen were retracing nature's footsteps. They were methodically tearing down what had just as methodically gone up. Although many mysteries about the growth of living things still remain, it is quite clear that there is a basic order and design. A seed doesn't just happen to grow into a towering forest giant. Certain conditions favorable to growth must be present so that the various stages will progress smoothly.

It would seem, then, that the most natural thing in the world is proper planning, whether something is being built up or being torn down, whether it is alive or inanimate, whether it is a tree, a building—or a composition! And since careful preparation is so essential, it is always puzzling to your teachers why you are often reluctant to spend the necessary time to organize your ideas before you write.

You hear about an outline almost as soon as you begin to write full paragraphs, way back in the lower grades. Your teachers stress the need for planning what you are going to say so that the final talk or composition will have the good sense and good form that every well-developed effort should have. It's old hat to you—the stories about the relationship between blueprints and houses, travel agencies and enjoyable trips.

You appear to be impressed with this logic when it comes to talking. You would be terrified if you were asked suddenly to stand up and deliver a five minute talk on some subject. You would consider this kind of assignment grossly unfair. A person needs time to think it out, you would say, to figure out the main points he wants to make. He has enough trouble even when he prepares his speech.

Yet when it comes to compositions, many students think an outline is a waste of time. They become impatient and want to get started at once. If their minds are blank when confronted with a topic, they would rather sit around and wait for an inspiration than spend the time working out an outline. It reaches the ridiculous at times. I have known students who rushed blindly into a composition and then, to satisfy the teacher's insistence on an outline, jotted down some notes *after* they had finished.

Yes, I readily admit that some people can and do succeed in writing excellent pieces without a moment's planning. But if you examined their ability closely you would discover three things: they apparently were born with a strong sense of order, they have trained themselves to formulate their ideas in their minds very rapidly, and they have a superior command of the language as well as a considerable background of general information. They can dispense with a written outline because they can think ahead fast enough and far enough to avoid going off the topic or underdeveloping the paragraphs. However, even these gifted writers know full well that for long essays or those requiring research they will do poorly unless they set things up first on paper. A professional author would not dare to submit an article or a story to an editor unless almost as much time had been spent in designing the piece as in writing it. The whole point is beautifully summarized in the words of one of the great English poets, William Wordsworth. Rather than subscribe to the popular and false notion that poets feel inspired by some sight or emotion and then promptly dash off an immortal lyric, he said:

"Poetry is emotion recollected in tranquillity."

Words destined to be well-remembered are not poured out. They are the products of thought, effort, and planning.

You can be sure of one thing. Without some preliminary thinking on paper, you will rarely produce the best composition you are capable of writing. You can be sure of another thing, too. A brief and simple outline, of the kind we will shortly discuss, will not be a waste of time; on the contrary, it will help you do the writing job right:

1. It provides the paragraphs for the body. It might be said that a composition should be prepared inside out. Unless you know what your main ideas are going to be, you cannot very well know where to begin or how to end. Therefore, the main purpose of the outline is to set up the middle of the composition.

The outline can be made to work almost by mathematical

formula. As a rule of thumb, you can assume that an adequately developed body paragraph will require about 100 words. Many good paragraphs are shorter, of course, and many others run into hundreds of words. But, on the whole, you can use the 100 word suggestion as a means for determining the number of middle paragraphs you should prepare in relation to the total number of words required.

For example, you have been asked to write 250–300 words on a given topic. Since you will want to leave at least 75–100 words for the beginning and ending paragraphs, you can readily see that two paragraphs in the body would be just about right, 100 words or so for each. Knowing this, you can concentrate on planning the best two paragraphs you can think of, rather than aimlessly writing a series of brief, pointless little paragraphs or cramming everything into one whether it fits or not. Naturally, you want your writing to sound free and spontaneous, and you may fear that this formula type of approach may prevent that. But once you have developed the technique, you will be amazed at how your mind will develop the habit of preparing main ideas in an organized pattern of suitable length without robbing itself of spontaneity.

2. The outline provides the material for the opening and closing paragraphs. Since one leads into the major discussion and the other brings it to a close, it is a relatively simple matter to set up a good introduction and conclusion once you have planned your body paragraphs.

Indeed, if you wish to extend the formula idea, you can use it here, too. If you plan to write two body paragraphs, you can expect to write four sentences in your introduction— one to suggest the main idea and purpose of the entire composition, one to hint at the contents of the first middle paragraph, another to refer to the second, and a fourth to help you lead into the body. The same device can be used for the conclusion. Exactly how this is done will be made clear to you in Chapter 5.

3. *The outline prevents wandering from the topic.*
When you have carefully planned what you are going to
write in a particular paragraph—and nothing else regardless
of how tempting it may sound at the moment—you won't be
able to introduce ideas that do not belong because you will
have imposed upon yourself a discipline that all writers
recognize as necessary to insure the logical sequence of
thoughts centered about one point at a time. Not only will
each paragraph have unity within itself but its contribution
to the topic as a whole will be improved.

4. *The outline helps you avoid technical errors.* It is
usually difficult, if not impossible, to do two things at once
and do them well. You will recall that the model compositions were judged on the basis of their form and content.
Whenever you write you are faced with the double job of expressing yourself with interest and good sense as well as correctness as dictated by acceptable usage. If, because you
have prepared a good outline, you do not have to think
about what you are going to say next, you can concentrate on
forming good sentences and avoiding careless errors in spelling and grammar. The driver of a car who doesn't know his
way gets into an accident easily. He can't keep his mind on
the road and its hazards because his eyes are searching for
signs to show him the right direction.

5. *The outline saves time!* Yes, it saves time; it doesn't
waste it. It may take you ten or fifteen minutes to prepare
your work and you may think you have fallen behind some
of the other writers who began scribbling away as soon as
the signal to begin was given. But you will eventually catch
up to them and pass them. You won't be stopping every few
minutes to wonder what to say next, nor will it be necessary
for you to cross out huge sections of writing because you
have suddenly discovered that you have wandered off the
subject. Once *you* begin it will be full speed ahead. If you
have ever watched a mile race, you are familiar with the
picture of the runner who dashes into the lead at the outset

and appears to be leaving everyone hopelessly behind. The eventual winner, who has planned his pace, inevitably passes the now-faded early flash and finishes strongly and confidently. Similarly, the outline helps you pace your writing so that the last part of your composition is as interesting and forceful as the beginning.

It is quite possible that the distaste some students have for outlines stems from the fact that they have been taught to approach the whole idea as if it were a jigsaw puzzle. The suggested procedure goes something like this:.

Let your mind roam at random about the subject.
Jot down any idea that occurs to you.
Eliminate the ones that don't fit.
Arrange the remaining ones in proper order.
Coordinate the ones that go together.

The trouble with this method is that you often bog down while you are playing the complicated game of shifting subtopics about. It does seem silly and time-wasting to let your mind blunder about up half a dozen blind alleys and then literally drag it back to where it should have been in the first place.

We're not going to prepare outlines this way. This method sounds all right, but it doesn't work for most students. Our technique is simpler and much more direct. It depends upon the same kind of mental direction and discipline that enable an expert to get to the core of a problem almost without a moment's hesitation.

When an architect is called in to plan a house, he doesn't begin by making aimless drawings on a piece of paper, hoping that one of them will look attractive to his clients. First there is a meeting to discuss the kind of house the buyers want. At least three basic questions must be answered:

What style does the family prefer?
How many rooms are necessary?

What features must be included in each room so that it best suits the needs of its occupants?

The answers to these questions lead to the plans from which the house is built.

As a writer, you are an architect with words. If you want to plan quickly and effectively, you, too, must learn to use questions to guide your thinking. They will help you force your mind to focus directly on the demands of the topic. They will lead you to an outline that takes into account the purpose, length, and major ideas of the composition you wish to write.

The key questions you must answer before you write a single word on any topic are also three in number. Memorize them. Use them regularly. Make the guide-question technique a habit. Your outlines will become the indispensable tools they should be for successful writing.

Question I: *How shall I handle the material?* Here is where you make your final decision about what you want to tell your reader and how you want to tell it. You should have partially answered this question while you were selecting your topic, if you followed the suggestions offered in the previous chapter. Now you review the situation. Have you narrowed the topic sufficiently to suit the length required? Is this a controversial subject that calls for a definite point of view? Will you have to get more information than you have? Are you going to *personalize*? Have you thought of an unusual approach? Can you get the point across in the form of a story, or will a vivid description do the job, or will perhaps a "how to" explanation be best? This briefing session you have with yourself points your thinking in the right direction and ideas flow readily when the actual writing takes place.

Question II: *How many paragraphs do I need?* Now, remembering that the outline prepares the material for the middle or body of the composition, you check the total number of words you will have to write. Let's say it is 300. You can subtract 100 words or so for the beginning (introductory) and ending (concluding) paragraphs, which you will add later on. That leaves about 200 words for the middle, or 100 for each of two body paragraphs. If you work it this way you will be using the formula technique suggested previously, a very effective way of training yourself to lay out paragraphs that are suitable both in number and length. Let me repeat, however, that the numbers are to be regarded by you as approximate, merely as yardsticks, and that variations are to be expected. Under certain circumstances it would be perfectly reasonable to write one rather full body paragraph of 200 words or three or four short, crisp ones of 50–75 words each. Whether you decide to use the formula device or to try some other arrangement, the main thing is that you must know in advance how many paragraphs you will use. Why is this so important? Think about the architect again for a moment. He has to know how many rooms there will be in the house before he can plan what to put into each one. Your paragraphs are like his rooms, and the contents of either one depend upon the number.

Question III: *What major ideas will each paragraph develop?* You are now ready for the written outline. Suppose you have decided to use two middle paragraphs, the topic being "Dating on a Dime." Your approach might be to present your material as if you were an expert and were giving advice to others. Since this is going to be a "how to" piece of writing, you decide that the best way to explain your technique is to follow a definite teaching pattern. First you will describe your method and then you will give an example to illustrate the point. Thus one of the middle paragraphs will talk about selling the idea to your date and the other about carrying it out. On a piece of paper you draw two lines near the top, like this:

            _____

On each line you write a major idea heading that will briefly

suggest the contents of a paragraph. The phrase used here
should be general in nature and no more than two or three
words in length, as in:

SELLING THE IDEA	CARRYING IT OUT

Now you think of the details that will help you develop
your paragraphs and will later be converted into sentences.
Use specific words or phrases to list the details! Expressions
like "how it was done, where it began" are of little value because they do not act as good reminders. The main purpose
of an outline is to enable you to do your thinking in advance
so that you can concentrate on forming effective sentences
and paragraphs when you get to the actual writing. If at any
point you forget what you had in mind, your planning has
been wasted.

Consider how most people remember humorous stories.
They try to keep the "punch line" in mind, the *specific* word
or remark that brings the laugh. Building up the story around
this key expression then becomes easy. Once a skillful hu-
morist has a peg on which to hang his sentences, he can concentrate on his delivery, choose his words carefully, let his
imagination have full rein, and introduce variations as they
occur to him in the telling of the story.

The details you insert under the paragraph headings must
work the same way. They must be so definite that as soon as
your eye looks at them your mind is ready to form the sentences that will develop the thoughts in the most attractive
possible manner. Thus, if you write "where it began," you
aren't helped very much because you must stop to think
about the place and try to recall what you had originally
wanted to say. What is worse, you may even forget the point
altogether (as people do with jokes) and you will be blocked
in the smooth flow of words that should proceed from a good
outline. On the other hand, a phrase like "Joe's room" or "the

back porch" sets the train of thought in motion again when you have to write the sentences based on this detail.

Getting back to our topic, then, you arrange the *specific* details underneath the paragraph headings. The order will vary with the type of material that is to be presented. If it is narrative, you will naturally want to put first things first; if it is argumentative, you may want to build up to your most powerful point at the end; if it is descriptive, you will want to organize the items into an easily followed form, like starting near the door of a room and proceeding around it from left to right or vice versa. Since ours is going to be a "how to" composition with some narrative aspects, the order of the details is obvious: the series of steps that lead to a successful date on a dime. So you put them in:

SELLING THE IDEA	CARRYING IT OUT
anti-spending line	exit parents
simple things of life	icebox raid
value of exercise	living room walk
need for conversation	music, talk
parents' night out	icebox raid, walk
arrival	

At this point, your outline is finished and you are ready to write. The two major ideas in the body have been laid out and you know exactly what you are going to say in the paragraph you will form for each one. You spend a few minutes thinking about an opening paragraph that will start the composition off with a bang. In the next chapter you will be shown how this can be done with consistently good results. After you have written the most interesting beginning paragraph you can think of, you are ready for the material prepared by your outline.

The idea heading for each of the middle paragraphs will usually serve as the topic sentence. We'll have more to say about this type of sentence later, too, and explain what its purpose is and how good ones are created. For the moment, however, let's assume you have started one of the middle paragraphs properly and have reached the specific details of the idea headings. This is where the outline proves to be most useful. The points you want to develop in the paragraph are right before your eyes. Now you can really focus on the sentences—correct ones, interesting ones, colorful ones, varied ones, the best ones you can write.

Your final use of the outline involves a procedure very similar to the one used in writing the beginning paragraph. The only difference is that now you must direct your attention to bringing the composition to a satisfactory conclusion. You take a quick look at your outline once more to remind yourself of the major ideas you talked about. Then you write the final paragraph that ties things together. This is another technique that will soon be explained in greater detail.

Suppose we pause now to examine how a student handled the outline we have just reviewed. As you read the composition, check back to the idea headings and details. Notice how smoothly they have been worked in, and make up your mind now that you will train yourself to do this equally well.

Dating on a Dime

Boys, step this way. If you can't keep up with your girl and are bothered by empty pockets, I'll let you in on a big secret. You can have a good time for a dime!

First you have to sell the idea to your fair lady. That's simple. Get her into a conversation on the material things in life, the silly way people throw their money around. She will soon agree that it takes more brains to have fun without buying it. Then play up the simple things. Discuss the lost arts of walking and talking. If you've done your English homework, give her a few examples from literature. The knockout wallop comes with the unselfish approach. Why not give the folks a night out? By this time, she's hooked.

When the big night arrives, get to her house early. Offer to do the dishes. That impresses the folks and gets rid of them quickly. Once you are alone, get busy.

While you work around the kitchen (she does the dishes, of course), inspect the refrigerator. There may be some odds and ends there that you like. After everything is shipshape, take a walk—from the kitchen to the living room. Sit around, play some records, and talk. If you don't say anything for certain periods of time, that's all right, too. Sometimes actions speak louder than words. If you get hungry again, take another walk—back to the icebox. You'd be surprised how quickly time passes. In fact, the only drawback here is that the folks always get home too early.

But you've had a good time. It hasn't cost you a cent. What about that dime, you say? Oh, you keep it in reserve. Occasionally there's a kid brother around who has to be paid off.

This illustration of a completed unit demonstrates how helpful a good outline can be. It supplies you with the ideas and simultaneously holds the material together. Getting your paragraphs set up becomes almost routine with practice. Once you have decided upon your approach and the number of paragraphs, the rest follows a pattern. If your handling of a topic is to be personalized, you pick the highlights of your experiences related to the subject. Two paragraphs—two highlights; three paragraphs—three highlights, etc. If you plan to express an opinion, you select your best arguments to form your major idea headings. If you want to tell a story, you break it down so that each significant change of time or place becomes a paragraph. If you have a description or explanation in mind, you divide the material into the important aspects or steps, as was done with the dating topic.

Putting down the four or five specific details under the idea headings shouldn't be much of a problem, either. Usually you choose the topic and the ideas that will develop it. If you have chosen properly, you are writing about a subject you know. It is reasonable to expect, then, that the key words or phrases you jot down to remind you of the contents of each paragraph will occur to you practically as fast as you can write them. Even if you have been assigned a single topic about which you know very little, the procedure is still the same. You do some research first. Then you proceed with your selection of your approach, your decision about the number of paragraphs, the idea headings, and the details under them.

To make sure that everything we have said about the outline is clear to you, here are a few more examples prepared and written by students:

OUTLINE EXAMPLE 1

Topic: *The Art of Baby Sitting*

QUESTION I: *How shall I handle the material?* The writer decided to talk about herself as a baby sitter and to tell the story of a typical experience.

QUESTION II: *How many paragraphs do I need?* Since the composition called for 300 words, the writer planned for two body paragraphs.

QUESTION III: *What major ideas will each paragraph develop?* Many things happen in the course of a five or six hour baby sitting session. It was the job of the writer to select the two ideas that would be most interesting to the reader and most thoroughly cover the topic. This is what the outline looked like:

	FEEDING	PUTTING TO BED
SPECIFIC DETAILS	pablum	changing diaper
	first spoonful	loss of pin
	refusal to swallow	refusal to sleep
	dress disaster	screams
	annoyance	picking up

The Composition

My phone rang. It was my charming neighbor who was inquiring whether my services as a baby sitter were available. Since I had been admiring a hat in the store windows for several days, this was an excellent opportunity to get the money to buy it.

I arrived in time for baby's feeding. Her mother gave me instructions before she left, but I wondered about that peculiar look she gave me in addition. I prepared the pablum. Smiling at the child, I pushed a spoonful into her mouth and met no resistance. This was going to be easy. The baby's mouth was full but she made no effort to swallow the food. Was something wrong? The thought had hardly left my mind when, with a hissing sound, the pablum slithered out of baby's mouth and landed in my lap. I might get that hat, I thought, but what about a new dress? The struggle went on until my patience was exhausted. I had to stop before I did things to baby that are against the rules.

It was time for the little dear to be changed and put to bed. Since I was a novice, I left the safety pins nearby. What a mistake! I pinned one side. I started the other—but where was the second pin? Madness almost gripped me. Had baby swallowed it? I was about to drop in a dead faint when I heard a yowl. There, sticking to a chubby little fist was the pin. I hurriedly finished dressing her and dropped her into her crib. I had been told that she went to sleep like an angel. How could she have changed into a monster so fast? She screamed. She kicked. She blasted away until I picked her up. Then it was quiet. We went through this battle about forty times. She won every round.

When mother arrived she found a happy baby pulling merrily away at my hair. I refused an offer of a glass of milk and, clutching the money in my hand, left quite rapidly. Safe at last! Lately I have begun to wonder just how important new hats really are.

OUTLINE EXAMPLE 2

Topic: *Faces in the Subway*

QUESTION I: *How shall I handle the material?* This writer decided to describe an actual ride during which he had the opportunity to study the faces of the other passengers. His approach was to be in the form of a thinking-out-loud report, a sort of soliloquy.

QUESTION II: *How many paragraphs do I need?* Although this assignment also called for 300 words, the writer decided to use three paragraphs in the body because he wanted to establish the setting of his experience first. You will see how this contributed to the mood of the piece.

QUESTION III: *What major ideas will each paragraph develop?* Here the author very cleverly chose to go from the general scene, to faces as a group, and then to one particularly interesting face. Hence his three idea headings:

	THE CAR	FACES	ONE FACE
SPECIFIC DETAILS	people sounds smells	unmoving emotion the look thought	his looks questions war tears

The Composition

The faces in the subway are stamped by the heel of life. Every morning and night I see the faces of sadness, vacant eyes staring at wild "Buy, buy, buy" ads. Of these faces I write.

I stand transfixed, entangled with legs and feet I cannot see. I stare into cavernous nostrils, bottomless ears, gaping mouths—and wait. Wait for what? For anything! I wait for the train to stop rocking and rolling, for a thought to distract me, for the smell of toilet water, halitosis, Pepsodent, Chanel No. 5, alcohol, and hair lotion to disappear. But all these smells linger, hanging close to the roof of the shaking car.

The faces linger, too. They are mostly unmoving faces. At times I detect a quiver of emotion in a pouting lip and I tremble, for this must surely be a madman. No one smiles in the subway. I see a multitude of people standing nose to nose, staring vacantly ahead. Tired faces question each other. Far down in the womb of the city I inspect the faces that inspect my face and the face next to me that inspects the face that inspects my face.

But there must be thought behind those faces. That man! There! He is clean shaven, has a prominent brow and thin lips. Where will he be an hour from now? What will he be doing? Is there some pain gnawing away at his stomach? Does he love someone? Does he know hate? Sorrow? Does he know of mud and blood, and voices in the night crying for mother instead of a medic? When was the last time a tear fell from that blue eye? Was it twenty years ago or last night? Does he know that I am watching him?

They cannot all be sad faces. Behind them there must be a spark of hope, a surge of joy. Surely the heel of life that stamped these faces must be padded with prayers and dreams. Some day I will solve the mystery of these faces in the subway.

OUTLINE EXAMPLE 3

Topic: *Among Relatives I Have Known*

QUESTION I: *How shall I handle the material?* The writer chose an autobiographical approach, selecting various periods in her life and analyzing them as they affected her relations with her subject.

QUESTION II: *How many paragraphs do I need?* This is an excellent example of how a writer uses brief, sharply etched paragraphs instead of the fuller ones that are more common. Ordinarily, two paragraphs in the body would have been sufficient for the length of this composition. But since the author wanted to present insight into several stages of her development, she quite justifiably preferred to skip too much detail and concentrate on quick impressions. Four middle paragraphs, as you will see, were not too many, and, in this instance, were not underdeveloped.

QUESTION III: *What major ideas will each paragraph develop?* The material traces the growth of an attitude and an emotion from childhood to the middle teens. Each period is flashed before your eyes with a detail or two, just enough to create the desired impression. The four idea headings:

	LITTLE GIRL	PIRATE STAGE	GROWING OLDER	RECENTLY
SPECIFIC DETAILS	voice	pirate novels	similarities	effort to understand
	laugh	Lafitte, Blood	selfishness	new insight
	terror	Father's eyes	fear of imitation	contradictions

The Composition

This little masterpiece is going to concern itself with someone I've "known" for a long time, and yet, until just recently, never really knew, in the true sense of the word, at all!

When I was a very little girl, the most awe-inspiring, frightening human being in the world was my father. His booming voice and boisterous laugh invariably sent me scurrying behind any convenient person or chair, whenever he came into sight.

Like all children, I went through many stages. One of them was the development of a tremendous passion for reading pirate novels. My father's swarthy complexion and irregular features constantly had me envisioning him as Jean Lafitte, Captain Blood, or some other daring, swashbuckling brigand. His eyes have never been quite right for a pirate's though! They're brown and very deep and calm, like twin streams in a mid-autumn forest.

As I grew older, I observed that we were too alike in many respects—two selfish, irresponsible, impulsive, quick-tempered scamps who really didn't care what happened to the rest of the world as long as **we** were safe and comfortable. I loved him as one would love a charming, naughty child, but I didn't want to **be** like him. The knowledge that I **was** seemed to create a constantly widening gulf between us.

It's only during the last year that we've made any real attempt at getting to know each other. On my part I've discovered an intriguing, many-faceted personality who can be shrewd and "hard-as-nails" one moment, then gentle and almost child-like in his trust the next. He can tell both sad and ribald stories with equal proficiency. He'll forget something that happened to him yesterday, but be able to recall, down to the smallest detail, an incident that occurred in Moscow, Paris, or New Orleans forty odd years ago.

Yes, we've become friends . . . good friends. I only wish my mother had lived to see it. It would have made her very happy.

Although each of the outlines you just reviewed was prepared for a 300 word composition, the number of middle paragraphs varied. This was done to illustrate to you the flexibility of the outline technique. The arrangement in Example 1, however, is to be regarded as typical and the one you should use most frequently. For the usual high school composition (250–300 words), stay with the standard paragraph breakdown: a beginning paragraph (50–75 words), two middle paragraphs (about 100 words each), and a final paragraph (50–75 words). Try variations only after you have begun to feel confident in your use of the four paragraph composition.

Of course, you may be in a school where a 500–750 word composition is the normal thing, or you may be required to prepare a 1500 word term essay on occasion. What do you do? That's right. You plan for more middle paragraphs. You may want to increase the size of the paragraphs by 25–50 words each, but this simply means the addition of a few more details under the idea headings for the paragraphs and the writing of an extra two or three sentences. The valuable thing about learning to plan your paragraphs in terms of the number of words required is that you develop the ability to handle any composition assignment regardless of its size. It's very much like those sweaters the women in your household (or you yourself) knit. A bigger size makes little difference. All it needs is a little more time and some extra wool. The basic pattern remains the same.

Here are some exercises that will test your understanding of the outlining principles we have been discussing. You will find the answers at the end of this section.

EXERCISES

1. You have been asked to write 300 words on "Teenage Drivers." Which of the following ways of handling the material would probably produce the most interesting paragraphs for your composition? Place a check in the space provided before your choice:

_____ a. A discussion of good and bad teenage drivers

_____ b. The history of granting licenses to people under 21

_____ c. What adults think of teenage drivers

_____ d. Why you consider yourself or a friend a superior driver to many adults

_____ e. The laws of your state affecting all teenage drivers

2. Below are three pairs of outlines. In each example decide which outline is superior because the idea headings indicate that the topic has been sensibly narrowed down and the details have been made more specific. Place a check in the space before the letter of your choice:

Topic: *Modern Medical Miracles*

_____ OUTLINE A

U.S.A.	Europe
East	Russia
Midwest	England
Far West	France
South	Italy

_____ OUTLINE B

Salk Vaccine	Heart Surgery
polio threat	TV demonstration
injection series	cutting through layers
reduction of victims	sewing tissues
fourth shot	sewing layers back

Topic: *Part Time Jobs*

——————— **OUTLINE A**

My Job	Why I Like It
tailor shop	extra money
preparing tickets	saving for college
bicycle deliveries	outdoors, meeting people
collections, tips	sense of responsibility

——————— **OUTLINE B**

Kinds of Jobs	Employment Laws
neighborhood	causes for enactment
business district	age requirements
messenger service	number of hours
delivery jobs	compensation

Topic: *A Memorable Football Game*

——————— **OUTLINE A**

Team Records	The Game
Home team	First quarter
Visitors	Second quarter
League standings	Third quarter
Coaches, players	Fourth quarter

——————— **OUTLINE B**

The Crowd And I	The Key Play
Our spirit	Score
Banners, food	Tense moment
Keeping warm	The end run
Cheers	Tearing down goalposts

3. Below are pairs of idea headings which represent the material that might go into one of the middle paragraphs of the composition on the topic. Select the ones which are superior because the details listed are more specific. Again place a check in the space provided before your choice:

Topic: *TV Westerns*

_____CHARACTERISTICS A	_____CHARACTERISTICS B
Setting	Main street, bar
Characters	Fast gun, challenge
Story	Marshal, villain
Climax	Slow walk, draw

Topic: *Sunday at Home*

_____MORNING A	_____MORNING B
Sleep	No alarm clock
Breakfast	Cereal, bacon, eggs
Reading	Sunday comics
Chores	Weekly room cleanup

Topic: *Keeping Teachers Happy*

_____ASSIGNMENTS A	_____ASSIGNMENTS B
After supper	When to do
Outline, review	How
Library sources	Extra work
Typewriter, pictures	The dressup

ANSWERS

1. d. Approaches *b* and *e* would probably be very boring to your readers or listeners; they have heard *c* before; *a* would sound as if you were preaching at them; *d* makes them feel you are their champion and one of them. Half the battle is getting the audience on your side.

2. "Modern Medical Miracles"—Outline B is definitely supe-

rior. It would be impossible to cover adequately the medical progress of two continents, whereas concentrating on two examples is much more reasonable. The details, too, are much more specific in the second outline.

"Part Time Jobs"—Outline A is better. The topic has been sensibly narrowed down, the details are more specific, and the approach is personalized.

"A Memorable Football Game"—Outline B is clearly superior. Nothing is duller than the review of a game in detail. Writing about sports is much more difficult than many students realize. Only by concentrating on highlights and human interest aspects can the telling of an athletic contest be made interesting.

3. "TV Westerns"—B
   "Sunday at Home"—B
   "Keeping Teachers Happy"—A

How Are Good Paragraphs Constructed?

Let's see how far you have progressed.
You now know how to:

§ select a topic that suits you
§ narrow it down in terms of the required words
§ try to take an original, unusual approach
§ plan an appropriate number of paragraphs
§ prepare idea headings for the middle paragraphs
§ list specific details under the headings

If you have mastered these techniques, you have hurdled the first big obstacle—knowing what to do *before* you begin to write. But, important as they are, these are only the preliminary steps. The final judgment of your work will be based upon how well you write the composition. This means we must now turn to the *how's* of the writing job itself.

I. PARAGRAPH STRUCTURE

Any discussion of writing improvement must begin with the paragraph because anybody who can learn to write a good paragraph can be taught to write well. Let these words sink in for a moment. They represent the most significant statement that can be made about the writing process and their basic truth is recognized by every authority in this field. There is no question about it. The paragraph is the key to all writing. It is the prime material with which you build compositions and, when the occasion demands it, longer essays, chapters, whole books. That's why it is essential that we take a long, close look at how good paragraphs are constructed.

In a recent television production of W. Somerset Maugham's *The Moon and Sixpence* appeared this remarkably clear definition of a sentence: "words put together in a definite order to give meaning to man's thoughts." You accept this as valid because you are accustomed by now to thinking of a sentence as being a single unit of expression, making sense independently when it stands alone and collectively when it appears with other sentences. To get the proper perspective of a paragraph you must look upon it, too, as a single unit. Instead of words it contains *sentences* which are put together to give meaning to man's *ideas* rather than single thoughts. There you have the core of the relationship between sentences and paragraphs. One expresses a single thought, the other a main idea toward which a number of thoughts point. Both, however, have basically the same construction.

Observe this:

Snow fell.

Despite its bareness and simplicity, this sentence states a fact, expresses a thought, makes sense. It contains a subject (what is being talked about) and a verb (that which helps us say something about the subject). If we wanted to enrich the meaning of this sentence and give it a more finished appearance, we might add some modifiers, thus:

The heavy snow fell steadily.

Although we have given a little more substance to the sentence, it is still a single thought, and it has its limitations as such. It cannot be stretched out indefinitely and therefore cannot by itself express in adequate detail what a writer has in mind when he wants to expand a thought. Other sentences must be added so that the thought blossoms into an idea, well-developed and broadened in scope—something like this:

> The heavy snow fell steadily. Rooftops soon were covered with the blanket-like whiteness that gives a clean, fresh look to a city. Trees began to sag beneath the weight of the clinging snow and reached long arms to the ground. Pavements and roadways became fused into one broad expanse and drifts began to pile up in doorways. Cars moved slowly, struggling in the slippery going as their spinning tires whined piercingly. Pedestrians, their faces hidden behind upturned collars, plodded along, dragging their feet as if they were wading through surf. Lights appeared in the gathering darkness. Still the snow fell—undisturbed, relentless, enveloping.

Now we have a paragraph. What has happened to the original sentence? It has become the indicator of the main idea (topic sentence), toward which all the other sentences point. Whereas a subject, a verb, and a few modifiers were enough to express the thought of the sentence, the paragraph requires a whole sentence to suggest the topic and a series of sentences to develop it. Note, however, that the basic pattern of these two units of expression is still maintained:

	Sentence	=	*Paragraph*
What are we talking about?	= Subject	=	Topic Sentence
What are we saying about it?	= Verb	=	Related Sentences
What are the finishing touches?	= Modifiers	=	Concluding Sentence

You can see why we say that when you write a good paragraph you do not just tack one sentence onto another, but you start with a thought and then expand it into an idea. To put it another way, we can return to our discussion of the outline. The idea heading becomes the topic sentence and the details become the related or supporting sentences. In fact, it should be possible theoretically to expand any sentence into a paragraph. We'll do that with some very ordinary sentences to drive home the point that it should be possible to reduce every well-constructed paragraph to a single core sentence.

Sentence

I'm going home.

Paragraph

I'm going home. I've been working hard lately and I'm very tired. Besides, it's getting late and it will be an hour before I get home. You won't mind, I'm sure. The party can go on without me. Say "good-by" to the others for me.

Sentence

Did you call me yesterday?

Paragraph

Did you call me yesterday? I was taking a shower when I heard the phone ring. Although I dashed out as quickly as I could, I didn't make it. Then I remembered that you had told me you would be in touch with me. Was it you?

Sentence

That was quite a crash!

Paragraph

That was quite a crash! I'll never know what makes people drive like maniacs on wet pavement. They see pictures about accidents, read grisly accounts of them in newspapers, but don't seem to understand that it can happen to them, too. I suppose they're convinced when they wind up like this.

There you are. It's really quite simple when you get the idea. Experiment with this concept until you can actually feel the unity that should exist in every paragraph. Take commonplace expressions like "I will not," "Don't talk to me," and "What time is it?" and try adding four or five sentences, enough to prove that you can expand a thought into an idea. After you have finished, check each paragraph to make sure it has a clearly defined topic sentence and related ones as well. We'll have more to say about the concluding sentence later, so that it is not being listed as an absolute requirement at the moment.

Now let's examine the basic elements of a paragraph, one by one, in order to help you learn the most effective ways of forming each.

A. *The Topic Sentence*

1. *Position:* You would expect the key sentence of a paragraph, toward which all others point, to appear at the very beginning, and it usually does. However, many writers place it elsewhere occasionally to give variety to their work or to create a particular effect in the paragraph. The latter reason for shifting the position of the topic sentence occurs most frequently when the writer is attempting to build up toward a climax. He may want to save the punch for the end, increase the suspense, and so may place the topic sentence last. At other times it may come in the middle of the paragraph if the purpose is to lead up to and away from it to create a feeling of balance. Here are some examples taken from student compositions. The topic sentence has been printed in **boldface** in each case.

a. Beginning

(This was the second paragraph of a composition on "Political Indifference in the United States.")

The American is exposed to windy assurances that there is nothing to worry about and is convinced of just that. *It seems to be typical of twentieth century man that if he makes himself believe something* it will come true. He is sure that problems arising in Europe, Asia, and Latin America are no concern of ours. He is so certain of the security of our position in the world picture that he withdraws into a little cocoon to play with all the toys our industry has made it possible for him to possess. His automobiles, refrigerators, or lawn mowers become more important to him than intercontinental missiles or H-bombs. Leave everything to the State Department, says he.

b. Middle

(This was the third paragraph of a composition on "My Kid Sister.")

She is good. She is good to her family, better to her friends, and best to herself. She is shrewd. She is shrewd with her teachers, shrewder with her friends, and shrewdest with me. **Oh, she has many admirable characteristics.** She is bright and alert. She is bright and alert with younger children, she is brighter and more alert with guests, and she is brightest and most alert with boys. Yes, she is like a human violin, responding sensitively to the touch of circumstance.

c. End

(This was the third paragraph of a composition on "Thoughts on a Rainy Day.")

Now the dark shapes are no longer friendly, but ominous and frightening. They mingle furiously with one another until we can't distinguish between them. It is impossible to tell which of the surging shadows has been cast by the brooding clouds and which by the open umbrellas clutched tightly by hurrying passersby. We become confused and troubled as are the ghosts we are creating. Their blackness whispers evilly of disaster, tears, and death. **We are depressed.**

2. Types: In addition to shifting its position from time to time, you can also vary your handling of the topic sentence by changing its form or impact. The great majority of your topic sentences will, of course, be rather direct suggestions or summaries of the contents of the paragraph. But, remembering that you must constantly work to catch the reader's interest, you will want to try the novel approach as often as you can. These are some types that have been used successfully by other students.

a. Change the pace with a very brief, compact sentence. Look back at the paragraph above that ends with "We are depressed." A three or four word sentence in a descriptive paragraph can be very effective, especially if it is thrown into a collection of longer sentences. It also goes well in a narrative paragraph when you wish to indicate a sudden turn of events.

b. Ask a question sometimes. If your material is personal and you wish to give it a conversational tone, a question will draw the reader into the discussion. It can be used with equally good effect when you are expressing an opinion or when you are attempting to inject humor into a factual paragraph. For example, in the following, taken from a composition on "Our Forty-ninth State," observe how the question helps set the mood:

> What do you suppose is the scarcest item in Alaska? Women! Men who run from the States to escape them find that the shortage is a serious problem. They can't find enough of the ladies to avoid. For the young woman back home, the opportunities in this land, devoid of ruffled curtains and home-baked apple pie, are readily imaginable. The ratio of males to females up thar' is approximately 25 to 1. Surely any bright, husbandless girl cannot fail to see the desperate situation behind such a statistic and the limitless horizon beyond it.

c. Launch a surprise attack! This is a sure attention-getter. An unexpected bit of information or an unorthodox approach, even if it shocks the reader, appeals to his curiosity irresistibly. I recall one student, delivering an oral composition on cheating, who started one of his paragraphs with this sentence: "We are nothing but a pack of thieves!" Moreover, I am sure you will agree that this arresting device added to the interest of the following paragraph taken from a composition on "Bringing Up Mother":

> I hate mothers. When you're little, they fondle and caress you. They feed you and watch over you to make sure you don't break your silly, little neck. They make you feel wanted. Then you get older and you start pushing them away. They want to share their experiences with you, but you know better. You battle them right down the line. One day you grow up. Suddenly, you discover how right they've been. I hate anybody who makes me feel ashamed and guilty.

Other types of unusual topic sentences will occur to you as you continue to make a conscious effort to pep up your paragraphs from beginning to end. Perhaps you will want to use a quotation to start things off, if it fits. Remember now, *if it fits!* Nothing is worse than ramming a familiar line or two into a paragraph despite its complete irrelevancy to the topic at hand. However, if it is apt, a quotation can give style to almost any type of material. Then again, you may want to try the poetic touch on occasion, something like the line Alfred Noyes used to begin one of his stanzas in "The Highwayman":

> *"Tlot-tlot,* in the frosty silence! *Tlot-tlot,* in the echoing night!"

Imitating sound and motion, particularly in a narrative, fires the imagination. Or you may decide to use a bit of dialogue to get your main idea started or a series of interjections, as one student did in a composition on "Problems of a Senior":

> "Marks! Marks! Marks! They dance before my eyes!"

The main thing is to mix up your attack, as the football phrase goes, and you will gain an important aid in sustaining interest in your writing. Let your topic sentence fulfill its dual purpose: suggest the contents of the paragraph, create a desire in the reader to go on.

B. *The Related Sentences*

These sentences represent the core of the paragraph. They point toward the topic sentence and develop the main idea. They are formed from the details that you have inserted under the idea headings in your outline. And this is the clue to making related sentences effective. Details!

The heart of your paragraph must be specific. It must take its cue from the topic sentence and feel both *limited by it* and *obligated to it*. Let's make this point a little clearer. Suppose you started a paragraph with this topic sentence:

A walk in the rain is not for me.

You would be expected to *limit* your material to a walk in the rain, not just any walk at any time. Moreover, you would be *obligated* to offer reasons why such a walk is not for you. It's a kind of proof that your suggested main idea is in fact what it pretends to be. It is also a means of preventing rambling, disconnected thinking.

Let's try it again. Your topic sentence is:

Building a television set from a kit is easier than you think.

You would be *limited* to television sets (not boats, radios, or cabinets) and *obligated* to present the various steps in such a way as to prove that the job is easy.

Again, you open with:

Work camps may be one of the answers to juvenile delinquency.

In this paragraph you could talk only about work camps and you would be expected to offer evidence that they have worked in the past or are being tried successfully at the time you are writing about them.

If your related sentences fail to stay within the limits set by the topic sentence and fulfill their obligation to it, you disappoint your reader. He feels cheated, may become confused, and reacts by losing interest in what you have written. Don't let this happen in your compositions.

Put in enough details to make every paragraph do what you want it to do. *Details* lead to interest. *Details* increase understanding. *Details* make your ideas acceptable, your opinions worth while, your explanations clear, your stories enjoyable, your descriptions picturesque, and your total writing effort superior.

Now, what we call details come in many disguises, and it doesn't matter much what their names are so long as you use them. Whether they are referred to as facts or statistics (to support an argument), examples or illustrations (to clarify an explanation), their primary function is, as we have stressed, to develop the topic sentence specifically. We are going to examine some of the more commonly used detail patterns. In your next composition, try out one or two of the suggestions that are new to you. Keep on testing all of them and you will soon get the feel of when it is appropriate to use a particular pattern in a paragraph. The examples have been taken from student compositions accepted for publication in the school literary magazine.

1. *Narrative Sequence:* When you tell a story in one of your paragraphs, the best way to present the details is chronologically, that is, in the order of time. Tell what happened first, second, and so on. When possible, try to group the details around some central point of focus so that the paragraph has unity. Get everything in—how you felt, what the background looked like, who was there. Here's how Tom Kelly did it in one of the paragraphs he wrote in which he pretended he was the inventor of the automobile:

> *I saw his hand drop. My foot touched the accelerator. The machine began to vibrate and the last mechanic jumped aside. With a tremendous shudder, we moved forward, slowly at first, but faster and faster and faster. I glanced at the speedometer, blinked, and had to look again. It was incredible, impossible, but after a quick*

check of the instruments I knew that the speedometer
was right. I was sure that my machine was a success. I
had proven that man could go as fast as he had dreamed.
I was traveling at 20 miles an hour. The automobile was
now a reality, and I was the first to drive it.

Did you notice the topic sentence at the end? Do you see
how even in a narrative paragraph, it helps to tie things together? Did you observe how the details, given bit by bit,
increased the suspense and sustained the interest?

2. Dialogue: Another effective way of presenting details in
a story is to let the characters talk and record their conversation. It makes the material sound alive and gives it a novel
touch. Here's a paragraph taken from Harold Haicken's piece
on a visit with his uncle who had just lost his wife:

> As we passed the second cornfield on Old Man Bry-
> er's place, he turned to me:
> "Remember how ya aunt use ta make apple pie?"
> "Yeh, I remember, Unk."
> "She made 'em good, eh?"
> "Yeh, Unk."
> "There's a deer, Pete! Ta ya left! Go ahead, you take
> it."
> "I see it!" I fired twice.
> "Ya missed. But I think the car jerked. Take the
> wheel. I'll get 'im." He fired, once.
> "Nice shot, Unk."
> "Thanks, but ya woulda got 'im if the car hadn't a
> jerked. Now I gotta skin it thin. Ya Aunt Lil use ta do
> that. I never had ta do it alone."

Did you see how well the dialogue carried the story, drew
a sympathetic picture of the uncle, and subtly indicated the
boy's reticence in the face of his uncle's grief? Did you notice
how the subject of the aunt is introduced early and how the
middle of the dialogue, even though it seems to concern itself with hunting, is basically pointing toward further development of the central idea, regret over the passing of a
loved one? You realize, of course, that in dialogue you are

permitted liberties with the language because you want to report faithfully how the characters talked so that their true identity is maintained.

3. Sense Impressions: When you write a descriptive paragraph in one of your compositions, your details must be presented in such a way that they create a picture in the mind of the reader. This means that you must try to stimulate as many of his senses as possible—sight, hearing, taste, smell, touch. A paragraph taken from Ellen Rudnick's story of a Hungarian child is a good example of this technique:

> Wide awake now, she remembered that she was alone. The child turned from the window and faced the staring cupboards. She found a piece of bread—the crust was hard—and, flicking off a caraway seed, she slowly munched it. As she aimlessly strolled about, her foot caught in the playthings which had occupied her before. Her little girl's body tumbled over and fell flatly to the floor. The piece of bread bounded out of her hands and flew into a dark corner to sit near a wizened pair of red shoes. Slowly she raised herself and stared at the scraped knee. Only the sound of a rolling spool of thread was heard. She watched small drops of blood ooze out of the scratched area, and suddenly she began to sob—lonely, heart-rending moans that rose from the very depths of the thin little chest. The cries shuddered through the misty-cold air and shook from wall to wall. She sobbed for gentle arms about her; for the sweetness and warmth of a mother.

Did you notice how the first and last sentences act as a framework for the central idea of the paragraph? Did you sense the appeal to your sight, sense of touch, your hearing, even taste (the crust of bread)? The faintly suggested smell in "misty-cold air"? Do you realize that these colorful details are, for the most part, presented in words that are very simple? Do you agree that you don't have to have a big vocabulary to describe a scene effectively?

4. *Comparison or Contrast:* If you were trying to explain what snow is to someone who had never seen it, you would have difficulty describing it directly. But if you talked about tiny pieces of cotton floating in the air, or suggested the feel of crushed ice, or mentioned the way down and feathers would settle on the floor of a room if a pillow were to burst open, you would have a better chance of making yourself clear. In a similar way, if you wanted to give a picture of the peace and quiet of a country road, you could sharpen the impression by indicating how different it is from a busy, traffic-choked main street. In one instance, *comparison,* you would be using what is familiar to your reader to develop an idea that was less familiar. In the other, *contrast,* you would be presenting an opposite concept so that your basic idea would stand out more vividly. In a piece on "You Can Have It," Eddie Martin developed one of the topic sentences we mentioned earlier into an effective body paragraph by using a combination of the comparison and contrast techniques:

> *A walk in the rain is not for me. I can't imagine why anyone would prefer soggy shoes, wet socks, and clammy clothing to a big, soft arm chair, a crackling fire, and a puzzling Perry Mason thriller. Who wouldn't trade a spattered nose and tightly closed lips for a mouth munching contentedly on peanuts and chocolate bars? I'm not a duck, I don't believe jackets are water repellent, and I'd rather take a shower without my clothes on. Sloshing about in puddles is for traffic cops and night watchmen. I like to do my walking when I can wiggle my bare toes in a thick, plushy carpet.*

Did you see how effective this device is for argumentative as well as descriptive and narrative paragraphs? Were you aware of the author's use of the comparison and contrast details in a balanced way so that each set heightened the effect of the other? Again, did you notice how the pictures are created by colorful, but simple, words?

5. *Evidence or Proof:* Whenever you write on a subject that calls for an opinion, explanation, or evaluation, you cannot expect your reader to accept what you say unless you support your statements with concrete evidence or proof. Generalities are all right at the beginning or end of paragraphs, but they become meaningful only when the material in between is specific. Get into the habit of cross-examining yourself. Don't leave doubts in the mind of your reader. Make the point. Then prove it.

Use *statistics* if you are dealing with numbers or quantities. Unless you are prepared to tell exactly how much or how many, you should not start a paragraph with a sentence like "Youthful crime is increasing" or "People are beginning to move back to the cities." If you haven't the facts at hand, look them up.

Use *quotations* if you want to add someone else's opinion to bolster your own. For instance, rather than make vague references to what some of your friends think about blind dates, quote them directly. Another person's actual words, especially if he is an authority, can often be much more convincing than your own.

Use *examples* or *illustrations* to clinch a point. It is the kind of repetition that is appreciated by a reader. It resolves his doubts and clarifies his own thinking on the ideas you have presented. Wouldn't you find it annoying if many of the suggestions made in this book were not illustrated by sample paragraphs and compositions? Think back to that paragraph written by a student about her younger sister who was "good to her family, better to her friends, and best to herself." Don't you agree that these statements could have been improved with a few examples of the behavior of the child?

Use *references* if you have a point of view that is shared by prominent people or authors. Give their names and summarize what they believe, and your own attitudes will command more respect. Suppose you are in favor of letting eighteen-year-olds vote. Perhaps a popular local citizen, a political figure, or a well known magazine writer agrees with you. Use this evidence; it is excellent support for your arguments. In short, back up what you have to say on a subject by relating it to the information you accumulate through reading, listening, and observing.

Here is a composition written on "American Schools, Wake Up!" Whether you agree with the conclusions or not, you will have to admit that an effort has been made to employ the factual approach so that each point seems to be supported by evidence or proof:

Are the Russians doing a better job in their schools than we are? Are they surpassing us in space research because their graduates have superior backgrounds and training? It would seem so, judging from some of the latest reports on the subject.

Some Americans are certainly not happy about the situation. A former principal of a science high school recently spoke about our "losing a greater battle than Pearl Harbor" in this educational race. An admiral criticized the softness of our courses of study before a nationwide audience. An M.I.T. professor had a college entrance examination used by the Russians translated into English and then gave it to some of his students. All freshmen failed, a few sophomores passed, and only juniors or better could handle the test satisfactorily. These are rather ominous straws in the wind.

According to a survey reported in "The New York Times," the Russian high school graduate is better educated in academic subjects at the end of his ten years of schooling than is his American counterpart at the end of twelve. A boy fresh out of a Moscow secondary school has taken courses in physics and biology for five years, chemistry for four years, astronomy for one year, and mathematics for ten years. This, of course, includes elementary training as well. In the United States, fewer than one third of the high school graduates have taken a year of chemistry, only one fourth have taken physics, and about one seventh have had advanced mathematics. In the Soviet Union algebra and geometry begin in the sixth grade, here in the ninth; trigonometry and calculus start there in the ninth and tenth grades, here sometimes not until college; there natural science begins in the fourth grade, here usually in the ninth. They start earlier and get more.

Russian students are marked on a point system. If one has attained an average of five, the highest, and permits his work to drop to a four, he must climb back up again. Otherwise he may find himself in the "Labor Reserve." This is a school where one learns how to work in the mines, transportation, or other menial occupations. American students can repeat if they fail and don't get thrown out of school if their averages drop. Our psychologists tell us it is bad to punish a child for getting a poor grade.

What are we going to do? Are we just going to stand by while Russia becomes the number one nation and we fall into second place? We must act now to improve our schools or we'll wake up some morning to find Ivan in control of the world.

Did you notice that the entire composition, in addition to following the factual approach, was also a running comparison? Isn't it difficult to shrug off statistics, quotations, and references? Are you studying the topic sentences and noticing how they set up the paragraphs?

6. *Emotional Reactions:* You recall that you were advised to write about yourself as often as you can, to personalize. When you use material from your own experiences, you are you own best authority. You were there! At such times, cold facts are not nearly as important as the glimpses you permit the reader into your inner self. In a story or a description, the final note of realism is introduced when you tell how you *felt* about the experience. Don't be afraid to let go. Your perfectly natural feelings of self-consciousness have no place in writing that pretends to be alive and interesting. You soon lose interest in a person who doesn't let you get to know him, and a composition that is just a matter-of-fact summary of a personal episode also fails to challenge attention.

Observe how Francine Brecher's frankness about her emotions made the following paragraph, taken from her account of a lost pet, so appealing to the sympathies of the reader:

I ran to the cottage and into my bedroom. I wept un-
controllably and spoke to my dog as though she were human. I made a move to take the puppy from her, only
to be stopped by an angry paw and gnashing teeth. By
this time, my mother had entered the room and, very
strategically, we removed the little dead puppy. I lost
myself completely in my grief. I snatched the puppy and,
quite foolishly, proceeded to administer artificial respiration. With gentleness and understanding, my mother
took the creature from me. We placed it into a potato
sack and walked to the corn field.

Would you be ashamed to be so open about your emotions? Wasn't that touch about the artificial respiration worth
a thousand words on how the grief-stricken girl felt?

This survey of detail patterns does more than tell you how
to develop the middle of a paragraph. It re-emphasizes the
big points we have made so far:

The best way to develop the topic sentence is to use details.

The best way to make sure you will use enough details is
to get into the habit of preparing an outline.

These are your guarantees of good paragraph structure
ALL THE WAY THROUGH!

C. The Concluding Sentence

You have been told several times now that somewhere in
a paragraph there ought to be what, for the sake of a label,
we call a *topic sentence,* which suggests the contents and
toward which all the related sentences point. This structural
design might be considered the minimum essential of a good
paragraph. Your use of a *concluding sentence,* however, need
not be quite as consistent.

There will be paragraphs for which you will find it impossible or undesirable to use a concluding sentence. For example, when the topic sentence comes last, as in several previous sample paragraphs, you will simply not have room to

write anything else. Or, in a narrative piece, you may not want to interrupt the suspense or the flow of action by stopping to summarize what has been said. This is particularly true when the paragraphs are rather short and a concluding sentence would really be an intrusion, as in the following:

> Arise! . . . Arise! . . . The cry of the people sounds weaker. . . . The guard's voice is hollow in the morning air. Standing up, I brush the bits of straw from my clothes.
> The door creaks; it isn't opened often. The guard is not singing now. He leads the way past doors closed tight. Does he really know the way . . . does anyone?
> The wagon rolls over the roughly paved street. How many cobble stones are there in the Boulevard? The walls are of faces now. The people wait.
> I am lifted from the wagon and down to the street. I cannot count the steps up to the platform. There are too many.

Did you notice that only in the first of the paragraphs quoted did a concluding sentence seem natural and useful?

Don't get the impression that a concluding sentence is rarely used. When you can fit one in to good advantage, and this is most of the time, you should. It ties the thoughts together, like a string around a package. It adds a finishing touch, like icing on a cake. It is a signal to the reader that you have completed your discussion of a main idea. What is perhaps most important, it prepares the way for the next paragraph.

Here are some of the more popular types of concluding sentences used by writers. In each of the sample paragraphs, the concluding sentence will be printed in **boldface** type.

1. *Standard:* The usual way a paragraph is brought to a successful close is by, in effect, a restatement of the topic sentence. It summarizes the main idea, thus fulfilling the primary purpose of a concluding sentence. Observe:

The anticipation yesterday was her greatest thrill. As she rushed to the beauty parlor for her wash, set, and manicure, she was sure that no one had ever known greater pleasure. She remembered reaching home, gulping her milk and cookies, dressing quickly. Sure enough, just as she was applying the finishing touches, the doorbell rang. She rushed downstairs and gaily tossed her glance at the mirror on the first landing. Everything was perfect! **She knew then that never again would she have such a feeling of anticipation and exhilaration, for this was a day like no other in the life of a girl who had just turned sixteen.**

Do you see how the last sentence both summarizes the central idea of the paragraph and enlarges upon the topic sentence? Of course, the paragraph could have ended with "Everything was perfect!" But it wasn't how the girl looked that was the main point. It was how she felt that needed emphasizing, and the concluding sentence did just that.

2. Short Sentence: You have doubtless realized by now that the unusually short sentence is a handy device to have around. It can be used effectively, as a change, anywhere in the paragraph. As a concluding sentence, its three or four words can help to bring the main idea into sharp focus:

(This was taken from a piece on an attempt at horseback riding. Prior to this moment, the writer had been trying to calm the beast by talking to it.)

People are still wondering how it happened. Some suspect that the horse was used to the long years of lazing around the stable and wanted to get back to his wife and children. Others maintain that he could put up no longer with my rhetoric. Whatever the reason, it still remains that the horse turned his nose in the direction of his home, and in this direction he bolted post haste. He stopped me in mid-sentence. The world raced past me, a fantastic fairyland of greens and browns and wind and sun. I said a small prayer into the horse's left ear (which was not as difficult as it sounds for I was sitting on his neck at this time) and the beast must have been a thoughtful old darling because he stopped, short. **I did not.**

Did you see how dramatically the few words at the end complete the picture? Did you notice, too, how the suspense introduced by the topic sentence is maintained to the last sentence and how the abruptness of the horse's action is matched by the size of the sentence. A longer one here would have spoiled the effect, wouldn't it?

3. *Foreshadowing*: Sometimes you may find it desirable to end one paragraph by referring partly to what has preceded and partly to what is ahead:

> It had begun on a cold, misty night not too long ago. The soldier had lain trembling in his bed of earth, whispering a prayer, hoping it would penetrate the murky clouds above him. He had prayed that what they had said was not true. There would be no trouble tonight. There would be no bursting of shells, no enemy advance, no fighting . . . no dying. He was alone and afraid. It was hard for him to pull a warm thought out of the cold night air. The hours had passed slowly, painfully. **No break in the sky had appeared; no light had shone upon the world.**
> And then there was light; the light of shells exploding in the distance, the light of shells exploding everywhere. . . .

Did you notice how the first part of the concluding sentence went back to the topic sentence, and how the second part went forward to the beginning of the next paragraph? Do you understand why it is called *foreshadowing*—casting its shadow before it, as does this concluding sentence, to suggest what is to follow?

There are other forms concluding sentences can take. Almost any kind of sentence you can think of can be worked in at the end of a paragraph. A question can be striking at times, as you may have noticed in the piece beginning with

"Arise! . . . Arise! . . ." An explosive expression like "Well!" or "Really!" has merit on occasion, especially when it summarizes how you feel about what you have said in the paragraph. A quotation can effectively point up the main idea, if you believe that some authoritative source is needed to support your conclusion.

Use whatever seems to fit the contents of the paragraph. As with all other aspects of writing, the main thing is to try to be original. And if a concluding sentence doesn't appear to be desirable at the end of a paragraph, don't force one in. Leave it out when it interferes. Put it in when it helps.

At this point you should stop reading ahead and go back over the entire section on how a good paragraph is constructed. Get the over-all view of how the basic unity and coherence of a paragraph are derived from the topic sentence, the related sentences, and the concluding sentence. Get this clear in your mind so that you will be ready for the special kinds of paragraphs we will now discuss—those that begin and those that end compositions of three or more paragraphs.

Bearing in mind what you have learned about the structure of a single paragraph, you can now turn your attention to a larger piece of writing which involves a series of paragraphs. In what way will the basic design of the longer composition differ from that of the short one? Actually, only in length. You still need a beginning, middle, and end.

Do you remember what we said about the paragraph's being a blown up sentence: the subject of one becoming the topic sentence of the other, the verb becoming the related sentences, and the modifiers becoming the concluding sentence? Well, the longer composition merely carries this idea one step further. Now the picture looks like this:

PARAGRAPH	=	LONGER COMPOSITION
Topic sentence	=	Beginning (Introductory) Paragraph
Related Sentences	=	Middle (Body) Paragraphs
Concluding Sentence	=	Ending (Concluding) Paragraph

Just as the main job of the topic sentence is to create interest and suggest the contents of the paragraph, so the purpose of the beginning paragraph is to get the composition off to an interesting start and to give the reader some idea of what the rest of the paragraphs will talk about. Similarly, the middle paragraphs point toward the introduction, and the concluding paragraph ties all the ideas together. Everything else, except for the length, is the same, too. There are different ways of beginning and ending compositions, at least as many as there are for varying the form of the topic and concluding sentences. And this is what we are going to examine in the next phase of our study of composition techniques.

One point you must not overlook. We will not give separate attention to middle paragraphs. We already have done that. Every word you read about the structure of a paragraph was meant to teach you how to write a good middle paragraph. It is only the beginning and ending paragraphs that have certain qualities of their own that need further discussion.

II. BEGINNING PARAGRAPHS

Everyone knows how important a first impression is, whether in a job interview, a talk with a college dean of admissions, or an introduction to a guest at a social gathering. It is somewhat of a trial period for two people who have the opportunity to size each other up and decide how well they are going to get along. The initial few minutes of such a meeting sometimes determines what the entire future relationship will be.

In the beginning of a composition, you are meeting your reader for the first time. If you have prepared an outline for the middle of the composition, you already have planned the main ideas that will develop the topic. Your immediate concern, therefore, is not with *what* you are going to say but with *how to get it started*. You want to make such a good first impression that the reader will become interested immediately and will be anxious to continue with what you have written. To accomplish this purpose, you must make every effort to launch your material in the most attractive way you can.

First, let's consider what you should not do! One certain way to create prompt boredom is to start with something like "I am going to write about . . ." You insult the reader's intelligence if you try to lead him by the nose into your subject. Let him figure the thing out for himself. Don't warn him that you are going to be tiresome.

Another undesirable method of beginning a composition is to write a single sentence that baldly announces the topic, such as "There are several reasons why I enjoy fishing." Is there even one reason why a reader should be interested in an approach that is uninspired, much too abrupt, and about as exciting as a page in a telephone directory? Such a sentence might conceivably do for a single paragraph, but not for a composition of some length.

There's something else you should avoid doing. Don't "come in out of left field." Don't waste time and space by leading up to your subject through a jungle of irrelevancies. Introductions are supposed to get you started, not to lay down a smoke screen. For instance, this is bad:

> When our forefathers landed on Plymouth Rock, they offered a prayer of thanks that they had come to a land where freedom was theirs for the asking. They pledged themselves to respect the rights and beliefs of others. Down through the ages, this has been the guiding principle of our great country. If this is so, why aren't teenagers given more freedom by their parents?

What has Plymouth Rock got to do with the rights of teenagers? Be interesting, get to the point, and don't take a trip around the moon before you do!

Good beginning paragraphs are not accidental, nor do they depend upon "gimmicks" or trick devices for their effectiveness. They are thoughtfully prepared by successful writers and deliberately designed so that they fit the tone of the rest of the paragraphs. If your composition is going to be written in a light, humorous, very informal vein, you must keep your introduction in the same mood; if you are planning to present serious arguments, you must begin in such a way that the reader will take you seriously from the very first word.

All this means that it is impossible to suggest any one way to begin all compositions. So much depends upon your topic, the nature of the contents, and your approach. However, the problem of getting off to a good start can be solved more easily if you become familiar with certain types of opening paragraphs that appear frequently in superior writing efforts, by both students and professionals. In this way you can provide yourself with a choice and avoid beginning every composition in the same old manner, as so very often happens.

A. Narrative

It is here that students should most decidedly follow the lead of professional writers. Recently I compared the opening paragraphs of several hundred student compositions with those found in about 100 articles in the "Reader's Digest." Among the latter, 40-60% of the authors used a brief bit of narration to catch the reader's interest. And this type of opening was not confined to articles that told a story in the middle paragraphs. On the contrary, most of them did not, as evidenced by such titles as "Driver Had Been Drinking," "Why Doctors Hesitate to Prescribe Antibiotics," "What Tomorrow's Army Will Look Like," and "Is Your Child's School Safe From Fire?"

Among the students, the figures were quite different. Those who wrote narrative compositions based upon incidents or personal adventures very often began their stories in the opening paragraph. However, fewer than 10% of the students who developed their topics through argumentation, explanation, criticism, or description thought of using the opening device that is most popular with the professionals. Perhaps, like most other students, you believe that only when you are telling a story from beginning to end should you use a narrative opening. As evidenced by the survey just mentioned, this assumption is not supported by the facts.

"All right," you say, "I think it's a good idea. But where do I get all the stories? And what about a topic, for instance, like 'Creating International Understanding'?"

That's easy. You have been told several times that the most fruitful source of material is what has happened to you. Regardless of the subject, you can generally come up with a personal experience that can be tied in with the topic if you think along narrative lines. You want to write about international understanding? Fine. Haven't you ever had a disagreement with a friend as the result of a misunderstanding and then patched up your differences? If you have, tell about it briefly and in the middle paragraphs apply the illustrated point on a broader scale to nations abroad. Is the topic concerned with accident prevention? Wasn't there a time when you got hurt because of carelessness? Tell about it. If you bend your mind to it, you will discover that there are very few topics for which you cannot recall a personal episode to help you get started.

Suppose you can't think of one of your own experiences. Look elsewhere. Your parents, relatives, friends—things have happened to them that you know about. You read stories in newspapers, books, magazines. Borrow from these second hand sources, if you must, but make a conscious effort to use the narrative beginning more often.

It is usually sure fire, provided you are careful. Don't be like some afterdinner speakers. They know the value of prefacing their remarks with an amusing anecdote to get the audience warmed up to the major contents of their talks. But often what they hope will be funny falls flat, or, what is worse, it has nothing whatever to do with the subject to be discussed. Make sure the story you use to begin a composition is suitable, is pertinent to the main ideas you plan to develop. Secondly, make sure you give enough detail, but don't drag it out. Remember, your introduction should be but a small fraction of the total length of the composition.

With these cautions in mind, study the examples that follow. Observe how effectively the narrative opening paragraph creates interest. Try to guess where the writers got their stories. Get into the habit of considering this kind of opening for almost any topic and you will have a valuable writing tool at your disposal. The first two examples were written by students, the last two by professionals.

Sample #1

Topic: *The Result*

(This student was attempting to show how ridiculous some television commercials are. This particular one involved a diagram intended to prove that one aspirin tablet gets into the blood stream faster than another.)

The tension was easily apparent. The silence which prevailed in the large room was broken only infrequently by orders to the cameramen as to their fixed positions. An oval circle of cameras and microphones surrounded the long table, and overhead in the balconies all eyes stared intently at the awe-inspiring figure on the table. His features were partly hidden by the long thin wires attached to his body. Recordings would instantly be made of the reaction of the glands, nerves, tissues, and muscles which would yield the indisputable answer. He had been carefully chosen for the experiment, and indeed it had been necessary if the experiment was to be a successful one.

Where do you suppose the student got this story from? He made it up, of course! You can do the same thing occasionally. It just takes a little imagination. Do you see how effectively the use of a false setting of scientific accuracy exposes the silly practices of some advertisers?

Sample #2

Topic: *Just a Card*

(Here is a perfectly delightful composition on the effects of a certain mark on the feelings of a hurt student as he gazes at his report card.)

He just sat there, motionless, too stunned to speak. His head ached, and wild, improbable thoughts ran through his brain. How could she have done this to him?

Notice how brief, how simple is this narrative opening. Yet how effective!

Sample #3

Topic: *Driver Had Been Drinking*

(Here's how a professional uses a brief narrative opening to start an article on the need for strengthening law enforcement agencies to combat drunken driving.)

Last November a Detroit driver wiped out seven lives. Befuddled by liquor, he was driving the wrong way on a four-lane divided superhighway in Ohio when he plowed head-on at high speed into another car.

Sample #4

Topic: *What Tomorrow's Army Will Look Like*

(In this magazine article, the writer breaks down his narrative opening into two paragraphs, a completely acceptable procedure if the story lends itself to it. The title makes clear what the middle paragraphs discussed.)

The two GI's hid in a grove of trees at the edge of a clearing deep in enemy territory. Hours earlier they had destroyed a particularly troublesome missile-launching site. Now they were anxious to reach their own territory, but certain they could never make it on foot, for fast-moving enemy patrols were hunting them.

One man stood watch; the other spoke softly into a walkie-talkie-type transmitter. Soon a big cargo-carrying airplane burst low over the clearing and paradropped a cylindrical canister about the size of two oil drums. Rushing to it, the GI's pulled out a piece of floppy, rubbery material and quickly spread it on the ground.

So that you won't be consumed by curiosity, the floppy material turns out to be an inflatable airplane. Do you see how this beginning can lead effortlessly into the major discussion of the latest equipment used by our armed forces?

B. *Direct*

Continuing with the results of the survey mentioned before, we find that over 80% of the students preferred to go directly to the heart of their topics in the opening paragraphs. Fewer than 30% of the professional writers used the direct opening, probably because they were more experienced in devising interesting beginnings, they wanted to avoid a standard approach, and they were consciously trying to exercise their imaginations. This fact would seem to indicate that until you master the techniques of creating unusual beginning paragraphs you should regard the direct opening as your "bread and butter" device, the one you can depend upon to get you off to a good start when you can't think of a more inspiring one. When young writers who have barely begun to develop personal styles discover that they cannot fly at a particular moment, they should have sense enough at least to walk.

The direct opening has much to recommend it on other grounds. It enables the writer to make full use of the outline. It immediately tells the reader what to expect and thus directs his thinking for him. It is relatively easy to construct. Let's see how it is done. We'll use one of the outlines we talked about in the previous chapter.

Topic: *Modern Medical Miracles*

SALK VACCINE	HEART SURGERY
polio threat	TV demonstration
injection series	cutting through layers
reduction of victims	sewing tissues
fourth shot	sewing layers back

With the outline before you, the entire beginning paragraph can be worked out quickly. In the first sentence you
suggest the topic as a whole. In the next few sentences you
suggest what each of the middle paragraphs will cover. Then
you compose a sentence to lead into the body of the composition, and you are done! It's as easy as that.

A word of caution. Notice that the beginning paragraph is
intended to *suggest* what follows. Let's emphasize that. You
suggest; you do not discuss the main ideas that will be developed in the middle paragraphs. Otherwise you will be
wasting your verbal ammunition and will have little left
later on when you will really want to concentrate your fire.

Based on the outline above, here is an example of a beginning paragraph using the direct approach:

> *Considering what they have accomplished in recent
> years, it is little wonder that many of our medical men
> are being referred to as workers of miracles. In their dedi-
> cated battle against disease, they have been advancing on
> several fronts. Among their most exciting victories have
> been the development of a vaccine against polio attacks
> and newly perfected methods of performing heart
> surgery. Thousands of people owe their lives to these
> valiant soldiers whose weapons are test tubes and guinea
> pigs, scalpels and sutures.*

Do you see how the topic is indirectly restated in the first
sentence? Do you remember what was said about the *topic
sentence,* that it *limits* and *obligates* the writer? Need you be
told that the same principle is observed in a beginning paragraph, that it suggests the main ideas to be discussed and
fixes the responsibility of the writer to fulfill his promise in

the middle paragraphs? What would have been wrong if the paragraph had been written this way:

> By reading about Dr. Jonas Salk and watching some television programs, I have become familiar with some modern medical miracles. I now know how a series of injections can make many people immune to attacks of polio. At first three were required, and lately a fourth has been suggested. Also, it is very interesting to watch doctors perform heart operations on television. The way they cut through the layers of flesh is hard to take at first, but when you get used to it you find it fascinating.

Yes, what is wrong most of all is that this opening paragraph *tells;* it should only *suggest!*

It is possible to introduce variety even in the rather standard opening we have been describing. You may want to insert a few questions to achieve a change of sentence form, as is done in this beginning paragraph based upon another of the outlines presented before:

Topic: *Part Time Jobs*

My Job	Why I Like It
tailor shop	extra money
preparing tickets	saving for college
bicycle deliveries	outdoors, meeting people
collections, tips	sense of responsibility

> Recently, when I found I had some extra time on my hands, I went out and got myself a part time job. I can truthfully say I'm glad I did. What's it like? Why do I enjoy it? Let me tell you.

Again, did you observe how the first sentence presented the general topic? Did you sense the conversational tone the writer was able to adopt by use of his questions? Do you see how the middle paragraphs are suggested, but not talked about?

Or you may want to vary the sentence length to avoid the
ordinary, as is done in the next outline-opening paragraph
example:

Topic: *A Memorable Football Game*

THE CROWD AND I	THE KEY PLAY
Our spirit	Score
Banners, food	Tense moment
Keeping warm	The end run
Cheers	Tearing down goalposts

*I shall never forget the football game we played against
Blakeville two years ago. The stands were full of crazy
rooters. One of our players did the impossible. I almost
fainted!*

Do you see how the series of staccato sentences is designed
to infect the reader with the enthusiasm and excitement of
the writer? Once more, did you observe the general topic
expressed in the first sentence, the suggestion of the middle
paragraphs in the next few sentences, and the last sentence
preparing for the body of the composition?

Here are a few more typical direct-opening paragraphs,
the first two by students and the last two by professionals.
Observe how, with only minor variations, they follow rather
closely the pattern of construction recommended for this type
of beginning paragraph.

Sample #1

Topic: *Threats to World Peace*

Beginning Paragraph:
    *An intelligent observer of the world as it is today no-
tices many dark shadows hovering over it. These ominous
shapes vary in size and intensity. They represent political, social, and religious issues which are threatening to
envelop us. Some cover various sectors of the globe, while
one monstrous figure totally encompasses the earth.*

Sample #2

Topic: *A New World of Electricity—The Solar Cell*

Beginning Paragraph:

The world today is confronted with many acute shortages, possibly the most serious being that of raw materials. Since, for the most part, it is raw materials that run our great electric generators, human ingenuity must provide some way for future generations to produce much needed electric power without dependence upon organic fuels. Scientists may have found the answer in something we see every day—the sun. As a substitute for man-made power, it has tremendous possibilities.

Sample #3

Topic: *Why Do Good People Suffer?*

Beginning Paragraph:

We are ever baffled by the injustice of the moral world. "Why?" is the most timeless and universal of all questions, as old as the first tear and as recent as the latest newscast. We can see a reason for scoundrels dying young, but why the untimely death of saints? We can justify a gangster's being stricken with disease, but why little children? We can accept adversity in the life of an infidel, but why in the life of the faithful? The Bible gives us answers to these questions.

Sample #4

Topic: *Fresh Water From the Sea*

Introductory Paragraph:

Since the first desperate human being dying of thirst stumbled to the sea, gulped mouthfuls of salt water and chokingly spat it out, mankind has dreamed of making salt water fresh. Not only the thirsty but millions of people such as those in the Middle East, where the sea actually washes up on the desert, have longed for a day

when sea water could be used to irrigate the dry land.
That day is coming.

C. Detailed

Even though facts, statistics, quotations, or other means
of concrete support are most effective when used to develop
middle paragraphs, they can often help you build up an
interesting beginning paragraph, too. In using details this
way to start a composition, you lend an air of authority to
your main ideas and establish respect in the reader's mind
for your opinions and conclusions. Be careful, however, to
bear in mind that in the introduction you must only *suggest*,
not tell. Don't squander important material at the beginning
and then find that you have to repeat yourself later on. Here
are four examples of the successful use of this technique:

Sample #1 *(student)*

Topic: *The Baby Sitter*

Opening Paragraph:
   From experience, I have learned that a good baby
sitter must be armed with the following weapons: one
pair of iron shins; one good pair of lungs (for screaming
for help), one and only one sweet face (for the benefit of
paying parents), and one pair of strong fists (for you
know whom). She must also keep on hand one hammer
with a flat head (for a flat head); one tourniquet, large
enough to go around a young neck; and one straitjacket.
If the night goes along as expected, some one may have
to take her home in the latter piece of equipment.

Sample #2 *(student)*

Title: *West of Broadway*

Beginning Paragraph:
   Wednesday is a special day. It is a day when in autumn
chilled leaves on sidewalks make joyful, crackling sounds;

a day when in winter the pristine snow is quickly turned to a lush of ugliness; a day when spring brings joys of love. It is an important day to those who come to lose themselves in the excitement of the theatre. It is the day of the matinee, the reduced price, the smell of Schrafft's and Helena Rubinstein. The time is two-thirty-five. Except for a few tardy patrons, the street after its casual excitement is calm.

Sample #3 (professional)

Title: *This Problem of Narcotic Addiction—Let's Face It Sensibly*

Beginning Paragraph:

Approximately 50,000 people in the United States today are narcotic addicts. They commit over one fourth of the nation's crimes. They infect thousands of others every year with this dread disease. Half of them are under 25. All of them suffer the tortures of the damned.

Sample #4 (professional)

Title: *The Private Life of the Cricket*

Beginning Paragraph:

One of the world's humblest voices has for centuries been prized in many lands. It is the cricket's—a chirp of contentment in the rusty summer grasses. Fiddler, ventriloquist, acrobat, fighter and optimist (even when chill autumn nights warn of his end), the cricket long ago jumped into the affections of mankind. "I love it for the many times I have heard it, and the many thoughts its harmless music has given me," says Dickens for us all in **The Cricket on the Hearth.**

D. Descriptive

Sometimes by providing a colorful background, you can make your ideas stand out more clearly. Of course, many narrative pieces begin with a description of the setting. But

the same device can be used even when the middle paragraphs do not tell a story. What you do is create a picture
in the mind of your reader so that he can more easily follow
your reasoning within the framework of the background you
have supplied.

Let's say you are planning to write about the elimination
of a slum district or an eyesore on the school campus. Why
not start by describing it in detail and then presenting your
arguments and suggestions? Observe how it was done in the
following four examples:

Sample #1 (student)

Topic: *Hurricane*

Beginning Paragraph:

The ocean was still. Over the depths came a soft
breeze, nudging the calm waters. The breeze was a quiet
thing as it traveled along, picking up more and more of
its fellows, growing into a torrential wind shouldering
along a mass of angry waves.

Sample #2 (student)

Topic: *God's World*

Beginning Paragraph:

You look up at the sky. The black clouds have blown
out the sun's golden rays. The soft warm wind has become cold and fierce. Trees that gently swayed in the
faint breeze now unwillingly bow their heads to a mighty
unseen master. The wind is howling out its anger.

Sample #3 (professional)

Topic: *How to Get More Out of Life**

Beginning Paragraph:

Take a look at the members of a certain American
family draped in front of the television set on a typical

---

*Reprinted by special permission from *Sports Illustrated.*

evening. Their bodies sag and often bulge. They nibble away at TV snacks. They are tired and tense—the certain harvest of a superstimulated, underexercised day.

Sample #4 *(professional)*

Topic: *Vulture Country**

Beginning Paragraph:

There are three essential qualities for vulture country: a rich supply of unburied corpses, high mountains, a strong sun. Spain has the first of these, for in this sparsely populated and stony land it is not customary, or necessary, to bury dead animals; where there are vultures such burial would be a waste of labor. Spain has mountains, too, and the summer sun is hot throughout the country. But it is hottest in the south, in Andalusia, and there the vultures hang in hordes in the roofless sky.

E. Conversational

Suppose your beginning paragraph suggests that you are going to write about several people. You have an excellent opportunity here to supply a real human interest touch. Have your chief characters talk! Dramatize your opening by using dialogue, as was done in these two examples:

Sample #1 *(student)*

Topic: *The Expert*

Beginning Paragraph:

It does not take a long time to become an expert. In fact it came quite naturally to me. I didn't even think I had any talent whatsoever until my mother approached me one day and said,

"Wouldn't you like to help me with the dishes?" Since she had a heavy frying pan in her hand at the time, I didn't think she was merely asking a question.

"Why, of course," said I. That was when I became

---
*Reprinted by special permission from *The Atlantic Monthly.*

an expert. I became an expert in getting out of doing the dishes.

Sample #2 *(professional)*

Topic: *Watch Your Conversation—Children are Listening**

Beginning Paragraph:

"What is the most neglected problem in family life today?"

"The way parents talk to their children and to each other in front of their children," says Dr. James H. S. Bossard, director of the William T. Carter Child Helping Foundation and professor of sociology at the University of Pennsylvania.

F. Unexpected

Occasionally it may be possible for you to use a technique that was suggested as effective for topic sentences—the element of surprise because the direction of your ideas takes a sudden turn contrary to the expectations of the reader. What you do here is save the twist until the very end of the beginning paragraph, with the first few sentences proceeding in what seems to be a perfectly normal fashion. Here are two good examples:

Sample #1 *(student)*

Topic: *On Doing Homework*

Beginning Paragraph:

How often I sit Indian-style on my bed, doing homework. I don't believe there is anything I hate more. But I really shouldn't take such an attitude. Where would I be without it? I would be out having a good time, that's where!

---

*Reprinted by permission of *The American Weekly*.

Sample #2 *(student)*

Topic: *Blind Date Blues*

Beginning Paragraph:

Fellows, are you tired of playing cards with the boys each Saturday night? Are such things as billiards in the pool hall, dice in the school yard, mugging in the alleys, fighting in the streets your only relaxation over the weekend? If so, boys, keep it up; you're doing fine.

Did you experience a mild shock at the contents of the last paragraph example? But did you want to read on? There, neatly summarized, you have the whole point of a good opening paragraph. Naturally, you wouldn't want to be guilty of bad taste just to start off in a sensational way. But the writer above is obviously joking and so can be a little more flexible about his material. The point is that he succeeded in attracting your interest, and that's why he surely can consider his composition well begun, particularly since he adhered to the other basic principles of good opening paragraphs:

> **suggested contents**
> **brevity (50–75 words, usually)**
> **the personal touch (when possible)**

Basically, what you should strive for consciously in your first paragraph is for the reader to think to himself: "I'm going to enjoy reading this."

III. ENDING PARAGRAPHS

Now we come to the other end of the composition. Assuming it is of average length, you have written three or four paragraphs and wish to bring matters to a close. You wouldn't want to announce your intentions by using a phrase like "In conclusion . . ." or "To sum up . . ." This would be too mechanical, too dull. You would want to sustain the interest of your reader to the very last word. You would have to be just as careful, therefore, to compose an effective ending paragraph as you were in developing the beginning and middle paragraphs.

First, you must end in such a way that the reader *feels* there is nothing more to be said. He shouldn't come abruptly to a blank space at the bottom of a page and wonder whether you had time enough to write everything you should have or you just ran out of words and ideas. The effect should be very much like that of a musical composition on an audience at a concert. If, after a final wave of his baton, the conductor must turn to bow before the applause begins, then it is very likely that the piece that was played, even if unfamiliar, had a weak, undefined, and unsatisfying ending. However, when a brilliant surge of music brings the score to an emphatic close, no listener has to be told that it is time to express his appreciation. He *knows* it's over!

Before discussing how to write good closing paragraphs, it is important at this point to advise you against using certain devices that unfortunately find favor with some students:

Don't expect a single sentence to do the job of a paragraph. Although occasionally this can be done effectively at the beginning or end of a composition, it is difficult enough for professionals and certainly not to be recommended for developing young writers. How flat and pointless it sounds when at the end you come to something like "That was quite an experience," "I guess some day the problem will be solved," or "What would you do?"

Don't repeat yourself. Don't belabor the same points you covered in the middle paragraphs. The writer of the following closing paragraphs had been describing how wonderful a relative of hers had been and how she could not understand why this aunt had died so prematurely. Despite the imaginative language and the literary references, the paragraph almost destroys the whole effect of the previous

material because, through repetition, the emotions are being
thrust upon you:

> I often wonder why so good, so very good a woman
> had to suffer so very much. Perhaps, as Poe says of his
> Annabel Lee, the angels in heaven envied us for having
> and knowing such a woman as she. But I suppose I shall
> never really know why she died at so young an age and
> why she had to endure so much suffering. Yet I do know
> the world was better off for having such a woman on it.
> She did not know multitudes and her goodness was felt
> by only a few. Nevertheless, those who were so for-
> tunate as to know such a woman can sincerely say:
> "She was a woman nobly planned,
> To warm, to comfort, and command."

Don't become coy or wishy-washy. You can't escape your
responsibility for writing a decent closing paragraph by in-
jecting a plaintive note that has nothing to do with what
came before or by hoping for the best when a clear conclusion or suggestion is called for. Imagine how frustrated a
reader feels when he comes across endings like these:

> Now as I think of each of my relatives and my rela-
> tionship to each, I wonder what they think about me.
> Don't you?

> The Supreme Court at the present time has been
> making very important decisions concerning segregation
> and many other issues. It is my firm hope that with the
> enormous power invested in it, the Supreme Court will
> solve successfully many of the problems facing our nation
> today.

Don't go off into a new direction. If your middle paragraphs have been properly developed, the main ideas in
them need to be focused. Starting a new train of thought at
the end throws everything into a state of confusion, as
happened in the following paragraph after a discussion of the
desirability of Alaska as our forty-ninth state:

Now that Congress has passed the bill and Alaska is our forty-ninth state, we can look back on Seward's purchase and thank him for making it. We have gained more than mineral wealth, water power, and other resources. Alaska is a strategic point in the defense of the whole western hemisphere.

Don't be irritating or smart-alecky. It is unreasonable of a writer to build up to a climax and then let his reader down, as did the writer who set a scene in a dismal room with five people seated around a table, apparently intending to introduce some action, but winding up with:

A man wearing a striped shirt bolted into the room and opened the window with a grand crash. With all the excitement of an opening symphony, the sounds of the wailing sirens staggered through the room. The front door of the apartment, left carelessly open, slammed shut with the force of a mighty wind entering the window. The man with the striped shirt bid good-bye to the seated suckers and, gingerly removing his gas mask, stepped through the open window, wondering . . . (as you are now).

(This kind of neither-rhyme-nor-reason ending is like a poor practical joke and most annoying.)

Don't become so lofty in your language and images that you leave both your reader and possibly yourself wondering what you are talking about. What follows is quite beautiful, but the secret of its meaning lies buried in the mind of the writer:

Then my thoughts, unhappy and plagued, are gone for a time as I am taken with watching a little bird which has decided to build his home in a tree not very far from where I sit. Again there is sunlight above and on the surface of my brook, but I do not revel now; I do not turn to dreams. There is time to dream later. I leave my little plot of happiness.

(This after the writer has been discussing how some of the

world's ills disturb her dreamy contemplation of a forest stream.)

To achieve an ending that is straightforward and well-proportioned, without being mechanical, dull, or contrived, you must have clear in your mind what you want to accomplish and then take pains to bring about the desired effect. By considering the topic you have selected and the approach you have chosen to handle it, you can readily determine what the general form of your concluding paragraph should be. For instance, if your composition is based upon a personal experience and you have used the narrative style throughout, imitate some of the techniques of our great short story writers. Save a few surprises for the last paragraph or dramatically tie together any loose ends of the story still remaining. If you have been arguing in behalf of a cause, suggest a course of action to the reader. If yours has been a piece that explained a process or system, indicate the final steps to be followed or crystallize the results obtained. If you have been mainly concerned with describing a person or scene, put the finishing touches to the portrait you have drawn. Let your final sentences take a definite shape and your reader won't ever be left hanging mentally or emotionally.

Now let's look at some examples of the recommended techniques for writing good ending paragraphs. For each one there will be two illustrations, the first by a student, the second by a professional. The material preceding the final paragraph will be summarized so that you will know what the writer was trying to finish.

A. *Narrative*

Sample *#1* (*surprise*)

Title: *The Punk*

Summary: This tells the story of a young hoodlum who has joined his gang in an evening's fun of slashing tires. On his return home, he finds his father stricken with a heart attack. The doctor seems to take an interminable time in arriving. Then the concluding paragraph:

> The doctor looked at him sadly. "Is that what you think, son? I'm sorry that you do. It's just that some punks slit my tires on Thirty-fifth Street, and I was delayed getting here. I didn't kill your father, son. They did."

Sample #2 *(tied together)*

Title: *Terrible-Tempered Mr. Mink*

Summary: This was a series of incidents, all designed to show how ferocious, despite his small size, is that fur-bearing creature that supplies us with pelts for expensive coats. The last paragraph here brought the situation up to date:

> Domestication has not altered the mink's attitude toward man. Even after many generations of captivity they remain the same savage beasts they are in the wild. Without so much as giving the food a glance a ranch mink will gladly bite the hand that feeds it.

B. Suggestive

Sample #1

Title: *Political Indifference*

Summary: After decrying the fact that the average citizen does not keep himself properly informed about local, national, and world affairs, the writer goes on to cite the dangers to freedom of this continued indifference. His conclusion suggests a line of action:

> What this country needs is some preventive medicine. There should be more public information releases by the government on the state of the union. Debates between opposite parties should be held on television, during the

evening hours, so that adults could watch and be informed. People should be encouraged to write to their congressmen and keep themselves in touch with what is going on in Washington. If these and other similar measures were followed, I believe the shameful title of this essay would find its way only into the pages of the history books.

Sample #2

Title: *Warning—Watch Out for These Five Stock-Market Come-ons*

Summary: This article described five swindles that unwary dabblers in the stock market can succumb to unless they are careful. Each item had its own conclusion, and the one that was used to end the statement on "Telephone and Door-to-Door Salesmen" was an excellent example of a short but effective ending paragraph that suggests a course of action:

> Don't buy securities from unknown salesmen who ring your phone or doorbell. Don't even talk to them.

C. Focused

Sample #1

Title: *My Dream House*

Summary: The writer described a rather huge place that she hoped one day to have, replete with all the latest gadgets. Then, in her last paragraph, she drove home the basis upon which her dream had been built:

> Altogether I expect my home to have twenty-two rooms, no more, no less. If you start to count you will find that I plan to have sixteen bedrooms. This will be a necessity for I also shall have seventeen children, all girls, who will be well-trained in the art of maintaining a home of this size.

Sample #2

Title: *Jim Thompson and the Busy Weavers of Bangkok*

Summary: An American adventurer finds himself in Bangkok after the Japanese surrender, and he is so fascinated by the people that he decides to forsake his former career as an architect. He becomes interested in the silk weavers of Thailand and organizes them into a company that in a few years exports enough of the material to earn great profits and an uplifted economy. His native partners are happy in the lovely house Thompson builds for himself among them, and the central point of the article is narrowed down to this:

> Their enthusiasm was a fitting tribute to Jim Thompson and the simple, man-to-man decency with which he sat down with a strange people and worked out a partnership which has made them prosperous by their own efforts. It is an example of "foreign aid" at its best.

D. *Miscellaneous*

There are other types of concluding paragraphs which do not appear as frequently as the ones illustrated above. However, each is quite effective when it can be worked into the development of the topic. You will notice in the samples that it isn't even necessary to summarize the contents of the middle paragraphs. The topic and the last paragraph are so well matched that the central ideas are suggested by the conclusion.

1. *Prediction:* After establishing your point of view, you end by telling what you expect in the future. This carries the reader a step beyond what you have said in the middle paragraphs and actually sharpens your main ideas.

Sample #1

Title: *Park in Winter*

Ending Paragraph:

I may see the park today and forget it. Months from now, when the trees' arms are full, and the earth has regrown its hair, and the flowers smell of sweet nature, and birds hum silly tunes, and people have awakened this sleeping thing—I will recall the park in winter.

Sample #2

Title: *Verdict Guilty—Now What?**

Ending Paragraph:

As more states adopt diagnostic centers directed toward getting the prisoners **out** of jail and back to work, the taboo on prisons, like that on mental hospitals, will begin to diminish. Once it was a lifelong disgrace to have been in either. Lunatics, as they were cruelly called, were feared and avoided. Today only the ignorant retain this phobia. The time will come when offenders, much as we disapprove of their offenses, will no longer be unemployable untouchables.

2. Contrast or Comparison: Whenever you write about something that happened to you a long time ago, you can always end your composition by briefly comparing or contrasting the past with the present.

Sample #1

Topic: *Memories of Home*
(written by a Hungarian refugee)

Ending Paragraph:

Eight months ago, when I arrived in America, I again found my blue sky. It is brighter, bluer, clearer than

*Reprinted by special permission from *Harper's Magazine.*

over my country. I hope, I wish, that some day the sky
over my country will be bright, too.

Sample #2

Topic: *Las Vegas: The Underworld's Secret Jackpot*

Ending Paragraph:

The state of Nevada derives some eight million dollars
yearly in taxes from legalized gambling—and another
ten million from sales taxes gleaned largely from the
tourists who come to be shorn in the casinos. This sum
pays more than half of Nevada's expenses and permits its
270,000 citizens to avoid personal and corporate income
taxes and inheritance taxes. But the rest of the country
is paying a high price for this free ride for the relative handful of citizens in our second least populous
state.

3. *Questions:* You would not expect questions to be a good
way to bring a discussion to a close, but, if used sparingly,
they can be helpful in summarizing your emotions or looking into the future.

Sample #1

Topic: *The Sound of Silence*
(after an atomic explosion)

Ending Paragraph:

Must I forever wander through this strange, new
world of silence, looking, listening? Would there ever
be a door open, an arm outstretched, a mouth to make a
noise I had to hear?
No one knows; there is no one to know. There is
nothing to hear but the great, foggy-grey sound of silence.

(A two paragraph conclusion is rather unusual, but it is likely to be necessary when questions are used.)

Sample #2

Topic: *Magnetic Tape: The Mind's New Tool*

Ending Paragraph:

And so the process of discovery goes on. Man's mind has a wonderful new tool. But like radio and TV, like paper and pen and print, tape can never be better than the mind that uses it. What are we going to say on tape, explore on tape, show on tape? There is the challenge. What is on our minds?

4. *Quotation or Dialogue:* A statement by an authority or a conversation can be a refreshing change in your efforts to think of novel ways of summarizing your main ideas. Again, as was pointed out with beginning paragraphs, make sure the quoted material is pertinent and does the job of ending your composition properly.

Sample #1

Topic: *Is Your Child's School Safe from Fire?*

Ending Paragraph:

Says R. C. Malmquist, president of the International Association of Fire Chiefs: "Approved automatic fire-detection systems should be mandatory in all schools." Donald S. Charles, immediate past president of that organization, adds: "I know of nothing that will pay a greater dividend on so small an investment."

The potential disaster inherent in 11 school fires a day, the wanton waste of 30 million dollars' worth of school properties annually, should alone convince us that no investment is too great if it will make schools structurally fire safe.

Sample #2

Topic: *Alone*

Ending Paragraph:

> He looked at me sort of hurt, yet understanding.
> "Sure you don't want to stay?"
> "I'm sorry, I can't."
> He walked out to the car with me. We shook hands
> and I took off. As I looked back, I saw him standing
> there, alone, waving after me.

This completes our survey of how good paragraphs are
constructed. By referring to this chapter frequently and trying out the various techniques in your compositions, you
will soon find that your written work will rapidly improve.
It must if you are persistent and consistent in your efforts.
You now know what to do. You know how to produce
superior work by proceeding in a series of orderly steps from
the choice of topic to the ending paragraph.

There are two general guides you must keep uppermost
in your mind:

§ You cannot depend upon chance or even inspiration to
produce a good piece of writing. It must be thought about,
it must be planned almost word for word, and it must be
controlled by the writer.

§ You must organize every paragraph within itself as well
as develop it for its contribution to the topic. An opening
paragraph, for instance, does what its name implies for the
total composition, but in its own structure, it should have a
beginning, middle, and end.

Now let's try some exercises to see how well you have
learned the structural elements of the three types of paragraphs that must appear in every composition—indeed, in
every piece of writing. Don't do them all in one sitting. Take
them section by section and review the principle involved as

you work with the exercise. (You will find the answers at the end of the chapter.)

I. In each of the following paragraphs, the topic sentence that appeared originally has been omitted. From the three choices offered for each example, select the one that you think was probably the original topic sentence.

A. *The earth is yawning before its long winter's nap. The winds of dawn have gathered to greet the day. Their symphony has awakened me. Before long I step out to meet the morning. I walk with the tall slender trees as my guide. As though they were my dreams, I tread softly on the crimson leaves. As I gaze above, only God's delicately made lace interwoven with pale blue sky can be seen.*

The original topic sentence for this paragraph was:
   1. It is October.
   2. Spring has come at last.
   3. How still it is at night.

B. *The white twin beds, the matching dresser and the pink accessories all were a young, wonderful part of it. She looked across to the white, plush chair where were draped the remnants of a wonderful evening. There were numerous frilly petticoats, two shoes which lay askew on the floor in front of the chair, and a fragile, frothy lace gown tossed haphazardly over all. The sweet sixteen corsage was still pinned to the bodice.*

The original topic sentence for this paragraph was:
   1. The room looked a mess.
   2. She lay awake, thinking.
   3. She gazed about her lovely, feminine room.

C. *Can that possibly be your reflection on the glass door? You hold the flame of the match under your chin. What has really happened to you in these last quick years? You used to be so beautiful. The light of your* match fades and dies in a kind of symbolism. The glow of your youth and beauty has disappeared just so. But there the difference ends; you can always light another match.

The original topic sentence for this paragraph was:
1. It is a hot and sultry day.
2. You stop in a hallway to light a cigarette.
3. You walk briskly through the heavy traffic.

II. In each of the following paragraphs, the sentences have been numbered. Select the one that you think is best suited to be the topic sentence:

A. (1) Cool breezes pushed their way through the open fields and through once populated cities and towns, but there was no one to feel and enjoy them. (2) Buildings still stood, but there were no people to enter or leave them. (3) Cars and trucks were still in the streets, but there were no people to drive them. (4) Humanity had done away with itself; all life had ceased.

B. (1) The two men entered a trim little room. (2) A little beyond was the museum. (3) The old man threw open the door and Peter stepped in, looked around, and stared in amazement. (4) He had been expecting the usual things: some stuffed birds, old coins, etc. (5) But this room was piled with the most broken, haphazard collection of junk he had ever seen. (6) Not one item in this muddle showed even a sign of being a decent antique. (7) The old man watched Peter.

C. (1) By this time, you must understand, the jungle is hot. (2) The tropical sun has risen from the horizon and is overhead. (3) If it happened to rain the night before, we are in an even worse fix—because then we must rub liquid soap on our clothes and skin. (4) When the jungle bushes and grass are wet from rain, or even from very heavy dew, they are full of leeches. (5) These little worms attack every man who passes by, bury their heads in his skin, and hang on for dear life. (6) The odor and taste of soap is the only thing that will keep them at a distance, and so, whenever we go into the wet jungle, we wash ourselves with plenty of liquid soap and leave it smeared over our skin and clothes.

III. In each of the following paragraphs, the original concluding sentence has been omitted. Select the most likely one from the three choices offered.

A. The raindrops seemed to have one aim, to cleanse the earth. They washed away the guilt of the sickly dog, the sorrow of the innocent rabbit. The drops fell with the gracefulness of love, the determination of a stubborn child. As they fell, they washed away the sins of man.

The original concluding sentence for this paragraph was:
1. It was a miserable day.
2. Rarely had there been so much rain during the month of August.
3. They left for him a clean, new slate, to clutter once again with his profound mistakes.

B. The traffic survey shows where how much road should be built. But the way the road should go must be decided by the designer. His job is to draw a line through the aerial picture that will require the least valuable land, the least amount of earth moving, the fewest drainage ditches and culverts, be the shortest distance, do the minimum damage to the value of the neighboring area, and provide the greatest service.

The original concluding sentence for this paragraph was:
1. Road-building is hard work.
2. One thing must be juggled against another.
3. Roads are laid down quickly these days.

C. Every student must pass a critical examination in English at the end of each semester during all three years. Standards of grading are inexorable. Failure to punctuate correctly, for example, may cause the student to fail the course. "Do you mean that one little old comma left out will flunk me?" one student asked incredulously. And I heard the teacher reply, "One little old cotter pin left out of your hot rod could make the difference between life and death."

The original concluding sentence for this paragraph was:
1. Youngsters learn thereby that a part of education is the mastery of infinite detail.
2. It is a very difficult course.
3. The rules in this school are too strict.

IV. In each of the following exercises, the sentences that appeared in the original paragraph have been scrambled and numbered. Decide what the proper order should be and then insert in the space next to each number the proper letter, using *a* to indicate the first sentence, *b* the second, and so on, as in this example:

_c_ 1. She answered it with a curt "Hello."
_e_ 2. It was Rhonda.
_a_ 3. It was on the evening of her second week at home.
_d_ 4. The sound of the voice that greeted her seemed to reach out with almost physical power, tearing through her.
_b_ 5. The phone rang.

A. ___ 1. She was very understanding, but it didn't happen again.
___ 2. I brought them here with me and shall keep them in my heart forever.
___ 3. The first section stayed in the same room, the second went to another.
___ 4. No, I won't ever forget those warm and wonderful memories.
___ 5. All of us, in a delightful mood, stood giggling and choking with laughter as our teacher searched for us, up and down the stairways!
___ 6. On one April Fool's Day, I remember, fifteen girls, instead of reporting to our room, hid in a corner of the hall.

B. _____ 1. I look in the mirror and see the beginnings of a beard.

_____ 2. Man makes elaborate plans for the future because he realizes that all too soon it will be the present.

_____ 3. Being drawn back into reality, I think of the future.

_____ 4. When I look back on the past seventeen years of my life, it seems like one day with many events crowded into it.

_____ 5. I plan for the day when it will be the present.

_____ 6. Only a minute ago I was learning long division; I thought high school was a hallowed place never to be attained.

C. _____ 1. No one knew what could be expected from it; but it was my own idea and my own invention, and I had to test it.

_____ 2. A warm beam of light had fallen upon my face.

_____ 3. My mind was bursting almost to collapse under the intense strain.

_____ 4. It was a bright sunny day when I awoke.

_____ 5. This morning might be my last; this was the thought that constantly went through my mind, for today was the day that I was to test the new machine.

V. Each of the following beginning paragraphs has been developed by one of the techniques listed below. In the space provided at the bottom of the paragraph, write the name of the technique used:

> Narrative
> Direct
> Detailed
> Descriptive
> Unexpected

A. In an idle moment the other day, I sat down to figure out just how much time I've spent talking on our "Today" show since it went on the air in 1952. The astonishing answer was—roughly 1700 hours! At an average speaking rate, that comes to more than 12 million words—enough to fill more than 120 full-length books!

B. Burglary, like all other professions, can be mastered only through continual practice. It is my hope that this article will be of use not only to those wishing to enter this field, but to practicing burglars (temporarily enjoying the hospitality of the state) who want to improve their techniques.

C. The night air calls to you from the broken pane of glass in the window. You walk over and stare out into the chill of December. Your ears tell you that the night is screaming for you to come. The hall closet door opens; you grab your coat and walk out into the loneliness of the night. The biting wind stabs through you. You start to walk and the echo of your footsteps makes a disordered pattern like the years of your life.

D. What do parents (a species which is considered outdated by the younger generation) think about teenagers going steady? Well, I hear about it plenty . . . from my dad.

E. In the sanctity and serenity of surrounding hemlock he rests. To the West, in the valley, the river where he swam in his youth goes to sea. Upon the hill is the house, the beginning of his journey and the end. Towering elms look tenderly upon the edifice. The lawn green flows over the earth. The oak with limbs heavy with age, where as a child he rested, shelters the soft sadness with its broad leaves. And the sky, a heavenly roof, rains its peace on this place, the place where a man found rest from the stress of a devoted life.

VI. Each of the following middle paragraphs has been developed by one of the techniques listed below. In the space

provided at the bottom of the paragraph, write the name of
the technique used.

> Narrative
> Sense Impression
> Comparison or Contrast
> Evidence or Proof
> Emotional Reaction

A. *She ran out of water and drank canned fruit juices
rather than take time off to go to the spring. She played
her beloved guitar, sang until her voice almost failed,
pounded her head, burned her hand with a cigarette—
anything to stay awake and alert. A married couple in
the next district were taken off their tower in hysterics
20 minutes before the mountaintop burst into flames.
Janny switched her radio to their frequency and so it
was she who picked up the frantic call from the nine-
man crew trapped below the abandoned tower.*

_____

B. *Some Indians do have legitimate grievances against
the U.S. government, and the Indian Claims Commission is an excellent place to settle them. The Potawatomi
tribe showed, for example, that in 1862 the government
took tribal land for a railroad right-of-way—without adequate payment. The Commission has seen to it that
present-day descendants received fair compensation* **with
interest for 94 years**—*a total of $359,460. Andrew
Jackson was so eager to protect the Union by a buffer
area against the Spaniards in Florida that in 1814 he
forced the Creeks to surrender 25 million acres without
payment. The Commission has held the United States
liable. In some other cases the United States has been
proved negligent in handling Indian affairs held in trust.
The Commission is correcting these mistakes.*

_____

C. *In the darkness, a man crept cautiously, his eyes
piercing the dense forest like a knife. The cry of a wild
animal made him start. He became frightened and
started to run. He stumbled. He turned around and
stared into the darkness, trying to see something where*

there was nothing. He was lost. Somehow, during the
attack, he had been separated from the rest of his company.

_____

D. Hadn't she realized how much this whole thing
meant to him? From the time he first had seen her, he
had been completely hers, devotedly doing her bidding,
always at her beck. Why, only the other day she had
smiled at him so tenderly, so proudly, and he had felt
so confident that everything would be all right.

_____

E. An outstanding example of the power of enthusiasm to bring out new capabilities was demonstrated by
the old Boston Braves. In Boston the team had been
drawing small crowds, had weak support and did very
poorly their last season in that city. Then they were
transferred to Milwaukee, where the enthusiasm of the
citizens for their new team was unbounded: they crowded
the ball park, 30,000 for each game, took the Braves to
their hearts, believed they would win. One could sit in
the stands and actually feel optimism, confidence, and
faith flowing from the spectators to the players. The
same team that finished in seventh place one year pushed
almost to the top of the league the next year, and last
year won the World Series. They were the same men as
before, but they were now experiencing and drawing upon
a new power that released hitherto unrealized abilities.*

_____

VII. Each of the following ending paragraphs has been developed by one of the techniques listed below. In the space
provided at the bottom of the paragraph, write the name of
the technique used.

> Narrative
> Suggestive
> Focused
> Prediction
> Comparison or Contrast

A. Last but not least, the good guest knows when to leave a party. Keep an eye on the clock (it's an unwise hostess who doesn't have one in view) and go when it tells you to go. Tell your hostess how much you have enjoyed her party—and be gone.*

B. The lean and gangling horseman, garbed in black, passed quickly out of sight. He did not look back. Alone and brooding in the forest clearing was a small tombstone, with the epitaph that said simply:

Born 1816   Died 1837
Beloved by All
Ann Rutledge

C. Sandys lacks his father-in-law's oratorical skill, but otherwise there are many similarities—the delight in working all night, the youthful rebelliousness, the utter certainty of the expert amateur. In the end, sheer competence and fierce determination may make him the Queen's first minister. If this should happen, few people, and certainly not Duncan Sandys, would be surprised.

D. The stakes are high for all of us. But if we are successful, if the railroads are stripped down and made muscular, as I am confident they can be, they will perform their mass-transportation function more cheaply and more efficiently than has ever been known before, I see an industry that will be continuing to pay—not spend—tax dollars. Finally, I see an industry growing in volume, increasing its employment and growing in the service that it renders to the public.†

E. The swift flowing stream of time cannot be slowed, but it can be put to better use. People who are poor in the gift of time can ill afford to waste any of it. We should try, to quote Longfellow, ". . . departing leave behind us footprints on the sands of time."

*From *How to Do It*, by Elsa Maxwell, copyright, ©, 1957, by Elsa Maxwell; published by Little Brown & Company.

†Ben W. Heineman, Chairman, Chicago and North Western Railway Company.

VIII. In the following selections, the original paragraphs have been deliberately fused into one. Decide where each paragraph break should have occurred. Underline the word that should have started each new paragraph.

A. *I can never forget the day I went swimming during the month of March. The sky was blue, but the temperature was a snappy 25 degrees. I am not in the habit of doing this but was tricked into it. Some friends had said I would not have the nerve to go swimming at that time of the year. Not wanting to be called a coward, I had accepted their dare. My friends and I piled into a car and drove to Coney Island after lunch. We arrived at the beach at about two o'clock in the afternoon. Five minutes later I had stripped down to my swimming attire, which consisted of an outfit worn by Navy frogmen. I ran into the water and remained in the pounding surf less time than it took me to dress. The ocean, I might add, was a bit cool, but I didn't mind it. My outfit was insulated for just this type of weather. After I came out of the water, I quickly ran into my car which was parked nearby and changed into some warm clothing. That evening I began to feel a little cold coming on. I called my doctor and told him the story. He prescribed some special pills that cost a dollar each. I was to remain in bed and take one of these pills every hour on the hour for twenty-four hours. One hour I was to take a pink pill, another hour the green pills, changing the procedure every four hours. After taking enough pills to feel I was loaded with buckshot, I recovered without any harmful results. Here is a word of wisdom to anyone who is thinking of going swimming in the month of March. Don't! You may enjoy taking pills, however. I know I don't. I can't look one squarely in its round little face.*

B. *How many parents have stood before me, after I have sentenced their children to prison, and asked, "Judge, what did I do that was wrong? I sacrificed for him, gave him a good life, put him through school. . . ." It's not what they* **did**; *it's what they did* **not** *do. They did not put Father in charge of the family. They did not teach their children discipline. A child must be disciplined to do things he does not want to do, if it's* in the best interests of the family, for that is how, realistically, the world will treat him when he gets older. The child does not want a do-as-you-please, "permissive" world. It makes him unhappy, confuses him. He wants the solid walls of rules and discipline around him, defining his world—giving him a large free area but telling him exactly how far he can go. In my boyhood I had that discipline, and I'm very glad I did. I was raised in a dismal slum on New York's lower East Side. My father ran a little dry goods store that barely made enough for us to live on. But he was the head of our house and I respected him. When I was 16 and he told me to be home at a certain hour, I got home. Many a teenager today roams until two or three in the morning, and considers his parent impertinent if he so much as asks whether he had a good time. A home where the father is not the recognized chief of the family is not much better off, to my way of thinking, than a home broken by divorce. Every time Mother overrules Father, undermining his authority and standing in the child's eyes, she knocks a piece off the foundation on which the child stands.*

IX. Here are excerpts taken from student compositions. Each contains one or more serious paragraph errors. Read the selections carefully and then answer the questions based on them.

A. Tears, if they are idle tears, are terribly foolish. What a waste of time! Women are usually guilty of this habit. At the drop of a hat they burst into tears. Mother cries to get her own way. They are idle tears that say, "You do as I say or I will be hurt." So the tears flow softly and quietly. It always works. I do as the tears ask.

My dog cries wetless tears. She cries when she is hungry or when she wants to be aired. Her tears are high-pitched and sweet. Their sound touches my sympathies. I am always quick to answer them. My aunt's tears are loud for all to hear. She cries for her husband. He is dead. She is alone. She wears her tears as she wears her dress of black.

*Reprinted from *This Week* Magazine, copyright, 1957, by the United Newspapers Magazine Corporation, with the permission of Mr. A. E. Hotchner.

What is the major error in the beginning paragraph?
What did the writer fail to do in the middle paragraph?

B. A dependable friend is not replaceable. He can always be counted upon when one is in or out of trouble. My buddy Dean is in this classification. Last summer when there was a serious illness in the family, Dean went out of his way to assist me in getting a ride to the hospital. He always sympathizes with me when I feel bad, and often takes me out to give me a good time so that I can forget my troubles.

On the other hand, Dean is dependable in another way. I can look forward to enjoyment when he is around. It is easy to relax with Dean who seems to understand me even when I am angry. He can hold an intelligent conversation or laugh it up a little.

Why is the first paragraph markedly superior to the second?

C. Yes, sometimes I find it amusing to sit in the subway and watch people's faces. Everyone's reveals a different character and I have learned a great deal from these people. Well, I am sorry; this is my stop. Good night.

Why is this ending paragraph spoiled?

D. Of course, April weather isn't the best, nor are the flounders the biggest, but like a fool I go fishing just the same. Then May rolls in. The weather still isn't good, but the weakfish in Peconic Bay put the flounder to shame. Weakfish are the most fun when caught with a spinning outrig. Every good fisherman must have some light tackle if he really wants to have fun. Even a one pound fish is fun with a light rod. By June, practically everything is in good shape, even the weather. My boat is kept on a trailer so that I can go from one bay to another, depending upon fishing conditions.

What major principle of paragraph construction has been violated here?

E. The therapy consisted of arts and crafts. Realizing that the children were moody, we had to be able to change or adjust the evening's activities at a moment's notice.

I tried to be impartial, but being human I found one child that I liked better than the others. She was a beautiful and affectionate child.

By just a quick look, how can you tell that these paragraphs both suffer from the same defect?

X. Here are two complete compositions. In a single sentence for each paragraph, summarize its major strength or weakness.

A. *The Trial*

I had a curious dream the other night. My life on earth had ended and I was flying to heaven, escorted by a band of angels. I kept wondering whether or not I'd be accepted behind the big, golden door which was getting nearer and nearer. St. Peter was at the door and, after his old, tired eyes had located my name in the register, he shook his head and said,

"You'll have to stand trial. The Punctuation Society has accused you of a life full of crimes against them, of repeated abuses and complete disregard of the laws protecting them."

And so it was that the case of Serge vs. the Punctuation Society was brought to court.

Judge Mark of Exclamation was presiding, and his cousin, Question Mark, was the prosecuting attorney. Question's opening remarks were very short, and soon the first witness was called. His name was Semi Colon. After curling up in the witness chair, he accused me of the odious crime of not knowing what two matched clauses were and not being respectful of his wife, Connie Junction. The next witness, Joe Bracket, violently protested that I had overworked him, even though my life had been void of quotations where he was most at home. And on they came: H. Comma, B. Period, S. Dash—smiling at the jury, looking at me with hurt eyes, and showing signs of the duress I had inflicted upon them. Their testimony was very damaging.

My good attorney, E. Teacher, finally had his say. He had calmed me down by mumbling something about his reputation being involved and that no power on earth (!) would keep him from getting me into heaven. He produced several witnesses who spoke well of me and who offered extenuating circumstances. There was J. Complicated Rules, who did an especially fine job of throwing some good will toward me. A representative from the Anti-Homework Society scored heavily in my favor when he proved how loaded I always was—with work, that is.

The trial lasted three days and finally the jury withdrew to its chambers. E. Teacher had a confident look on his face; Question Mark's grin was just as evident. The court room was tense. The public gallery occupied by my classmates was apprehensive.

I was acquitted. The jury ruled that the Punctuation Society had its rights on earth but was not recognized as infallible in heaven.

I woke up that Sunday morning and remembered I had to finish those miserable exercises on page 143. Can't wait to get to heaven!

B. *Lost and Found*

I was on my way home one afternoon when I saw a little black dog, dragging a leash and rushing toward me. It was obvious that he was lost. He was running so wildly and he looked so frightened. I stopped and, as he passed, I stepped on the leash and the little fellow came to an abrupt halt. Before he could recover, I had him in my arms. He was exhausted and quite upset, but after a few moments he relaxed. He was a tiny black and white dog, beautifully marked. His collar and leash showed evidences of considerable wear, and he wore two small discs that tinkled like bells, and he had an identification tag. His name was Mike, and he lived just a short distance away. I decided to take him home.

It was a lovely house, with a well-cared-for lawn and beautiful trees. I hesitated for a moment on the front walk. Just then the door opened and a chorus of voices called out his name. Mike leaped from my arms and yipped with joy. He dashed toward the open door and ran in circles, in and out of the anxious arms that reached out for him. Finally, he was captured. After much petting and scolding, he was taken away to be fed.

I met so many wonderful people at Mike's house, people who lived nearby but whom I had somehow never before had the chance to know. We are friends now and see each other often. And we all agree that Mike is the most popular dog in our community.

ANSWERS

I.   A. 1   B. 3   C. 2

II. A. 4   B. 2   C. 4

III. A. 3   B. 2   C. 1

IV. A. 1d, 2f, 3a, 4e, 5c, 6b
     B. 1c, 2a, 3e, 4b, 5f, 6d
     C. 1d, 2b, 3e, 4a, 5c

V.   A. Detailed   B. Unexpected   C. Narrative
     D. Direct   E. Descriptive

VI. A. Sense Impression   B. Evidence or Proof
     C. Narrative   D. Emotional Reaction
     E. Comparison or Contrast

VII. A. Suggestive B. Narrative C. Comparison, Contrast
     D. Prediction E. Focused

VIII. The following words should have begun new paragraphs:
     A. My friends . . .
        That evening . . .
        Here is . . .
     B. It's not . . .
        A child . . .
        In my boyhood . . .
        A home . . .

IX. A. The beginning paragraph should have ended at "burst into tears." "Mother cries . . ." should have started the first middle paragraph. Remember, the beginning paragraph suggests, usually.

The middle paragraph should also have been broken into two, at "My aunt's . . ." Two separate ideas, two paragraphs!

   B. The first paragraph gives an example and details to illustrate the point made; the second is full of unsubstantiated generalities.

   C. The last two sentences ruin this paragraph. They represent a weak effort at coyness that winds up sounding childish.

   D. The paragraph lacks unity, as evidenced by the absence of a topic sentence to tie things together and the constant drifting from one thought to another.

   E. They are much too short and underdeveloped.

X. A. 1. The first paragraph would have been an excellent example of an interesting, narrative beginning if it had stopped at "nearer and nearer"; "St. Peter" should have started the first middle paragraph.

   2. What is the second paragraph here shows fine detail and imagination and is very good indeed.

   3. The same can be said for the next paragraph, with its continuation of the well-developed narrative sequence.

   4. This one, too, is very good as it plays up the emotional aspects of the trial.

   5. As a change of pace, this short paragraph is quite acceptable, since it achieves its purpose of announcing the verdict and there would have been no point in padding it.

   6. The ending paragraph is just right for this type of

composition, since it maintains the tone of the piece and ties things together neatly.

B. 1. Again we have an excellent narrative type of beginning paragraph spoiled by being extended beyond where it should have stopped: at "looked so frightened."

2. The second paragraph shows good emotional tone and colorful detail.

3. The last paragraph is a fine example of the focused type of conclusion.

What Language Tricks Should You Use?

Let's return for a moment to our comparison between building a house and writing a composition. The way the foundation, walls, partitions, and roof are put up determines the soundness and durability of a house. However, a solid framework will not in itself attract most buyers. Their interest is aroused mainly by the finishing materials that have been used—the stone, brick, or shingles of the exterior; the paint, paper, or wood paneling of the interior; the style and texture of the appliances.

Similarly, you achieve structural soundness in your composition by choosing an appropriate subject, adopting a valid approach, dividing your material properly into paragraphs, and adequately developing each one. But to make sure that what you have written will attract the interest and attention of the reader, you, too, must supply certain finishing touches. You must learn to use language tricks that can add to your writing the color, style, and appeal you want it to have; can make the difference between ordinary and superior work; can, as you learned in our analysis of student compositions in Chapter 2, help you *put in* what so many writers leave out. The five suggestions that follow have been called *tricks* because they work like magic to lift your composition out of the dull and the routine.

I. MAKE YOUR PARAGRAPHS AND SENTENCES READ SMOOTHLY!

A good piece of writing moves along like a well-oiled machine. There are no sudden stops and starts, no sputtering, no unevenness. Each paragraph flows *from* the one preceding it and *into* the one following it. Within each paragraph, the sentences repeat the same pattern, following one another easily, in a clearly connected way, toward the central idea. The professionals call this kind of smoothness *continuity*. Achieving it is not very difficult at all. It is done with words or phrases strategically placed to form the links in the chain of thoughts and ideas.

A. *Continuity Between Paragraphs*

Observe the words in **boldface** type in the following excerpt. They illustrate how the writer established continuity right at the start of his composition. The last sentence of the beginning paragraph is picked up and carried forward by the first sentence of the middle paragraph:

> The sky above the quaint little Swiss winter resort was covered with heavy, sad-looking clouds. The air was crisp and cold, and, although conditions were perfect, few skiers were out on the snow-covered hills. But **my father** had decided that this should be **the day** when he would **go skiing** with his ten year old **son.**
>
> **We** didn't have to wait long in front of the sun-tanned wooden hut which housed the **ski lift's bottom station.**

Do you see how the beginning paragraph ends with a sentence that clearly tells the reader what direction the composition will take? And do you see how the first sentence of the next paragraph picks up the idea and carries it forward by using "We" and "ski lift" to tie in with previously mentioned "father," "skiing," and "son"?

Variations of the same technique are used to develop continuity among the middle paragraphs. A word, phrase, or sometimes a whole sentence in one paragraph directs the mind of the reader to go back very briefly to what was said and then forward to what is about to be said. That is really all there is to the trick of getting paragraphs to follow one

another smoothly. It is what a good teacher does in class—
quickly reviews the previous day's lesson before proceeding
with the new one. Now study the way the writer maintained
continuity throughout the rest of his composition:

We didn't have to wait long in front of the sun-tanned
wooden hut which housed the ski lift's bottom station.
Presently, we were standing side by side on the track,
waiting for the hook, shaped like a reversed clothes
hanger, to be put under our seats by an attendant. We
slid a few yards and—whoop, there went the hook snap-
ping in the air. This meant we had to start over again.
Once more we stood next to each other, waiting. The
awkward maneuver worked even worse the second time
and we stumbled to the ground. Again we tried—and
went sprawling. Finally we decided to **travel separately.**
    Alone, it went beautifully, and, with no effort at all,
I was carried up the steep, long mountain. The white-
capped fir trees looked down on me with a friendly smile,
as if to say, "So you finally made it!" I glanced behind
me to see whether my father was following me, but there
was no sign of him. "Well," I thought, "I'll meet **him
at the top.**"
    Five minutes, ten minutes later—no **father** was being
pulled up the **last steep stretch of the track.** Apparently, he couldn't even ride the ski lift alone. After at
least another twenty people had made it to the top, I decided not to wait any longer and descend by myself. But
which way? It was the first time I was on this mountain
and the way down was not marked. The only solution I
could think of was to **take the same route I had used
to go up.**
    There was no trail **along the track of the ski lift**
and the snow was soft, deep, and dangerous. The slope
was getting so steep that I had to take off my skis and
try to stagger downhill. With every aching step, I sank
to my knees. As if my misery wasn't complete, it began
to snow with thick, clinging flakes. Soon my legs were
numb and I could barely move. I must have tortured
myself for half an hour when I heard a yell. It was one
of the attendants from the bottom station. He guided
me out of the drifts and, after a short rest, took me down
the wide, easy trail **back to the hut.**

Once I was **deposited before a roaring fire,** my boots were off in no time and I began to thaw out with a cup of hot tea. My father, rather guiltily, put a heavy hand on my shoulder and said, "Next time, son, you won't have to fight both me and the slope."

That's how it's done. You repeat an important word used in the previous paragraph, or you refer to the main idea just developed, or you simply use an expression that bridges the gap between paragraphs (called *transitional words,* like *on the other hand, in the first place, however,* etc.), and you establish the continuity that makes your composition read smoothly. Here are a few more examples, with the key expressions in **boldface** type.

Example 1

Mountains disappear and in their stead great cities extend their towers of steel and concrete heavenward. White, fleeting man-made birds streak through the clear azure. Spans of metal and wire appear over great chasms and wide rivers. Through the hand of man the paths of great bodies of water are diverted and arid deserts are turned into fruitful, cool, green plains. With each passing breath, man walks further onward and upward, leaving the shadows of his ignorance and stupidity behind him. Only glory is felt; the entire world seems **to hum with existence and achievement.**

The humming, however, is not unbroken. Occasionally the pitch of advancement that seems to exist so inherently in the human race is broken. Pain is where only love should be; hunger exists when plenty might abound; the light of the gleaming white sphere, high in the sky, dims and flickers. War breaks out; hatred runs amok. There is **faltering; there is regression.**

But then, as quickly as it began, it is over. The light resumes its intensity, with perhaps a bit more brightness . . .

Example 2

I heard the girl moaning in pain. And yet I could do nothing for her. I felt my own fear and agony. We were all in this together. **We had known** what we were doing.

It seemed ages since I'd left the ones I loved, and
I was cold and hungry. Many of us were groaning aloud
and pleading for mercy. But there was no mercy. Soon
it would be my turn to be taken. I hoped I could control
myself until then, contain my fear, go with pride and
dignity, walk through under my own power. It would be
as if a door were flung open to me and I would be
whisked away to . . .

I had been **suffering so long.** My arms and legs
were numb with cold and pain. But, they whispered,
it would soon be over. How I waited for that one blessed
moment when it would be over. But, perhaps, I shouldn't
have said that. How could I know what was to be? The
world beyond those doors might be more horrible than
this one I was leaving.

But, **whatever it was,** I thought, let it be quick.
Anything but this, this torment, **this waiting.**

At last. They're coming for me. The end is within
sight. It's my turn. Oh glorious moment. Now if this
kid would get his elbow out of my ribs, I might be able
to get on the bus in one piece.

Example 3

(From the delightful *Please Don't Eat the Daisies* by Jean
Kerr[*])

The Everest of my ambition is to teach my children
the simple precepts of existence—"Keep your fingers out
of the plate," "Don't wear your underwear to bed,"
"Keep out of federal institutions"—and somehow arrive
at middle age with my larynx intact. But no matter how
I struggle to keep my voice out of that piercing upper
register which, I am told, only dogs can hear, my boys
can always discover a **chink in my armor of control.**

For instance in the morning, when I spring down
the stairs jaunty in my husband's old dressing gown, I
brace myself against the dazzling sight of all those eager,
ill-scrubbed faces. I tell myself that it is quite natural for

[*]From *Please Don't Eat the Daisies*, by Jean Kerr, copyright, ©, by Jean
Kerr; reprinted by permission of Doubleday & Company, Inc.; published in
Great Britain by William Heinemann, Ltd.

children to be cheerful at 7 A.M. I resolve that I am going to remain calm. Calm, do you hear? **Calm. Discipline can come later** when we are all up to it.

So I find three lost shoes, put a new cover on Colin's speller, comb the house for 32 cents' milk money, and untie Gilbert, who has been strapped to a chair with a cowboy belt while I was looking for the money. All this time I am exuding such syrupy good humor that the children are awed. **I hear myself saying coolly:** "Just because he ate your crayons is no reason to hit him on the head."

When they are finally seated at breakfast, I watch the twins spell out their names in butter on the plastic place mats but I refuse to get riled. When they all decide to make sandwiches of boiled egg and cereal, I remind myself that after all, they're just Little Boys. Then I notice Christopher stirring his orange juice with an old pocket comb. At this point everything snaps and my wild, sweet soprano can be heard for miles.

B. Continuity Within Pargaraphs

Since the related sentences of a paragraph should point toward the topic sentence, you can readily understand how good continuity can contribute greatly toward the smooth development of the main idea. Here, too, a word or phrase that echoes the previous thought or makes some reference to it does the trick for sentences. Once again, observe how, in the following excerpts, the words in boldface type provide the links in the chain:

Example 1

Five spindle-legged chairs perched upon the dirty floor in a circle like storks about to fly off. Within the **circle of chairs** stood a square table, high and mighty, determined to keep the floor down. Set upon the **table** was a dilapidated felt covering with charred holes at the corners and a bald spot in the center. A heap of soggy lima beans lay on the **bald spot** and sweated the moisture of the air. The nooks, crannies, and corners of the **room** were stock still, staring longingly at the walls. The paint and plaster from the cracked **walls** rained down like leaves in autumn. A baby in an **adjoining room** screamed spasmodically, sending a shiver into the particles that floated through the heavy air.

Did you notice how skilfully the writer directed your attention toward the center of the room, the furniture therein, then the adjoining walls and ceiling, and finally a room next door—all the while maintaining a strong sense of unity because of the excellent continuity? Of course, you won't always want to repeat a word from a previous sentence to make the connections, but, as was said, it can be done in other ways, too. The next two examples will show you the great variety of ways that are available for developing continuity between sentences in a paragraph.

Example 2

The dance was all too quickly over. Settling a silk scarf over her hair, Terry shivered, not in reaction to the crisp autumn air, but in delicious anticipation that the **best of the evening** was yet to come. **After a brief discussion** among the small group of Les' friends, the unanimous decision seemed to be for eating at a restaurant described as "that little place with the green lights on Route 9 that has such great fried chicken." The thought of a **drive in the country** and dinner at a **cozy, intimate restaurant** with Les sent Terry's heart soaring.

Example 3

Then there is teaching. **This is the profession** my family and friends believe I will one day enter. **Perhaps I will,** for in the twelve years I have attended school I have often thought of how interesting it would be to teach history. **Besides,** people tell me it is pleasant work and well suited to a young girl. **This,** I have no doubt, is true, and I am genuinely attracted to the field. **But** there is a big **but** that lies in the way.

II. AVOID POINTLESS REPETITION!

Sometimes writers and speakers deliberately repeat words to create a special dramatic effect or to reach a climax. You are probably familiar with the technique so dear to the hearts of politicians who thunder:

"I say that these conditions are intolerable. I say that the time has come to change them. And I say the time is now!"

Or you have read material in which the writer used repetition to promote humorous effects, as did the student in the following:

> As the door opens, you are greeted by a girl who isn't pretty, isn't ugly . . . just pretty ugly. Immediately, she takes you into the living room to meet her father who is polishing his double-barreled shotgun. You soon learn that he makes his living polishing double-barreled shotguns—and shooting them!

However, unless you are pointing toward a special effect, try to avoid repetition. Nothing can kill interest more quickly than the monotonous appearance of the same word in every other sentence. There is no excuse for it because our language is rich with synonyms, and thinking of an alternate expression takes but a few extra seconds. A fairly safe rule is this: If at all possible, do not use a key word more than twice in the same paragraph. Here is a typical example of deadening repetition:

> People who oppose world government say that there is no proof that such an idea would work. The supporters of world government contend that this may be true, but wasn't the United States formed from thirteen individual sovereign colonies? The thirteen sovereign colonies who found it was becoming increasingly difficult to survive

with different types of legal tender, different laws, and
different trade regulations delegated a portion of their
own sovereign powers to an outside government to control all of the colonies equally. This may not be proof
that a world government may work, but it gives an example of a similar type of problem which was solved in
a similar manner and has worked for nearly two hundred
years.

Now notice what happens to the paragraph when the two
simple cures are supplied:
Eliminate when you can!
Substitute when you can't!

   People who oppose world government say that there
is no proof that such an idea would work. The supporters
contend that this may be true, but wasn't the United
States formed from thirteen sovereign states? These
independent colonies, who found it was becoming difficult to survive with different types of legal tender, laws,
and trade regulations, delegated a portion of their powers
to an outside body which could exercise equal control
over all. This may not prove that such a plan would
work internationally, but it gives an example of a similar
problem and solution which has worked for nearly two
hundred years.

Note how the repetitions were eliminated:
   Sentence 2:   "of world government"—eliminated
                  "individual"—eliminated
                  "states" substituted for "colonies"
   Sentence 3:   "independent" substituted for "thirteen
                       sovereign"
                  "different" eliminated twice
                  "sovereign, government, colonies"—
                       eliminated
   Sentence 4:   "internationally" substituted for
                       "world government"
                  "type of" and "similar"—eliminated
Besides the actual word eliminations or substitutions, it was
necessary to change a construction here and there, but the

improvement in readability of the paragraph is, I am sure you agree, well worth the effort involved.

An even more serious type of pointless repetition involves the contents of a paragraph more than it does the individual words. The writer, instead of developing his material through detail and example, keeps saying the same thing over and over again. Although he writes a lot of sentences, he makes no progress beyond his opening remarks, as you can see in the following:

> If I were to be asked, I would say that a true friend is a kind of person who can tell you what he thinks straight to your face and really mean it. A true friendship calls for honesty. Being honest in your judgment creates true friendship and influences people. In other words, say what you mean and mean what you say. Don't say a thing to your friends which you think would please them and yet don't mean it. In other words, give him the praise he deserves and tell him his mistakes which need correcting. Thus, by telling him exactly what you think and meaning it, you help him to improve himself.

Elimination or substitution would not help much here because practically nothing but the topic sentence could be retained. The paragraph needs major surgery and a complete rewrite job, with emphasis upon specific illustration to develop the main idea. Watch out for similar empty repetition in your own compositions. It happens all too often.

III. MIX UP YOUR SENTENCES!

Before the 1900's, most essay writers favored long, complicated sentences, densely punctuated. This type of structure often made it difficult to follow the main ideas and contributed very greatly to the dryness that is associated with some classics. As you can see by the two illustrations that follow, very little change in style occurred for hundreds of years:

> They do best, who, if they cannot but admit love, yet make it keep quarter; and sever it wholly from their serious affairs and actions of life: for if it check once with business, it troubleth men's fortunes, and maketh men that they can no ways be true to their own ends.

—52 words—"Of Love" by Francis Bacon (1561–1626)

> Say what you have to say, what you have a will to say, in the simplest, the most direct and exact manner possible, with no surplusage:—there, is the justification of the sentence so fortunately born 'entire, smooth and round,' that it needs no punctuation, and also (that is the point!) of the most elaborate period, if it be right in its elaboration.

—63 words—"Style" by Walter Pater (1839–1894)

(Note that Pater didn't follow his own advice!)

The turn of the century brought ever-increasing emphasis upon brevity and clarity as the keynotes of a good writing style. Most modern authors prefer simpler, shorter sentences, averaging under twenty words. They get their effects not by heavy phrases and massive punctuation but by mixing up the form and pattern of their sentences, knowing that any design, if repeated often enough, contributes to dullness.

As a student, you have long since learned the standard sentence types in our language—the simple, complex, compound; the declarative, imperative, interrogative. The names, however, have probably been meaningless to you because you haven't realized the important point about these types. It isn't that they exist; it is that to become a superior writer you must consciously try to use them so that your paragraphs will have variety in sentence structure as well as in words and ideas. You must make yourself aware of the fact that you cannot start and finish every sentence the same way without creating monotony. You must learn to break up the pattern of an unending series of declarative statements featuring the most common English sentence order—subject, verb, modifiers. Such sameness takes the spark and life out of a composition almost as surely as repetition does.

Any sentence can be rephrased or redesigned so that its basic thought is retained but its form is changed. It is your job as a writer to keep track of your sentence structure and put in variations as you go along. Note how many different ways the writer could have arranged the following sentence, taken at random from a student composition:

Original Sentence

The melancholy strains of the last dance number floated about her ears, like a soft spring breeze caressing her thoughts.

(This is certainly a perfectly good sentence, with balance and color. But if it were the fifth in a series of similarly constructed sentences, it would lose some of its effect because of the monotony of the design of subject, verb, modifiers.)

Variations Possible

(Inverted)

Like a soft spring breeze caressing her thoughts were the melancholy strains of the last dance number floating about her ears.

(Exclamatory)

The melancholy strains of the last dance number floated about her ears. How like a soft spring breeze caressing her thoughts!

(Interrogative)

The melancholy strains floated about her ears. Was it the last dance number? Or was it really a soft spring breeze caressing her thoughts?

(Dialogue)

"It's like a soft spring breeze caressing my thoughts," mused Linda, as the musical strains of the last dance number floated about her ears.

(Short, crisp)

Now came the last dance number. The melancholy strains floated about her ears. It was like a soft spring breeze. It caressed her thoughts.

There are other variations possible, and you are limited only by what your mind and imagination can invent. But do you see how it is done? Sometimes you take part of the second half of a sentence and put it up front; or you change an ordinary statement into a question or an exclamation; or you make several short sentences out of a long one; or you combine some short ones into a long one. You must be like the star baseball pitcher who keeps the batter off balance by "mixing up his stuff." You don't want to fool your reader, of course, but by mixing up your sentence structure you will certainly have a better chance to keep him interested.

Notice how much sentence variety contributes to the mood and humor of this excerpt, a continuation of the paragraph from "Blind Date," quoted a few pages back:

After answering some pointed questions about your family, your prospects, your intentions, you escape from her apartment and, in order to save your hard earned money, you suggest a nice stroll through the park. She appears to be the long-haired intellectual type, so you use your best lines on her:

"I think that I shall never see
  A poem lovely as a tree."

Looking up at you rapturously through her shabby eyebrows, she murmurs,

  "Uh, huh."

The hours crawl by like hours. Four steak sandwiches, 22 ice cream sodas (double scoopers), and 2 large pizzas later, she suggests a late movie. She obviously thinks that she's worth more than the eleven dollars you have already spent on her. You kill that idea!

  "No," you say. "I'm going hunting tomorrow."

How can you tell her that it will be for the friend who fixed you up with this date?

Here's an example of how effective sentence variety can be added to a paragraph simply by a few changes in form:

Original Paragraph

One day every six months, my friends and I have a baking day. We gather in one house and really go to town. We always have the whole house to ourselves. We take down the cook book and select what we wish to make. We spend a lot of time doing this. We can't seem to agree on what to bake. We have to hold an elimination contest to see whose suggestion will be the winner.

Altered Version

One day every six months, my friends and I have a baking day. After gathering in one house, which we always have to ourselves, we really go to town. The cook book is taken down and the selection of what we wish to make begins. What a lot of time it takes to do this! You want to know why? No two of us can agree on what to bake. Eventually, to see whose suggestion will be the winner, we have to hold an elimination contest.

IV. GET RID OF LANGUAGE WASTE!

Most editors, when asked for advice on how to put life into a style, will say briefly and pointedly: "Cut! Cut! Cut!" This advice is based upon sound reasoning. Long-winded sentences, in speech or in writing, slow up the movement of ideas and rapidly bore the reader.

You must learn to use the editor's blue pencil, too. Go over your sentences and cut out what is unnecessary. Make them get to the point. Make every word in a sentence do a job. Get rid of those that just lie around doing nothing. Don't be like the insufferable sleep-talker who never says in ten words what he can say in a hundred.

Take that sentence by Walter Pater. Not only is it complicated, but it is much too wordy. Had he followed his own advice, he might have phrased it thus:

Say what you have to say simply, directly, and exactly.

Let's study a few more examples. Some use too many words; others are too pompous:

Uncut: *There were some of the boys who were saying that they wanted to leave just about after the sun rose.*

Cut: *Some boys wanted to leave at dawn.*

Uncut: *In view of the fact that the game of baseball is considered by everybody to be our national pastime, many millions of people come to view this sporting event during every one of the seasons it is played.*

Cut: *Because baseball is our national pastime, millions of people watch it played every season.*

Uncut: *Judging by the frequent outbursts of laughter that emanated from the audience, it appeared to regard Mr. Crowley as a very funny comedian and offered him a salvo of applause with a great show of vigor.*

Cut: *Judging by the laughter of the audience, it considered Mr. Crowley a very funny comedian and applauded him vigorously.*

Uncut: *(Similar to some of the wartime signs posted in the middle '40's)*
Illumination of these premises is required to be extinguished prior to the departure therefrom of the occupants thereof.

Cut: *Put out the lights before you leave.*

Uncut: *In my opinion I believe I can safely say that I certainly do like to experiment with new recipes very much.*

Cut: *I certainly like to experiment with new recipes.*

Observe what happens to the first three paragraphs of the following student composition when the blue pencil is applied liberally:

Original Version

There are a great deal of ways to have effective money raising projects. It would take me at least one hour to explain them all. Since I have only fifty-five minutes left, I shall elaborate upon only one.

The first question that may pop into someone's mind is: "Why do we need effective money raising projects?" That question is answered in just a few short sentences. We need effective money raising projects to raise money. We need the money to buy things. For example, we may have to buy a new college wardrobe, a summer outfit, gifts for Father's Day, and that darling bathing suit in Lacey's window.

Both of us know that the only way you can get a new wardrobe is by not having any other clothes. The following project has proven very effective. The first thing you must do is rip or burn all of your clothes. (If this isn't successful, the rest of the plan is worthless.) Second you must make sure that your father has eaten a good meal. Then you must make the innocent statement: "Dad, I have nothing to wear." When your father wants to prove how hysterically funny this is and proceeds to go to your closet, he will find out that you weren't fooling when you said what you said in the first place.

Cut Version

Many effective money raising projects exist. Since time is short, I shall elaborate upon only one.

Why do we need these projects? We have to buy things! It may be a college wardrobe, summer outfit, gifts for Father's Day, or that darling bathing suit in Lacey's window.

We know that you get a new wardrobe only when you don't have other clothes. The following project has proven very effective. First, rip or burn all your clothes. (If this isn't successful, the plan is worthless.) Second, make sure your father has eaten a good meal. Then say, "Dad, I have nothing to wear." When he wants to prove how hysterically funny this is and goes to your closet, he discovers that you weren't fooling.

Remember, now; don't let your paragraphs get overweight. Keep the sentences trim and attractive. Get rid of high-calorie bombast and excess words.

V. CHOOSE YOUR WORDS WITH CARE!

London, December 9, 1749

Dear Boy,

It is now above forty years since I have never spoken
nor written one single word, without giving myself at
least one moment's time to consider, whether it was a
good one or a bad one, and whether I could not find out
a better in its place. . . . . . I will freely and truly own to
you, without either vanity or false modesty, that whatever
reputation I have acquired as a speaker, is more owing to
my constant attention to my diction, than to my matter,
which was necessarily just the same as other people's.
When you come into Parliament, your reputation as a
speaker will depend much more upon your words, and
your periods, than upon the subject. The same matter
occurs equally to everybody of common sense, upon the
same question; the dressing it well, is what excites the attention and admiration of the audience.

This is what Lord Chesterfield said in a letter to his son
over two hundred years ago. And yet his advice is as useful
and fresh as if it had been given yesterday to a high school
English class. What wisdom there for the developing young
writer!

It's not so much *what* you say that counts, but *how* you say
it. On any given topic, most students with intelligence and
imagination will come up with similar ideas. The differences
in quality of the compositions will be found in the language
they use—and language means words. That's why it should
make a difference to you whether a particular word you have
chosen is "a good one or a bad one." And that's why you
must constantly strive to "find out a better in its place." Before discussing the kinds of words you should try to use, let's
take a brief look at some you should avoid.

Don't use stale language. Most of us are lazy by nature.
It is easier to copy and imitate rather than tax our own
brains in an effort to be original. Thus when someone creates
an unusually effective expression, we very often appropriate

it for our own purposes and then use it to death. For instance:

eats like a horse	talks a blue streak
face like an angel	flat as a pancake
cooking with gas	dead as a doornail
you can say that again	crazy as a loon
slick as a chick	right down the line
Now, you're talking	as big as all outdoors
the $64 question	hard as nails
lay it on the line	as large as life
pretty as a picture	red as a beet

Whoever said these first had reason to be proud because at one time these expressions were sparkling and witty. However, because of constant repetition, they have become flat and meaningless, like hundreds of other overworked phrases. They are the mark of the unimaginative and lazy speakers and writers who cannot or will not think for themselves. If you want your sentences to sound as if you had written them, follow this general rule: What has been used before by many isn't worth being used by you.

Don't try to show off. Suppose you have done a lot of reading and have acquired quite a vocabulary. That's very good; it's one of the basic objectives of a good reading program. But words should not be used to impress; they must fit and be the right ones for the thought you are trying to express. There will be occasions when an unusual word will be the only one that helps you say what you have in mind; that's when you use it. However, when something can be said beautifully and simply, don't destroy it by doing what the writer of the following passage did:

There is a fortifying essence that floats around a clear brook during the earliest morning hours that cannot be found inside any man-made structure. There is a majesty around a towering monolyte that no palace, however ostentatious, can afford. The spirit of the outdoors exerts a permeating influence on a person whenever it invades one's soul.

How artificial has become the cool breeze near a quiet stream at daybreak! Never come to your reader in a cap and gown when he expects to find you wearing slacks and a tweed jacket. Oddly enough, the same writer shows that he is capable of using "big" words appropriately in the same paper. You won't find his language objectionable now because the words are creating the pictures he wants you to see:

> This spirit changes the shapes of clouds from reckless horsemen to gigantic ships, from seductive maidens to grinning gargoyles, from sinuous sylphs sailing celestial seas to grotesque creatures from outer space. It streaks dazzling ornaments on the blue skies, paints green undulating prairies on the desert sands, transmutes emerald leaves into golden and scarlet draperies to embellish autumn days, and covers the naked earth with a blanket of immaculate white during the long, frozen winters.

There's your main point. Any word is good so long as it projects the image or sentiment on the right level. What Francis Bacon said about studies can also be said about words: ". . . to use them too much for ornamentation is affectation."

Don't overdescribe. In an effort to present a striking picture, some students become so obsessed with the search for descriptive words that they seem to strain for the effect after a while. Note how the sentence in **boldface** type below overdoes it and spoils what is otherwise an outstanding bit of colorful writing:

> The weather! Today is a gray blanket, dull, depressing, pushed close to a body too drained to resist. Even the birds fussing in the trees are fluttering about to be sure the hot coverlet does not slip. Not a gasp of air can be had. **Sticky eyelids press on heavy eyeballs to force from sluggish memory the coolness of an evening**

sky. *Say the cool words—mint, water, swimming, shallow—before the heat can change them into tepid, panting syllables. Is all memory burned? Has the gray blanket suffocated all lively thought and pleasant fancy? Are all blankets gray?*

Create images by all means, but you need not be microscopic about them. It is understandable why some critics have said that all adjectives should be abolished.

All right, then, what are the good words, the right words, the words that fit? There is no set formula that will cover all writing situations. But there are some general guides that you should find useful.

Use words that are alive. Living things have definite shapes, sizes, names; they feel, taste, smell, move about; they cry, laugh, snarl, jump for joy. Your words should give life to your sentences by helping the reader see precisely what you see, feel what you feel. They should not be vague and indistinct. "Person, walk, building, merriment" are dead compared to "boorish oaf, stomp, ramshackle hut, cackle." Of course, you will frequently be talking about things like justice, honesty, power, delinquency, compassion—none of which you can actually take hold of. But you can make these ideas come alive in your examples and details, where you can use the words that fill the mind with color, warmth, and sharp outlines.

Here are two student compositions written on the same subject, "As I Gaze Out the Window." In the first one, the writer doesn't seem to have seen anything, judging from the lifeless words he uses. Compare his effort to the second selection, which makes you feel as if you were there, too:

A.

Upon glancing out the classroom window, I realized from the outlines of the tall buildings off in the distance that one doesn't have to go far to find a great piece of

work. Here, amidst the traffic and people, we have pieces
of architecture that took years of planning, hard labor,
and thousands of dollars. Although I'm not very familiar
with the surrounding neighborhood, I imagine all types
of worthy projects, works of art, and plans for future generations are taking place in these structures. One, off in
the distance, seems as if it would have as much aesthetic
value as it does functional.

B.

A heavy sky, lit by unseen fires, hangs limp and thick
and wet beyond the park. With sloth-like arms it enfolds
itself languidly around a building top, leaving to the eye
no more than a flat and aging pen-and-ink that shifts
from gray to darker gray and back again. Blowing hard,
I put a hole in it and see the sun squirt sparklers on a
half-drowned tree, hear suddenly the song of one lone
bird pipe echoes through the arch below.

You notice that the words that make the second paragraph
attractive are composed mainly of one or two syllables; certainly they are not big or long. They have been put in the
right places, so that the language has punch and style. You
can do it, too. Make the nouns in your sentences suggest
things that can be recognized in a particular way rather than
as a general class. Let your verbs provide movement, action,
emotion. Say things positively. Instead of "The facts were
given by my friend in a way that showed he didn't care what
happened," say "George blurted out the truth defiantly." Let
your adjectives and adverbs, when you find it advisable to
use them, add color and detail to the picture you are creating. A good way to practice is to take ordinary sentences
and try to build them up into lively thoughts. Here's what
some students were able to do with two such sentences:

Original Sentence

The woman was angry.

Variations

The shrill-voiced matron screeched in piercing tones
at her wilting spouse.

The short, dumpy shrew, red-faced with rage, wheeled on her tormentor.

Kate's torrent of angry words flooded the room with venom.

Original Sentence

The tree was tall.

Variations

The majestic spruce towered over its lesser neighbors like a lighthouse above dark and jagged rocks.

The gnarled oak stretched leafy arms languorously toward the sky.

The graceful poplar seemed to play tag with the drifting clouds.

Let the words be simple and bare when the beauty is in the thought. When you talk of concepts that are common to all human beings, you don't have to dress them up. State the point cleanly; let the reader marvel at your wisdom, not your flowery language. An excellent example of this kind of writing is found in *The Fighting Cock,* by the French playwright Jean Anouilh:

> Whether a man lights his house by pressing a switch or rubbing a tinder box, you can't tell me it makes the slightest difference to what is in his heart. Human beings have never changed . . . and they never will. They can blow up this planet or organize it in any way they like, but the real problems will remain what they have always been. You're handsome or you're ugly. You're bright or you're a fool. You've got some honor or you haven't.

Or this from a student composition:

> I could do without the idiot whose sense of humor leads him to believe he is funny when he makes jokes about my size. Now, I realize I'm not thin. When I walk in Central Park the horses neigh for fear I might hire one of them to go riding. I realize this and try to be broad-minded, but when people make jokes at my ex-

pense and my parents chide me for my weight, it gets under my skin. Go ahead; say it: there's plenty under my skin already.

Don't be afraid to let go. If you feel in a poetic mood and would like to write about some inner emotions, forget about the self-consciousness that makes people cover up most of the time. Come out with it; you'll feel better afterward, and you will probably produce a superior piece of work. There's nothing wrong with poets. Whitman, Sandburg, Frost—every one a he-man, and yet unashamed to let the reader glimpse his sensitive mind. Observe how in the two selections that follow the students who wrote them did let go and produced superb paragraphs:

White Is for Brides
(*written in 1943*)

White is for brides. White is for brides after the war. Black and brown and red are for war. Sorrow is gray and pale blue, making an end to contentment and hope. Hope is white and pastel pink and warm yellow. Hope is candles and good music on Sundays, and sounds of a man shaving in the morning. I hope I am a bride after the war.

I am very much afraid. Mud, and stupidity, and responsibility, and no women, and killing, make men different. Am I a defeatist? Will I be happily married in spite of myself? I am still young, young enough to daydream, young enough to wonder; old enough to have contemporaries who are dead and cold in the terrible sea, and whose minds have become accustomed to the racking noise and movement of a stuttering machine gun. I am too old and too young. I am too naive and too sophisticated. I want to grow up quickly, and yet I am frightened of growing up quickly.

Has youth always struggled? Has youth always questioned? Has youth always found the answer? I hope, but I am afraid.

(Did you notice the deliberate but effective repetition?)

Apple Orchards in Maine

I'm hungry for something. I don't know what it is, but there's a gnawing inside, a thirst for something, a void.

There are apple orchards in Maine, I think. They say there are apple orchards in Maine. Cool greenness, the tang and vigor of cold ruddy apples in the fresh northern air; is that a Maine apple orchard?

That's what I want to see, to know, to have beauty and greenness and freshness in my reach. I want to know what exists beyond my own small sphere. I want to see beauty and life outside of here.

I want to feel the surge of the sea beneath me, to rise and fall with the waves. I want to wing smoothly over fleecy clouds and jagged mountains; I want to glide somberly under the ocean, along coral-paved paths. I want to jolt along in a bumpy bus through the sidestreets of small towns. I want to cross the desert like a shot of silver, to the thump of a locomotive. I want to walk on my own legs through valleys and in wooded mountains.

Do those things exist? Will they wait for me? Will the beauty wait?

As you see, when you write from the heart, the words come a little more easily. And again, they aren't complicated, rarely used, obscure; they are sharp and alive.

Now let's try some exercises to see how well you have learned the language tricks. You can compare your results with the suggestions made at the end of the chapter.

A. In each of the composition excerpts below, underline the word or phrase that ties together the paragraphs. Then underline the word or phrase that acts as a bridge between the sentences within each paragraph.

1.

The days are past when a workman labored from early morning to late evening, at a dollar a day, to obtain an ordinary living. His modern counterpart is more likely to work for at least a dollar an hour, eight hours a day, and five days a week. Even the lowliest worker, therefore, has leisure time nowadays. How this time is spent should be given careful consideration by everyone.

Our society recognizes the value of increased freedom from toil. According to doctors, rested minds and bodies function better and can produce much more. But does rest mean loafing or doing nothing at all? The answer of authorities to this question is an emphatic "No!" They say that doing something different from the daily routine can be even better for one's health than lounging on a couch. For instance, the accountant who plays tennis or builds cabinets in his workshop creates a stimulating balance in his activities. Similarly, the steamfitter or ball-player can derive benefit from a game of checkers or a crossword puzzle or a good book. It is a change, not necessarily relaxation, that is most helpful.

2.

A new-born baby girl is unaware of the world about her. So far as she is concerned, existence consists of sleeping, drinking milk from a bottle, and being changed. The helpless tot doesn't hear very well, sees rather poorly, and cannot speak at all. Certainly, the phenomenon of sound has not yet interested her.

After a few weeks, her sensitivity toward sound awakens. Apparently, she begins to be conscious of her parents' voices. They talk to her and she looks back as if she understands. Later, she becomes interested in toys that make noise. At first, a new rattle from grandma frightens her. But she gets used to it and shakes it at all hours. Yes, she seems to say, sound is fun.

At three months, she becomes keenly aware of special sounds about her. A puppy's bark, the television set in another room, the thunder on a stormy night, the chatter of birds on a bright, sunny morning—all these have a visible effect upon baby. One day she discovers that she can make her own sounds. She laughs when she is tickled, cries when she is hungry, and gurgles to herself in the secret language of infants. Now sound has become part of her inner and outer life.

B. Using substitution or elimination, rewrite each of the following paragraphs to correct the needless repetition:

1.

I can remember the time when I was about seven years old. It was Christmas time. My mother took us to Macy's shopping as she so often did at Christmas time. Signs of Christmas could be seen everywhere, especially Santa Claus and his reindeers. Since Christmas time was the only time we ever visited Macy's, we got very excited at the sight of Macy's. We thought Macy's was the main office of Santa Claus and his reindeers. We regarded it as such and had fun doing it at Christmas time.

2.

One of the main reasons I desire to become a lawyer is that a lawyer commands respect from people of all professions. After I become a lawyer, I shall strive hard to follow a lawyer's code of ethics. I am trying to become a lawyer because I am fascinated by legal things in our society and enjoy law immensely. I feel I shall make a good lawyer.

3.

The submarine will also be used a great deal commercially. With the many underwater deposits of minerals and oil, the submarine will be able to be used to dig them out. Moreover, the submarine will be able to transport these resources anywhere in the world. Submarines will be able to pick up many gallons of oil, for instance, in special plastic trains and then bring them anywhere in the world. I believe that submarines will also be used to transport passengers. A trip along the ocean floor in a submarine should be very exciting.

C. The paragraphs below have been deliberately written so that the sentences are overlong and complicated. Rewrite them with the aim of introducing as much sentence variety as you can. See how close you can come to the way each paragraph was written originally.

1.

The girl sitting on her right tapped her on the shoulder and said that she thought Lisa shouldn't eat so much because if she were as short as Lisa she would try to stay thin and besides the other girls had just been saying that if she ate less . . . She stopped abruptly as she caught sight of Lisa's outraged stare since Lisa had been listening to her uncomprehendingly and the tears came rushing to her eyes but she held them back and all of her be-pompadoured neighbors parted their over-red mouths in uncertain smiles as Lisa sniffed and thought what did they know anyhow.

2.

The writer is amazed but not amused by the fact that so many people answer questions with questions like when asked whether there is homework they also ask why they should know, or when asked whether they like a girl they want to know whether one is kidding, or when asked about a date they want to know why not. Such people are as popular with the writer as Republicans are in Georgia.

3.

This is my first formal dance, thought Sylvia, and this is the night I've spent half of my childhood dreaming about and the ballroom looks as beautiful as I imagined it would be so that an author would describe this as a picturesque scene with gaily dressed girls and smiling men. I wonder what I am thinking of and why I am trying to deceive myself since I'm the only girl here who hasn't danced and I'm a wallflower which is a horrible name but maybe if I stand closer to the center of the floor some one will ask me to dance but if I do the other girls will see me and they'll be certain to joke to their partners about some girls being able to obtain a perfect mark in Latin but not having a boy to dance with but I'll have to take a chance.

D. Each of the selections below was taken from a student composition that wasted language. Rewrite each one and get rid of the extra words.

1.

From my point of view, I would like to say that this unusual person is unusual to me only because of the kindness and help and encouragement she has shown to me in the past. A person such as she is is rare in our modern society as it exists today.

2.

I was born the youngest of three children. By the time I had reached the age of six years, my sister was no longer home because she had gone away and gotten married and my brother wasn't there either because he had gone away to a military school. Thus I was the only child left at home with my parents.

3.

I must admit that I felt better when I realized that the pain had not been inflicted on purpose but that it couldn't be helped. This made me come to the conclusion that some cures are not possible unless there is a little suffering involved in them.

4.

There is also the question of why there weren't more lifeboats to accommodate so large a number of people who were there. It would be possible to say that this was criminal negligence by the people who were in charge of such things.

5.

If you are a person who has a vivid imagination, then you are a person who is never lonely. It is this ability that can help you dream of exciting trips that you might take some day in the future. Also, you can sit down and read a good book and picture yourself as if you were right there where the action of the book is taking place even if you have never been there.

E. In each of the paragraphs below you will be told, in as plain language as possible, what the situation is, who the people involved are, and what is happening. Rewrite the paragraph, trying to use language that will make the material come alive. Then compare your results with the paragraph as it was actually written (printed at the end of the chapter).

1.

A girl is sitting in a school lunchroom, her face showing that she is not very happy. She unwraps a package and finds two sandwiches which don't look too appetizing, a rather ordinary cookie, and an apple. She sighs as she looks at her food. Then she pities herself for living in such a dull world and having to eat such poor food. She could have been alive at another time and been a famous lady. She could have spent her time making herself beautiful and eaten unusual foods. She wonders why she must do only routine things and why no romance is in her life.

2.

A child thinks of the days when she and her brother played with boats made out of long pieces of wood. Other little pieces of wood were used as people. The bathtub was the sea and in it the ships traveled. All kinds of exciting adventures took place. Her brother's boat did not sink but the other boats would be sunk.

3.

Mike has taken his father's car and is driving his date for the first time in traffic. He finds it is not easy to talk and pretend to be calm with his girl friend while concentrating on the cars about him. There are lights, other drivers, cabs. Suddenly he goes through a stop sign. A look in the mirror tells him he has been spotted by the police.

Suggested Answers

A. Between paragraphs: 1) this time, increased freedom from toil
2) not yet, after a few weeks, sound is fun, special sounds

Between sentences: 1) *First paragraph*
his modern counterpart, therefore, this time

> **Second paragraph**
> according to doctors, but
> does rest, this question,
> they say, for instance, simi-
> larly, it is a change

2) **First paragraph**
> so far as she is concerned,
> the helpless tot, certainly

> **Second paragraph**
> apparently, they, later,
> at first, but . . . it, yes

> **Third paragraph**
> all these, one day, she
> laughs, now

B.

1.

I can remember when I was about seven. My mother took us shopping to Macy's, as she often did at Christmas time. Signs of the holiday were everywhere, especially Santa Claus and his reindeers. Since we never visited the department store otherwise, we got very excited at the sight of it. We thought this was the main office of the jovial gentleman and his steeds. We had fun thinking it so.

2.

A main reason I desire to become a lawyer is to command respect from people of all professions. After I am one, I shall strive to follow a proper code of ethics. I want to do this kind of work because I am fascinated by and enjoy law. I believe I shall make a good member of the bar.

3.

The submarine will also be used commercially, perhaps to dig out the many underwater deposits of minerals and oil. Moreover, it will be able to transport these resources anywhere. For instance, large quantities of oil can be picked up in special plastic trains and distributed widely. It may be possible, in addition, to transport passengers. A trip along the ocean floor should be very exciting.

C.   **1.**

The girl sitting on her right tapped her on the shoulder with a stinging forefinger.

"Say," she cried, "why do you eat so much? Really, if I were as short as you, I'd try to stay thin. The girls were just saying that maybe if you ate less you'd . . ."

She stopped abruptly as she caught sight of Lisa's outraged stare. The poor thing had been listening uncomprehendingly. The tears came rushing to Lisa's eyes, but she held them back. Her be-pompadoured neighbors parted their over-red mouths in uncertain smiles. Lisa sniffed. What did they know anyhow?

2.

It's amazing, but not amusing. Hordes of people make up the type. They answer questions with questions.

Q. "Do we have homework?"
A. "How should I know?"
Q. "Do you like that girl?"
A. "Are you kidding?"
Q. "How about a date?"
A. "Why not?"

These are the people who have as much chance of being popular with me as a Republican in Georgia.

3.

This is my first formal dance, Sylvia thought. This is the night I've spent half my childhood dreaming about. The ballroom looks as beautiful as I imagined it would be. An author would describe this as a picturesque scene with gaily dressed girls and smiling men. What am I thinking about? Why am I trying to deceive myself? I'm the only girl here who hasn't danced. I'm a wallflower. Maybe if I stand closer to the center of the floor someone will ask me to dance. If I do that, however, the other girls will see me, and they'll joke to their partners about some girls being able to obtain a perfect mark in Latin but not having a boy to dance with. I'll have to take that chance.

D.   **1.**

This person is unusual because of the kindness, help, and encouragement she has shown me. Such a person is rare in our society.

2.

I was the youngest of three children. By the time I was six, my sister was no longer home because she had married and my brother had also gone away to military school. Thus I was the only child left.

3.

I felt better when I realized that the pain couldn't be helped. I concluded that some cures are not possible without a little suffering.

4.

Why weren't there more lifeboats to accommodate so many people? This was criminal negligence.

5.

If you have a vivid imagination, you are never lonely. You can dream of exciting trips you might take some day. Also, you can read a good book and picture yourself right there where the action is.

E.   **1.**

Betty sat in the school lunchroom, a look of discontent on her round young face. Her grubby brown hands began unwrapping a brown paper-covered package. She discovered two soggy cheese sandwiches, a crumbling oatmeal cookie, and an apple. An audible sigh escaped her lips as she regarded the meal spread out before her with distaste. Her mind traveled over familiar channels as she wondered why it fell to her lot to live in such a drab world and eat such tasteless food, when she should by rights have lived in the time of Marie Antoinette, or better still, Helen of Troy. Ah, for the olden days when girls were delicate, sheltered creatures who could devote all their time to making themselves lovelier, and dine on nectar and sparkling champagne. Why, oh why, was she a poor girl who wasn't allowed to do anything more exciting than homework, and for whom no lad ever held doors?

2.

She was thinking back, back to the time when she and her brother used to play boats. The long pieces of wood were the ships. The small pieces that fitted into the notches of the boats were the people. The bathtub was the vast and wonderful sea, the exotic ocean, murmuring of distant lands and gray dawns. Oh, the strange and perilous journeys that these vessels traveled! The storms that shook them, the pirates that plundered them! But always they were guided safely home under the sure pilotage of her brother's hand. The wonder of it! His ships never sank. It was only the enemy bark that overturned swiftly, the horrible hand of revenge sweeping down and destroying in a moment the proud lift of a queenly bow. And the people aboard would sink slowly to the bottomless deep.

3.

Mike hadn't figured on so much driving, but if that's what she wanted, it was fine with him. Traffic got heavier as they approached the midtown section. It wasn't easy being witty and suave and watching lights and pedestrians at the same time. Can't afford to slip up tonight, Mike. Stay under the limit. Watch the lights, the signs. Where'd that fool come from? He coulda hit us. What'd she say? Yes, Paula. Wow, almost scraped that cab. Didn't realize traffic'd be so bad tonight. Darn, he'd done it. Right through that stop sign. What kind of idiot are you anyway, Mike? Quickly he glanced into his rearview mirror. The familiar green and white job with the red revolving light on top had cut out from behind another car a block behind.

Why MUST You Revise?

A Declaration by the Representatives of the UNITED STATES OF AMERICA. in General Congress assembled

When in the course of human events it becomes necessary for one people to dissolve the political bands which have connected them with another, and to assume among the powers of the earth the separate and equal station to which the laws of nature & of nature's god entitle them, a decent respect to the opinions of mankind requires that they should declare the causes which impel them to the separation.

We hold these truths to be self-evident; that all men are created equal; that they are endowed by their creator with equal rights, that among these are life, liberty, & the pursuit of happiness; that to secure these rights, governments are instituted among men, deriving their just powers from

This facsimile of the opening sentences of the Declaration of Independence has been reproduced to dramatize another important principle in writing: *First words are rarely the best words.* As you see, Thomas Jefferson, the writer of the famous document, made frequent revisions before he was satisfied with his sentences.

So does any writer of any worth. Go to the library sometime and ask to see other original manuscripts. You will be astounded at the numerous deletions, insertions, and corrections that were made *even after an author had apparently decided upon his final copy.*

The picture of a writer sitting at a typewriter surrounded by torn or crushed pieces of paper is no exaggeration. The graceful phrase, the vivid description, the witty dialogue don't come in a flash and then get poured out on the spot. The general shape and direction of the material, yes; this does reveal itself rather suddenly at times. But the word patterns have to be worked on, in the manner of a skilled cabinetmaker who goes over and over a piece of furniture until he produces the fine finish he wants.

That's why the professional writer regards his initial effort as only the beginning. To get his material to sound just right, he knows he will have to rewrite—and rewrite—and rewrite. He may have to spend as much as an hour on a single sentence! Why, I just checked my own manuscript (which I always write out in long hand first). I counted over fifteen changes that I made in the paragraphs that appear on this page alone. Heaven knows how many more there will be before the editor and I are satisfied with the final result.

You can see, then, why it is reasonable to say that you should not let your composition stay as it is the first time you write it, why you should not be in a hurry to hand it in. Instead, you should get into the habit of starting with a rough draft and then polishing it up as much as you can in the time available to you. If you want your compositions to reflect your best ability, you have no choice. Think of the problems you face when you first put your ideas down. You have to make sure that you stay on the subject, that your paragraphs are properly developed, that you record a thought as quickly as possible before you forget it, and that you have generally satisfied the required number of words. You are concentrating on getting the general form of the composition to take shape. However, handing in a paper that hasn't been worked over is like appearing in public with half your clothes on. You will be recognized, but you surely will not make a very good impression.

In all this talk about revision, one problem stands out that can be solved only by you. You readily accept the need for "fixing up" your work. Doubtless you were convinced even before you read this chapter. But getting you to discipline yourself to put into regular practice what you know is necessary is something else again. It's much the same as with the outline. Young writers are impatient to begin, and then can't stand the sight of what they have written after they have finished. On the one hand you tell yourself that you will waste time if you don't plan carefully. On the other, you take a "What's the use?" attitude and tell yourself that you won't be able to make many improvements anyway.

Perhaps there was some justice formerly in both your conclusions. If you didn't know how to prepare a useful outline quickly, you may well have been wasting time when you tried one. You can't, however, fall back upon that excuse any longer. There is nothing difficult or time-consuming about the method you learned in Chapter 4.

In the matter of revision, too, you may have become discouraged because you were going about it in the wrong way. If you just read your paper over and hoped you would find some errors, you couldn't make many improvements. If you don't look for something specific, you won't find it. You must train yourself to be systematic about your revisions, to read your paper over several times, *each time with a different purpose in mind.*

Before we discuss the various re-reading steps, let's settle the question of time. In an examination you are fighting the clock. You usually have about an hour to begin and end a composition. You have all you can do to finish, let alone revise. In Chapter 12 I'll show you how to apportion your time so that even under such conditions you will have some time left for revision. We can agree, however, that when you write a piece at home you are not pressed as a rule. You can afford an extra fifteen minutes or so to get the job done right. It is on this assumption that I present you now with a four step program that will help you raise the quality of your compositions—if you use it!

Write your rough draft with spaces between the lines to leave room for revision later. Work quickly and concentrate mainly on getting your ideas down on paper in as attractive and orderly a fashion as you can. Don't worry too much about mechanical errors. You'll get to them in time. When you have finished writing, go over your work *four times*, each time focusing on a different problem. Once you have mastered the techniques, you will be able to handle the various steps in about 20 minutes or less for every 300 words you write. Here's how it's done.

√ First Reading—Check Your Paragraphs. Pretend someone else wrote your composition. Just try to get the general flow of the ideas. As you read, check each of the following:

1) Does the opening lead smoothly into the middle? If not, add what is needed to establish better continuity.

2) Have you indented for each paragraph? Where you haven't, insert this symbol (¶) at the point requiring the indentation.

3) Does one of the paragraphs sound disorganized because it is missing a topic sentence? Write one in then and there, but make sure all the other sentences point toward it.

4) Are there any sentences in the middle of a paragraph that don't belong, that have drifted away from the main idea? *Cross them out.* Don't try to tie them in somehow; the result is usually no improvement.

5) Check with your outline. Have you failed to put in a few details you had planned for? Add them, but do not disturb the continuity between the sentences.

6) Does your concluding paragraph really conclude? Does it give a final charge of interest? If it doesn't, rewrite it.

7) Have you stayed within the limits of your topic? It may be too late to do anything about this if it is an examination. But few teachers will object if you alter the topic just a bit to accommodate your ideas better.

✓ *Second Reading—Check Your Sentences.* This is the heart of your composition. Poor sentence structure leads to dullness and an unsatisfactory rating. Take your time about this phase of your revision.

1) Have you maintained good continuity between sentences? Insert a word or phrase where it is needed.

2) Have you put the periods and other stop signs at the end of legitimate sentences? Read each sentence aloud (you can learn to do this without uttering a sound). Listen for fragments and run-ons. If you have a weakness in this area, take care. This is by far the worst mistake you can make. It may even be necessary for you to sacrifice some of the other items to concentrate almost all your attention on this problem if experience has proved to you that you make a few sentence errors in every composition. Most teachers will automatically fail a paper that has more than one sentence error in it.

Don't take any chances. If a sentence looks rather long and complicated, and you aren't sure whether it would pass, don't try to patch it up. Break it up into smaller units. Then read each one aloud again. Be very careful of bits you have added as afterthoughts while you were writing. They can turn out to be fragments, like these:

I looked back over my shoulder. *Which was a mistake.* Some of us were lying on a mat at the edge of the pool. *Just talking and eating popsicles.*

3) Do you have enough sentence variety? Check to see that you haven't followed the monotonous pattern of subject, verb, modifiers, in almost every sentence. If you have time, and you will when you write at home, try some of the suggestions made before about the use of dialogue, questions, exclamations, inverted order, etc.

✔ *Third Reading—Check Mechanical Errors.* It is your responsibility as a writer to make a continuing effort to improve your ability in spelling, punctuation, usage, and other mechanical aspects of composition. It would be an intrusion on my part at this time to try to give you a rapid review of all the errors it is possible to make in any one piece of writing. It can't be done profitably in the space available here, nor would it be wise even if this book were to be doubled in length. Good habits must be developed over the years through persistent effort. They cannot magically be acquired by reading once again a few chapters on the correctness of expression that your English teachers have been patiently trying to explain and drill since you were seven years of age. To stop now to go over the thousand and one petty errors that are made in the use of our language would throw the emphasis in the wrong direction.

A high level of competence in mechanics is, of course, indispensable. You must redouble your efforts, if you are weak in fundamentals, to absorb the instruction given you daily in your English classroom. You must do independent review, also, in the many fine textbooks on good usage that are available in school and out. It is your job. No one can do it for you. Get this straight once and for all: until you write with reasonable accuracy, you cannot hope to receive satisfactory grades, no matter how well-designed, interesting, and creative your compositions are. Indeed, you can master every chapter in this book and still fail if you can't spell, punctuate, or write a grammatically sound sentence.

We will concentrate on the seven errors that college instructors agree are most commonly found in papers written by students fresh out of high school, the mistakes that lead to an F in freshman composition. These do not include sentence structure, which we have already talked about. Get busy and do something about any one of them that is interfering with your success in writing. So far as our revision program is concerned, in this, your third reading, look out for:

1. *Spelling*—If a word doesn't seem right, look it up in a dictionary at once. Keep a private list of words you misspell and study one a day faithfully. On an examination, where no references are permitted, my advice is quite simple. Change the word, and check the doubtful one at another time. Some instructors regard more than two spelling errors on a paper as sufficient grounds for failure.

Be alert to the simple little words and problems that account for many mistakes. Is it *its* or *it's* that you want to use; *your* or *you're, to* or *too, boys* or *boy's, tables* or *table's?* Have you put in capital letters where they belong? What about names and titles? They count, too, you know. Never, but never, try to cover up a spelling uncertainty by deliberately making your handwriting illegible at one syllable. The marker is well aware of such tricks and will be doubly resentful. Don't use words you have heard somewhere but haven't bothered checking. Some silly-looking spellings often result this way. Keep your language as simple as possible if you are a poor speller. Your ideas will be clearer anyway, and you won't run into so many difficulties. For a complete attack on the whole problem, you might get a copy of my book *Six Minutes a Day to Perfect Spelling.**

2. *Punctuation*—The primary purpose of all punctuation is to aid understanding. Using too many marks, therefore, can be more confusing than not using enough. As a matter of fact, current practice is to keep punctuation marks at a minimum. Your best guide, then, is to *use a mark only when it is required.* If you can't think of a rule to justify a comma or a semicolon, for example, don't invent one. Just keep on writing.

We have already mentioned periods and other stop signs. These are really part of sentence structure, and require no further comment. We can pass right on to the comma, which is the most frequently used internal mark of punctuation. With this one it is particularly important to remember: When in doubt, leave it out! These are the five most common uses:

---

*Published by Washington Square Press, Inc., New York (W 50, 35¢).

Series—three or more words, phrases, or clauses running
        consecutively

§ The closet was cluttered with old shoes, several tennis rackets, and some fishing equipment.

§ My routine consisted of getting up at six, washing
and dressing in fifteen minutes, and then driving almost
twenty miles.

§ Part of the crowd was already on its feet, other spectators were struggling to get up, but all were roaring
words of encouragement.

Introductory—words, phrases, or clauses appearing before
        the subject of the main clause

§ Consequently, we decided to stay overnight.

§ Without a moment's hesitation, he plunged into
the river.

§ Since the guests were beginning to arrive, I rushed
upstairs to dress.

Parenthetical—expressions that are added to a sentence but
        are not essential to the main thought

May I leave it out?	Yes.
Do I use commas?	Yes.
May I leave it out?	No.
Do I use commas?	No.

§ The ancient Ford, one might say, had seen better
days.

§ A person who gets so angry is probably guilty of
something.

§ Mr. Forbes, who gets so angry, is usually guilty of
something.

§ The beginning, I'm sure, will not be too dull.

§ The package, however, did not arrive.

§ Bill Thompson, an old friend, will come for the
weekend.

Direct address—repeating the reference to the person addressed for emphasis

§ You, boy, get your feet off.

§ We both know, Ellen, how hurt you are.

Conjunctions—with *and*, *but*, and *for* when the subject in the second clause changes

§ I hadn't meant to come late, but the traffic on the parkways was heavy.

§ The snow fell gently at first but soon became a blinding storm.

§ The starter suddenly raised his gun, and the runners tensed for the breakaway.

Don't put a comma in because you think there should be a pause. In reading aloud, it is often appropriate to stop momentarily for breath intake or for added emphasis, but this does not mean that a mark of punctuation is needed each time this is done. Follow the rules, not your impulses about commas.

As for the other marks—semicolons, colons, parentheses, brackets, dashes, quotations—if you use any, be sure they belong. I must repeat that it is your responsibility to learn how to handle punctuation, to practice until you can apply it correctly and automatically. A few cautions, however, are worth discussing here:

Semicolon—The most frequent use is in place of a conjunction between independent clauses. But you can't use this mark between any two clauses; the second must *grow out* of the first, be closely connected to it, or you are guilty of a sentence error.

> **Right:**   The rain had stopped an hour before;
>   the streets were quite dry.
> **Wrong:**   The rain had stopped an hour before;
>   I was getting hungry.

If you aren't certain that the two clauses are related closely enough, use a period and don't look for trouble.

Dash—This mark indicates a sharp break in the construction of a sentence like this.

§ We were just turning the corner—stop that, Tommy!

§ They will get here soon—if they ever do.

The mistake made by inexperienced writers in using the dash is that they become so fond of this mark that they pepper their papers with it. Like the exclamation mark, when it is used too often, the effect is lost. One dash a page is more than enough. Another thing is this. Students sometimes try to make dashes take the place of legitimate punctuation and are subsequently very unhappy about what is done to their papers by the teacher.

Exclamation—Again, don't overdo it. A startling statement now and then may help, but if the exclamation mark appears in every other sentence, you produce a "Cry wolf" situation. The reader stops being impressed. Besides, you can't create artificial excitement by a punctuation mark. Words and ideas do it properly.

Quotations—At one time quotation marks were used for slang expressions and other colloquialisms. Nowadays, if the language is appropriate for the tone of the composition, you need not single out particular expressions. Should a phrase be doubtful in your own mind, rather than use quotation marks, leave it out altogether.

Remember, if you are writing dialogue, you must paragraph each time there is a change of speakers.

Watch out for sentence errors in dialogue. They count just as much here as in the rest of the composition.

3. *Agreement*—Check every subject and verb to make sure that singular nouns or pronouns have been matched with singular verbs, and plural with plural. Be on your guard for these:

§ There **were** a torn sweater and an old pair of socks on the bed.

§ The main ingredient **is** crushed pineapples.

§ It is one of those gadgets that **are** very popular these days.

§ Every one of the spectators **was** chilled to the bone.

§ A list of papers, books, and pamphlets **was required** on the last page.

§ Neither the players nor **the coach was satisfied.**

§ Neither the coach nor **the players were satisfied.**

§ Along the dock **were** boats of every description.

4. Reference—Every pronoun you use must refer to a clearly identifiable antecedent. Don't do this:

> My mother and sister came in at that moment. She began to scold me before I could say a word. Then she joined her, too.
> (Who is "she" or "her"?)

Do this instead:

> My mother and sister came in at that moment. Mom began to scold me before I could say a word, and Sally joined in, too.

Be sure, also, to check the agreement of references:

§ Each of the players was assigned **his** own locker.

§ A store that does business that way will close before **its** lease runs out.

Don't introduce a pronoun if it has nothing in the previous sentence to refer to, as in this example:

§ We had lots of fun in Canada. **They** have the best hockey players there. (Wrong)

§ We had lots of fun in Canada. The best hockey players live there. (Right)

5. Dangling Expressions—Every modifying word, phrase, or clause must be clearly attached to the word it modifies. *Not this:*

§ He only had about thirty cents.

§ Having walked for several hours, the house was still not in sight.
(Did the house walk?)

§ The suspect was brought into the station by the detective, wearing handcuffs and looking a little dazed.

But this:

§ He had only about thirty cents.

§ We had walked for several hours, but the house was still not in sight.

§ The suspect, wearing handcuffs and looking a little dazed, was brought into the station by the detective.

6. Verbs—One of the problems here arises out of what is called sequence of tenses. Once you have started a paragraph in a particular time, you must stay in that time until the end, and not do this:

He came into the class several weeks after I did. At first he didn't seem to notice me. Then he starts to look my way and borrows things every chance he gets.

The paragraph should have progressed this way:

He came into the class several weeks after I did. At first he didn't seem to notice me. Then he **started** to

look my way and **borrowed** *things every chance he* **got.**
(Since the paragraph was begun in the past tense, it
should have stayed there.)

Another problem with verbs arises out of your use of
irregular forms:

Present	Progressive	Past	Perfect (has, have, had)
see	seeing	saw	seen
do	doing	did	done
lie	lying	lay	lain
lay	laying	laid	laid
drink	drinking	drank	drunk
cost	costing	cost	cost
begin	beginning	began	begun

These are but a few examples. There are more than one
hundred others like them. You simply have to learn the
principal parts of the irregular verb forms by practicing sample
sentences containing them until your response is automatic.
In a composition, if you aren't sure of a form, don't use it.
There is always another verb that will serve as well.

7. Consistent Structure—Here, too, the problems fall into
two categories. The first involves the *person* that is used in
the paragraph. As with the sequence of tenses, if you have
committed yourself to the third person (he, she, it, they,
etc.), you can't suddenly switch to the second (you), as
this writer did:

> A visitor to New York City would be amazed at its
> wonders. Most out-of-towners want to see Greenwich
> Village, a city within a city. The visitor can enjoy the
> cafés, art galleries, and shops. Or you can go uptown to
> Times Square to see movies, plays, and penny arcades.
> In the summer you can go to Coney Island, or the
> newcomer can watch major league baseball in Yankee
> Stadium.

(Each "you" should have been "he.")

The second error in consistent structure occurs when the writer fails to maintain what is called *parallelism*. Note these:

Wrong: The drill consisted of passing, dribbling, and a layup shot.
On the farm I enjoyed most the milking of the cows, the feeding of the chickens, and to take a walk down the road after dinner.
She was tall, frail, and wasn't dressed very well either.

Right: The drill consisted of passing, dribbling, and **shooting a layup.**
On the farm I enjoyed most the milking of the cows, the feeding of the chickens, and **the taking of a walk down the road after dinner.**
(This would be even better if it read " . . . milking the cows, feeding the chickens, and walking down the road after dinner.")

Parallelism is just another example of the matching principle in our language. When you join constructions or run them in series, each of the elements must be of the same design. The first exercise above was changed because there were two participles (or gerunds) followed by a regular noun. All three should have been the same. In the second one, the infinitive phrase did not match the others, and in the third a clause followed two adjectives. Thus, the latter must be changed to fit and becomes:

She was tall, frail, and **poorly dressed.**

We have reviewed the major errors you should look for when you read your paper over for the third time. Whether you find some of these or others that we haven't discussed, you will make progress in your efforts to clean up your work mechanically only if you pledge now *never to commit the same mistake twice*. Look it up; work on it; get rid of it!

√ Fourth Reading—Check Language Interest: The last time you go over your paper, your objective is to dress it up so that your language makes the material interesting to read. You must eliminate the dull spots and find the best words to express your thoughts and ideas.

1) Look for needless repetition. Count the number of times a particular word or phrase has appeared in a paragraph. Use the methods of elimination or substitution to correct the possible monotony.

2) Streamline your sentence structure so that all waste words are removed. Try to make your statements direct, concrete, and positive.

3) Make at least five changes per paragraph insofar as individual words are concerned. Pick a noun here, a verb there, and exchange it for a word that is more colorful, more active, more emotional. Set your mind to it, and you will have little trouble thinking of better words than the ones you used originally.

Four readings sound like a lot of work. They aren't, really. If you are faithful and careful about the preparation of your outline, try diligently to follow the suggestions about good paragraph and sentence structure while you write the rough draft, you will have very little to do during the first two readings. As your mechanical competence in usage improves, the third reading will reveal only a few corrections. When you find that most of your time is spent on the fourth review, you will have reached the ideal point in revision. You may even be able to combine some of the first three steps and go through the paper only twice and do the bulk of your rewriting in the pepping up of your language. Whatever you do, try never to hand in a composition that hasn't been roughed out first.

The exercises in this chapter will be confined to a single student composition that you will be asked to revise in accordance with the plan just presented. This is how we will do it. The original composition, with all the mistakes, will be shown to you. The lines will be numbered so that reference to the sentences can easily be made. Read the paper and jot down what changes you would make in the paragraph structure. Then go over it a second time and correct any sentence problems, again recording the revisions you have made. During the third reading, make note of mechanical errors that need attention, and finally, during the fourth reading, improve the language (at least five changes per paragraph). Rewrite the composition after you have done the work of revision. Only then should you compare your results with the ones at the end of the chapter. See how close you came to the second version of the original that will be presented last.

ORIGINAL COMPOSITION

Fishing Can Be Fun

1   Fishing can be fun and it is for me. With the right
2 equipment and some good luck, that is. Owning a small
3 fourteen foot boat and a fifteen horsepower engine, fish-
4 ing is my weekly sport during the warm summer months.
5 When I pick up the paper and read the outdoor column in
6 the beginning of April and see that the flounders are once
7 more in the bay, I simply flip. Then the fever hits you
8 and all the tackle is pulled out for necessary repairs.
9   Of course April weather isn't the nicest, nor are
10 the flounders the biggest, like a fool I go fishing
11 just the same. Then May rolls in. The weather still
12 isn't the nicest but the weakfish in Peconic Bay puts
13 the flounders to shame. Weakfish are the most fun when
14 caught with a spinning outrig. Every good fisherman
15 must have some light tackle if he really wants to have
16 fun. Even a one pound fish is fun with a light rod. By
17 June, practically everything is good, even the weather.
18 My boat is kept on a trailer so that I can go from one
19 bay to another, depending upon the fishing conditions you
20 are looking for.
21   However my greatest enjoyment is July. Then its good-
22 bye to the bay and the devil with the weather. When the
23 bluefish come in I am lost to everything else. Bluefish
24 are the most fun to all fisherman. Then its offshore to

25 all and out to the acid grounds, where most of the big
26 blues hide. I caught one twelve pounds two summers ago
27 and I shall never forget it. This blue jumped water about
28 eight times before I finally gaffed him into the boat.
29   Yes, fishing can be fun. You may get soaking wet,
30 hooked in a finger by some unexperienced nearbye dope,
31 bit by a fish or even catch your thumb in a skimmer
32 clam as I did once. But just think of the fun you have.
33 Telling those humerous tales to friends and hearing of
34 their experiences. Well, I enjoy fishing anyway.

Before indicating the revisions, I want to point out that
ordinarily the rough draft would be written or typed with
ample space between the lines to provide for writing in the
changes. But the limitations set by the size of a page in a
paperback book make that impractical here. You understand,
I'm sure, that in your own work you would not have to list
the changes; you would make them right on the paper. The
numbered lines should enable you to follow recommendations
easily enough and the rewritten composition at the end will
act as a summary.

⩒ First Reading—Paragraph Revision

1) Eliminate *With the right equipment and some good
luck, that is* (l. 1, 2). No development of this point is made in
the body of the composition; therefore, it shouldn't be introduced in the opening paragraph. (Incidentally, did you
notice that this piece is a fragment, not a sentence?)

2) Insert a topic sentence at the beginning of Paragraph
II to add unity:

> With my rig all set, I am ready for the early season
> thrills.

Otherwise, there is no clear-cut central idea.

3) Eliminate *Weakfish . . .* (l. 13) plus everything else
up to *with a light rod* (l. 16). These three sentences have
drifted off the main idea of the paragraph.

4) Add a few details to Paragraph II because it sounds
like a reading of the calendar:

> (l. 11) after *just the same.* To be truthful, I come

home chilled, half-drowned, and empty-handed sometimes during the rainy part of the spring.

(l. 11) after *May rolls in.* Sudden downpours, squalls,
and freezing mornings are still a threat, but the weakfish . . .

(l. 17) after *is in good.* The skies are clear, the waters are calm, and the fish practically leap out demanding to be caught.

5) Add a concluding sentence after (l. 28) to bring Paragraph III to a better finish:

I wish July were twelve months long.

6) Eliminate *Well, I enjoy fishing anyway* (l. 34) to avoid
a wishy-washy ending paragraph.

✔ Second Reading—Sentence Revision

1) Add continuity (l. 18):

This is when my boat is kept . . .

2) Correct run-on error (l. 10). Add *but* after the comma
to connect the two clauses legitimately.

3) Correct fragment (l. 33). Write it thus:

. . . fun you have telling those . . .

4) Change sentence beginning *But just think* . . . (l. 32)
to question:

But won't you have fun . . .

This will aid sentence variety.

✔ Third Reading—Mechanics Revision

1) *Spelling:*

it's for *its* (l. 21)

it's for *its* (l. 24)

inexperienced for *unexperienced* (l. 30)

nearby for *nearbye* (l. 30)

humorous for *humerous* (l. 33)

2) *Punctuation:*

Add comma after *you* (l. 7)

      ”   ”   ” *Of course* (l. 9)

      ”   ”   before *but* (l. 12)

      ”   ”   after *However* (l. 21)

      ”   ”   ” *in* (l. 23)

Remove comma after *grounds* (l. 25)

Add comma after *fish* (l. 31)

3) *Agreement:*

    put for *puts* (l. 12) (*Weakfish* is being used in a plural sense.)

4) *Dangling Expressions:*

    Change (l. 2) to read:

    I own a small . . . engine, and fishing . . .

5) *Verbs:*

    bitten for *bit* (l. 31)

6) *Parallelism:*

    caught by your thumb for *catch your thumb* (l. 31)

√ *Fourth Reading—Language Revision*

Paragraph I:

1) Eliminate *and it is for me* (l. 1). It is obvious and therefore unnecessary.

2) Eliminate *fishing is* (l. 3) because it is repetitious. Add . . . *can enjoy my weekly sport* . . .

3) Eliminate *the beginning of* (l. 6)

4) Change position of *in April* to follow *the paper* (l. 6) because it follows time more logically when it refers to when the paper is picked up.

5) Add comma after *April;* eliminate *and, in* (l. 5)

6) *me* for *you* (l. 7) Actually this correction belongs under consistency of structure (Third Reading), but you will often find that you pick up an error even when you are looking for other things. That's the value of more than one reading of a paper.

Paragraph II:

1) *is rather fickle* for *isn't the nicest* (l. 9)

2) *I keep my boat* for *my boat is kept* (l. 18)

3) *life behind a rod and reel becomes beautiful* for *practically everything is in good* (l. 17)

4) *I* for *you* (l. 19)

5) Condense *depending upon the fishing conditions I am looking for* to *depending upon conditions* (l. 19)

Paragraph III:
  1) *occurs in* for *is* (l. 21)
  2) Eliminate *to all fishermen* (l. 24)
  3) Eliminate *offshore to all and* (l. 24)
  4) Add *that weighed* after *one* (l. 26)
  5) *He* for *This blue* (l. 27)

Paragraph IV:
  1) *is fun* for *can be fun* (l. 29)
  2) *listening to* for *hearing of* (l. 33)
  3) *their lies as well* for *their experiences* (l. 34)

REVISED COMPOSITION

Fishing Can Be Fun

Fishing can be fun. I own a small fourteen foot boat and a fifteen horsepower engine and can enjoy my weekly sport during the warm summer months. When I pick up the paper in April, read the outdoor column, and see the flounders are once more in the bay, I flip. Then the fever hits me, and all the tackle is pulled out for necessary repairs.

With my rig all set, I am ready for the early season thrills. Of course, April weather is rather fickle, but like a fool I go fishing just the same. To be truthful, I come home chilled, half-drowned, and empty-handed some-times during the rainy part of the spring. Then May rolls in. Sudden downpours, squalls, and freezing mornings are still a threat, but the weakfish in Peconic Bay put the flounder to shame, and I must try out my light tackle. By June, life behind a rod and reel becomes beautiful. The skies are clear, the waters are calm, and the fish practically leap out demanding to be caught. This is when I keep my boat on a trailer so that I can go from one bay to another, depending on conditions.

However, my greatest enjoyment occurs in July. Then it's good-bye to the bay and the devil with the weather. When the bluefish come in, I am lost to everything else because these babies are the most fun. Then it's out to the acid grounds where most of the blues hide. Two sum-mers ago I caught one that weighed twelve pounds and I shall never forget it. He jumped water about eight times before I finally gaffed him into the boat. I wish July were twelve months long.

Yes, fishing is fun. You may get soaking wet, hooked in a finger by some inexperienced nearby dope, bitten by a fish, or even caught by your thumb in a skimmer clam as I did once. But won't you have a time telling those humorous tales to friends and listening to their lies as well?

Did you notice that as this composition was rewritten a few more changes were added, especially in Paragraphs II and III? This is really the final suggestion about revision. Even after you have made your alterations on the rough draft, you may still see something else if you rewrite carefully. That's fine. Your last copy will be that much better.

At this point you may be thinking that I, a professional teacher, would naturally find many things to improve in any paper, whereas a student might not spot half the possibilities. Suppose this is so. Wouldn't you say, however, that a revised composition with just 50% of the potential improvements would still be vastly superior to the original and certainly worth the effort involved in rewriting it? And certainly worth a higher rating?

For added practice in this section, you might try revising some of the numerous paragraphs and whole compositions that have been used in this book for illustrative purposes. See whether you can lift the quality of an ordinary or unsatisfactory sample to a superior level.

How Do You Prepare the Final Copy?

Let's go back a bit to the point where you have completed the last re-reading and revision of your rough draft. You are now ready to write the copy that you will hand in. Will its outward appearance affect the grade you get?

Technically, it shouldn't and, if teachers were machines, it wouldn't. But teachers, like other human beings, react to compositions the way they, and we, react to people the first time we meet them. The smooth dressers attract us, and the sloppy ones repel. Certainly Shakespeare understood our nature when he said, "Apparel oft proclaims the man."

Keep this in mind, then. The person who rates your paper tries to be completely objective and yet cannot help being more favorably impressed with neatness and good form than with carelessness and disorder. The estimate of your composition actually begins the moment your teacher sets eyes on it. If it looks outwardly good, you have stimulated a positive feeling; if it is a mess, you have handicapped your material and it will have to be very superior to overcome the bad first impression. The truth is that a beautifully prepared piece of work will often get a higher rating than it deserves just because of its attractive appearance. I therefore cannot over-stress the importance of handing in a "well-dressed" final copy. The suggestions that follow will help you achieve this aim.

Paper

Your school may require a particular size and quality of paper for compositions. If it does, use it. This is no place to show your independence of spirit. If you aren't given special instructions, the 8″ x 10″ or 8½″ x 11″ size is expected, lined for longhand and a good bond for typewriting. Avoid legal cap (8½″ x 14″) unless requested to use it, and never use odd pieces of paper that are either too small or outlandishly large. Your composition should stand out by virtue of its words and ideas, not by its peculiar physical shape. Moreover, the papers for each class must be kept in sets by the teacher, and the irregular sizes are sources of irritation because they make filing difficult or may slip out of the packs.

Ink

First of all, use it. Leave your pencil behind with the rough draft. Either black or blue ink is satisfactory, but stay away from the fancy colors. Your teacher will probably want to use red or green for marking so that it stands out against the color you use. If you use a ball-point pen, and it would be better if you didn't, try not to make heavy impressions on the paper because it may turn out to look as if someone had walked on it with hob-nailed boots.

Now I want to let you in on a secret. A teacher subconsciously gives a typewritten piece of work that extra edge I mentioned before. Somehow the printed word influences people more strongly than the handwritten one. Of course, on examinations you can't help yourself. But on other occasions, use a typewriter if possible. However, watch out for typographical errors, which will not be accepted as alibis for poor mechanics. Do the job neatly. Disorganized typing is much worse than careful longhand.

Headings and Spacing

Here again many schools have standard types, and you should use what is expected. Failure to do so shows an indifference that will be reflected in your mark. If you have a choice about headings, something like this will supply the necessary information:

Name of Student, Section   Teacher's Name
English Class   Date
                        (Skip a line.)
                            Title
                        (Skip a line.)
¶ Indent for the first paragraph . . .
(Do not skip spaces between lines in the text for longhand.)
                (Use double spacing for typewriting.)
        (Do not skip extra spaces between paragraphs.)
¶ Indent for the second paragraph . . .
                        Etc., Etc.

Margins

Leave margins on all four sides of your paper—top, bottom, left, and right. About an inch to an inch and a half is ample for each. Teachers appreciate margins because it gives them room for corrections and comments. Besides, the paper looks as if it had been framed and is accordingly more attractive.

Miscellaneous

In the title, unless otherwise instructed, use capital letters always for the first word and for all others except articles, short prepositions and conjunctions, and words in direct quotations used as titles. The only punctuation used is a question or exclamation mark, but no period.

If you have been asked to supply references for your composition, list them at the end, preferably on a separate page. For books, give the title, author, publisher, copyright date, and pages or chapters read. For a magazine, give its name, the edition (year and month or volume and number), the title of the article, the author, and pages read. Remember: if you quote anybody else's words, you must use quotation marks.

Even an innocent oversight can be legitimately regarded as plagiarism.

You may have to make last minute corrections. Do so without ruining your paper. Your teacher will prefer a paper slightly marred by a correction to one that has clean errors. Draw a single line through the unwanted word or phrase and write the new material directly above it. Should you have to revise more than a few words, it would be best to rewrite the page.

Get your work in on time. Even if you are sick, send it along with a friend. Whether your teacher penalizes you for tardiness or not is beside the point. You cannot expect your late paper to be marked with the same sympathy and interest given the ones that came in when they were due.

Don't handicap yourself by submitting a slovenly written final copy. Take pride in the appearance of your compositions and you will find that you are increasingly less guilty of careless errors. Neatness breeds correctness.

How Are Literature Questions Answered?

It's time to pause again, to look back before we go ahead.

You have learned how necessary it is to follow a step-by-step procedure to turn out a good composition.

You know that the final quality depends upon what you do about:

> The topic
> Its scope
> Your approach
> An outline
> Paragraph development
> Language interest
> Revision

Now, if you get one more point clear in your mind, you will be well on your way toward meeting all of your writing needs.

It is this. Not everything you write is called a composition, but *everything you write that is a paragraph or more in length must be handled like a composition*. For instance, there are the papers you have to hand in that are based upon the things you read or watch—the answers to literature questions, the book reports, the dramatic reviews. Can the same techniques of writing covered in the previous chapters be used here, too? Not only can they, but they must! And our next objective is to show you how.

I. *The Literature Question*

Perhaps you have often wondered why teachers insist upon training you to write about the books you read. Unless you become a professional critic, you say, you won't ever be expected to do this in adult life. Yes, but if you do any reading at all after you leave school, if you go to see motion pictures or plays, or even if you watch only television programs, you will talk about them with your friends. As an educated person, you will be expected to be able to say somewhat more about a production or a book than "Great," "Swell," or "What a waste of time!" The experience you gain in answering literature questions will enable you to criticize and evaluate intelligently, to offer reasons for your likes and dislikes.

So much for the *why's* of literature questions; let's get back to the *how's* of answering them. We can do this best by first examining the official rating suggestions issued to teachers on a recent state examination in high school English:

Literature

Judge literature answers primarily on content, but expect adequate technique of composition.

In general, require that a pupil in his answer (1) meet the requirements of the question, (2) show familiarity with the piece of literature he is discussing, (3) demonstrate his power to judge and to generalize with clearness and forcefulness of expression, (4) use specific references in support of statements made, and (5) show adequate technique of composition.

Item 1 is very significant. It tells you that you must address yourself to the problem presented in the literature question and that a re-telling of the story is not the way to do it. Indeed, later on in the instructions, the teacher is told to allow a maximum of half credit for any answer that is "merely a plot synopsis or a summary."

This is quite reasonable. Suppose some friends and you had just come out of a theater after seeing a play or motion picture. What would you be least likely to discuss? The plot, of course. Wouldn't it be absurd for one of you to tell the others what had happened in something all of you had just seen?

Similarly, in class you have presumably read whatever it is you have been asked to write about, and so has the teacher. Surely nobody wants you to tell the story merely to prove you have done the reading. This fact could be established much more easily, if needed, by a short answer test. No, what the teacher wants to know is whether you can express an opinion, can analyze, can compare—and that's what a literature question tries to find out.

Item 3 suggests why some schools refer to it as a Power Question. Your answer must demonstrate your *power* to think and express yourself with originality and your *power* to prove that what you have said can be supported by direct references to the book. This is the way in which you are trained to tell why you like or dislike what you see, hear, or read.

Note also that "adequate technique in composition" is mentioned twice in the instructions. You are expected to handle your answer like a composition, in every sense of the word, with or without the label. The only difference is that there is not much freedom of choice for the writer because his prime responsibility is to meet the requirements of the literature question. However, this actually makes the preliminary work of composition move more rapidly since much of the planning is dictated by the question. Thus, the topic, scope, and approach are quite definitely suggested in advance. But the rest of the steps should be followed just as if the answer were a regular composition. Let's see how it works with an actual question that appeared on an examination not long ago:

The Question

When we tire of the humdrum world in which we live, we like to escape into a more fascinating world created by the imagination of a great author. For each of two worthwhile books (one novel and one play) describe the kind of world to which you have been transported and show how the life there differs from that with which you are familiar. Give titles and authors.

Handling the Answer

The problem suggested by the question is actually your topic. In this case, you are expected to show how you were able to find escape in several things you read. The scope is clearly limited to a novel and a play. The approach is given to you by the words "differs from that with which you are familiar." Obviously, you will have to discuss these books from a highly personal point of view.

It is imperative that you prepare an outline for an answer to a literature question. For one thing, it will help you avoid making costly mistakes. Remember, if you are asked to write about a novel, and you pick a biography or a short story, you will receive very little credit for your answer. Here is what the outline would look like for this question:

No.	Type	Title—Author	References
1.	Novel	*Arrowsmith*—Lewis	jungle, natives Dr. Gottlieb death of wife
2.	Play	*Macbeth*—Shakespeare	Duncan Malcolm duel

As you see, the outline reminds you of the number of books you must talk about and helps arrange them by type,

title, and author. The last column does the real job of the
outline; it suggests the contents of the paragraphs. You notice
that three references to the text are recommended for each
paragraph "in support of statements made." This is about
average for full-length books. For shorter pieces—lyric poems,
essays, short stories—it might not be possible to use more than
one or two references because of the limited material.

The development of each middle paragraph of any answer
to any literature question should now be clear:

§ The first sentence should refer to the problem of the
question and give the title and author of the selection. This
makes a very tight topic sentence, doesn't it?

§ The related sentences should use the specific references
suggested by the outline to develop the main line of reasoning
of the writer as he demonstrates his ability to discuss the problem of the question.

§ The last sentence of each middle paragraph should
clinch the main point. This implies an emphatic restatement
of the attitude of the writer toward the problem.

Further paragraph development is the same as for a regular composition. As usual, the outline prepares the material
for the middle paragraphs. The introductory and concluding
paragraphs must be added later. In a literature question, the
problem presented practically dictates what direction the beginning and ending paragraphs will take.

Note: Some schools, even when two or more books are to
         be discussed, permit the students to leave out the in-
         troductory and concluding paragraphs. If this is so
         in yours, simply handle each book in a separate
         paragraph and follow the suggestions made above
         about middle paragraph development.

You can see how language interest is maintained by studying the answer below that was written for the question we
have been analyzing.

Answer to Literature Question

We would all like to be able to step onto a magic carpet and be whisked away to some far off place of adventure and romance when the cares of the day become overwhelming or life seems dull and uninteresting. How fortunate we are at such times since we need merely reach casually toward the nearest book shelf for the means of escape from our monotonous surroundings.

I can still remember how, at a time when there seemed to be little purpose in my existence, I came across the vivid pages of "Arrowsmith," by Sinclair Lewis. Suddenly, I had left the confining canyons of a big city and had been transported to a dense, teeming jungle. Instead of battling my way through a crowded bus, I was helping to test a medical theory and was working heroically to save the lives of simple, suffering natives. I even forgot about homework as I joined Dr. Gottlieb in his never-ending search for truth and accuracy. I grieved with the good doctor over the death of his wife and applauded his decision to dedicate his life to research and service to mankind, even as I, a useless adolescent, might some day do. Yes, the pages of this American classic became more than a magic carpet. They opened my eyes to shining dreams.

Similarly, when I am looking for escape, even a tragic play like "Macbeth," by William Shakespeare, can provide me with the private life of a Walter Mitty. My rather severely cut jacket and straight-lined pants are replaced by plumed hats, chain mail, flashing swords, and steel armor. I am a nobleman, not a teenager, and I seek to free my land of a bloody tyrant and his ruthless queen. Rushing about the castle announcing the murder of Duncan, convincing Malcolm to return to Scotland at the head of an army, or dueling the villain to the death are all adventures that happen to me, not alone to MacDuff. Petty squabbles with my friends or silly radio programs fade from my sight and mind as my pulse quickens with each new experience. The immortal bard has not only written a play, but has added a chapter to my own life, which has through the magic of his pen become so greatly enriched.

It is indeed a pity that some people find no pleasure in reading books. They miss so much because a book is not really a means of escape. It is just another way of living.

Comments

1. You can see how the beginning and ending paragraphs do little more than restate the problem of the question and suggest how the writer will handle it. Moreover, if these paragraphs were not required, I'm sure you understand how easy it would be to eliminate them.

2. Note how each middle paragraph has the tight topic sentence which cleverly inserts the title and author into the projection of the main point of the answer.

3. Observe, also, that the *specific references* are given in just enough detail to prove the point made but not at such length as to lose sight of the argument because of overstress of the plot.

4. Do you see how the clinching sentence at the end of each middle paragraph ties things together?

5. Incidentally, you should work with a rough draft in your answer to a literature question since, as we have repeatedly maintained, it is a composition. When you revise, look for the usual things but be especially careful of two things in addition:

- Don't forget the quotation marks around all titles if you are writing in longhand.
- Avoid sentence fragments when you mention the title and author, like this:

Wrong "Hamlet" by William Shakespeare. This play caught my interest . . .

Right "Hamlet," by William Shakespeare, caught my interest . . .

6. Did you note that a definite effort was made to use effective language and to vary the sentence structure?

Now let's look at some examples of single paragraph answers to literature questions:

Question

People make adjustments with varying degrees of success to certain factors in their environment. These factors may be their physical surroundings, other people, or the customs and traditions of the society in which they live. From the novels and full-length plays you have read, choose a total of any **two** books. In **each** case show by definite references to what extent a person in the book was successful in adjusting to one or more of the above factors. Give titles and authors.

Answer A

The great tragedy of Eustacia Vye, the brooding beauty in Thomas Hardy's "The Return of the Native," was that she was unable to make a successful adjustment either to her physical environment or the people about her. She would have loved being a lady of high fashion in Paris or London; instead she found Egdon Heath closing in on her more and more relentlessly. Scorning the village folk and their petty problems, she sought escape in the arms of Wildeve, only to find him a faithless wretch. In Clym Yeobright, she thought she had at last met the man who would free her and take her back with him to the glamorous metropolitan life he had known. Her great disappointment in him, his illness and his inability to tear himself away from the heath, inevitably drove her to the watery grave she found with the equally unstable Wildeve. Eustacia could not adjust, nay **would not,** and was therefore doomed to a life of unhappiness from the start. She taught me a valuable lesson. I will continue to reach for the stars, but, if need be, I will settle for and do my best with less.

Answer B

I felt very sad when I read in Eugene O'Neill's "Beyond the Horizon" how unsuccessful Robert Mayo was in adjusting to his environment. I could appreciate his desire to travel and leave his father's farm where he had spent the greater part of his life. But events conspired against him and he somehow could not fight back. His unfortunate marriage to Ruth, Andrew's heart-broken departure, his father's death, and the difficulty of scraping out a living from unyielding land challenged his ability to adjust. Robert, lacking the strength and knowledge of agriculture his father and brother had possessed, succumbed to the forces about him with hardly a struggle. I would have tried to be less impulsive in the first place, especially with Ruth, but once I had made the mistake I would have tried to improve my lot. I would have made an effort to learn more about farming so that I could meet my problems rather than be conquered by them.

Do you see how the first sentence in each paragraph mentions the problem of the question, the title and author of the selection, and the approach of the writer? Did you count at least three references to support the statements? Do you agree that the "clincher" at the end is necessary to round out the discussion? Did you observe the personal touch introduced into each answer?

Your success in answering a literature question rests mainly on your interpretation of the question, your analysis of the requirements, and your selection of references to support your arguments. It is really like writing any paragraph. You have to focus sharply on a main idea and then develop it through details. A few additional hints should be helpful:

1) Learn what various words mean as they are used in literature questions, like *modern* (written since 1900), *recent* (in the last 25 years), and *current* (within the past 5 years). Get a good book on literary forms and clarify for yourself the differences between fiction and non-fiction writing, novels and biographies and plays, essays and short stories, lyrics and narrative poems, verse dramas and epics.

2. If no set number of words is suggested in the question, keep in mind that the average full paragraph has 100-150 words. This total would apply to discussions of the longer works—novels, plays, biographies. For poems, essays, and

other shorter pieces, 75-100 words would be enough. You can also guide yourself by the number of credits assigned to the question. About 10 words a point should be satisfactory: 30 points-300 words, 20 points-200 words, etc.

3) Try to get yourself into the answer, as did the writers of the last two examples. It is interesting to note this statement in the official marking instructions mentioned before:

"Although *length* should not be considered a substitute for *strength*, an abundance of details and illustrations and *direct application to personal experience* serve to amplify and enrich the answer."

To improve your interpretation of questions, practice by reading as many as you can and jotting down briefly what the requirements are, after this fashion:

Sample Question #1

In writing a short story, an author, like a motion picture producer, creates a setting and an atmosphere that help to produce the effect he wishes. In other words, the place where something happens, the background, is important to the story. From short stories you have read, choose **four** and show by definite references how the author in each case created the desired setting and atmosphere and made it important to the story. Give titles and authors.

Requirements

I must use 4 *short stories* (not novels, plays, or anything else).

The plot is completely unimportant except as it is aided by the background.

My main discussion must be about the place where the action took place and how the author made it a factor in the development of the plot (the way Hardy uses Egdon Heath in "The Return of the Native").

Since there are four works, the individual paragraphs will have to be kept under 100 words; otherwise I'll never get finished. My sentences have to be concentrated and I have to hit the highlights only.

Sample Question #2

The basis of man's spiritual strength lies in freedom. His choice of an action frequently changes the whole course of his life. Illustrate the importance of choice in human life through references to characters met in literature. If you base your discussion on full-length books (as biographies, novels), use **two** books; if upon shorter selections (as essays, poems), use two selections as a substitute for each full-length book. Give titles and authors.

Requirements

I can use only *two* selections if both are novels, long plays, or biographies; I can use *three* if one is full-length and the other two are short; I must use *four* if all are short, like essays or poems.

I must show how one of the characters in each selection made an important choice of action and how it changed his life. I will get a personal note in by suggesting what I would have done had I been the character.

My references to the plot must be confined to occasions that describe a choice of action and the effects it had.

Now try it yourself with these questions when you have some spare time:

1. Biography may serve the reader through
   a. giving him a better understanding of human nature
   b. acquainting him with the spirit, purpose, and methods of successful people
   c. informing him of many pursuits and interests
   d. making historical events live

Choose **two** biographies, and show how each is useful in

one or more of the ways suggested. Mention authors and titles.

2. The reading public today is turning more and more to non-fiction literature to keep in touch with the contemporary world. Choose from your reading (excluding novels, short stories, plays, and poetry) **two** books of non-fiction and explain by specific references how each has brought you into closer contact with the world about you, with outstanding people of modern life, or with recent developments in the arts, in politics, or in science. Give titles and authors.

3. Great literature stimulates our own thinking. Select **two** essays and **two** poems and show how each has awakened in you a new thought or developed a half-formed idea. In each case, give the title, author, and enough of the ideas to illustrate how it has influenced your thinking.

4. The conduct of fictitious characters, like that of real people, results from such emotions as greed, ambition, fear, love, self-sacrifice, jealousy, hatred, revenge, patriotism, civic pride, and a desire to reform. Choose any **four** of the following—a play, novel, short story, biography, narrative poem—and show how in each the actions or course of action of some character resulted from one of these emotions. Give titles and authors.

5. People in novels, full-length biographies, and books of true experience often struggle against the forces of nature, such as bitter cold, intense heat, snow-fast mountains, the sea, storms, or the terrors of the wilderness. Choose **two** books from the types mentioned and show by definite references how a person in each book was or was not successful in the struggle. Give titles and authors.

6. A person's actions are often influenced by a strong trait of character. Choose **one** important person from a novel and **one** from a play, and show by definite references how this statement is true. Give titles and authors.

7. Some characters in novels and plays show in their actions fairness and consideration for others; other characters show unmistakably that they place their own welfare and desires above those of others. Support this statement by contrasting specific actions of **two** characters, each from a different novel or play.

8. Certain poems have a lasting appeal because of their important ideas, vivid pictures, or effective expres-

sion. Choose **four** poems and show by definite references
that this statement is true.

We will bring this section to a close by giving you a few
more model answers to literature questions. Study both the
questions and the answers carefully in relation to the suggestions made before and determine how the various recommended techniques have been employed.

Question

A novel or play cannot be regarded as successful unless at its conclusion the main character meets a fate
that seems to be the natural result of what he has done
or shown himself to be. Referring to the main character
of **one** novel and the main character of **one** play, show
by definite reference to each book that the above statement is true. Mention titles and authors.

Answer

(Fully developed type, including introductory and concluding paragraphs)

"As ye sow, so shall ye reap." The Bible tells us that
the final outcome of a person's life can be predicted on
the basis of his early behavior. Certainly, we have count-
less examples in real life of people whose service to mankind (or careers of crime) can be traced as far back as
their childhood. Great literature, too, is rich with stories
of men and women whose fate in the final chapters is
consistent with their deeds in the earlier ones. In fact,
a book may lose its claim to immortality if the ending
is not a natural result.

One of the reasons "Ethan Frome," by Edith Whar-
ton, has become a classic American novel is the success
with which the author makes clear, in the final chapter,
that the picture of despair is consistent with the pattern
of life that emerges from the study of Ethan's approach
toward his problems. When he somehow becomes en-
meshed in a marriage to Zeena, whom he doesn't love,

and sacrifices a promising career, one can see that there is a serious character weakness in the man. This lack of will power is further evidenced when he can find no way out of his desperate interest in Mattie Silver other than to let her go. Ethan's crowning act of futility, which turns a suicide pact into crippled misery, points toward unhappiness and frustration as the outcomes. Surely, his repeated failures to work himself out of his troubles make the ultimate hopeless anguish inevitable, and it is clear that the author has brought her story to a logical conclusion.

Similarly, when I read "Macbeth," I was not surprised at all when Macduff came striding back from battle bearing the head of his arch enemy. Throughout this great tragedy, Shakespeare repeatedly presents evidence that uncontrolled ambition coupled with violence must reap a harvest of destruction. The murder of Duncan by the Thane of Glamis is merely a prelude to a series of horrible crimes. Once Macbeth has succumbed to the bloodthirsty demands of his wife, and has allowed his moral fiber to be destroyed, he has marked himself as one who will perish by the sword since he has lived by it. The murders of Banquo and the family of Macduff, victims of a mad lust for power, are signposts on the road ahead for the crazed monarch. He held life cheaply, and in the end found his own snuffed out as if it had been a flickering candle. I was quite overcome by the tremendous dramatic force with which Shakespeare showed that what happens to people is the product of their deeds.

How often has this concept been duplicated in real life! Hitler and Mussolini rose to power on the broken backs of defenseless people and saw the day when their callous disregard of humanity was relentlessly destroyed. They surely met a fate that was the natural result of what they had done.

Comments

1. "Macbeth" was deliberately used for the second time to show you how the same book can be selected for a variety of questions, provided you interpret properly.

2. A concluding paragraph, when used, is most effective if the points made previously are applied or compared personally to the life of the writer or some well-known public figure.

Question

The enjoyment or appreciation of literature often depends on the mood of the reader. From the poems and essays you have read, choose **four** selections (using at least one poem and one essay). In each case show by definite references how the selection chosen would appeal to a person in one of the following moods: gay, questioning, sad, discouraged, serious, sentimental. Give titles and authors.

Answer

(Individual paragraph type, without separate introductory and concluding paragraphs)

§ Robert Frost's "Stopping by Woods on a Snowy Evening" appeals to me when I am in a serious mood. I sympathize with the poet's feeling of regret that man is so occupied with affairs of living that he leaves himself no time to enjoy the beautiful and fascinating world of nature. I, too, have longed to stop and watch. One day I sat above an ant hill—like Gulliver over the Lilliputians —marveling as the little creatures tugged and strained over a bread crumb until they got it down the hole. I could have sat for hours gazing at this other world, but soon a sense of guilt reminded me that, like the man in the poem, I had "many promises to keep," and much to do and had better move on. Frost's poem evokes a sense of some inner loss when man places value on only material things.

§ I suppose the reason Robert Frost's "Mending Wall" appealed to me when I first heard it was because of my own thoughtful mood about my "walls." "Something there is that doesn't love a wall . . ." My walls are not of stones and boulders, but it still seems as if some force of nature is against them. I am not trying to mend my walls—quite the contrary, I would like to tear them down. I must have known while I was building them what I was walling in and what I was walling out, but the reasons have long since disappeared and the walls remain. "Mending Wall," which I have read many times now, tells me beautifully that I am right when I want my walls down.

§ Edgar Lee Masters' "Abel Melveny" aroused a very deep emotion within me as I read about a man who acquired things of great value but never made use of them. The poem opened a window to a closed chamber reflecting a strange pattern in my own life of which I was unaware. I have been in the habit of acquiring many books but I seldom read them. They are meant for the future, a sort of insurance that I will some day be educated. I thought of this as I read about Abel Melveny's grinders, shellers, mills, rakes, ploughs, and threshers— bought but never used. I have come to realize that there is a touch of this strange man in all of us. Who doesn't have at least one dusty carton full of dreams stored in a dark corner of a closet? The poem helped answer some questions about me to me.

§ Anyone in a gay mood would probably be delighted with Christopher Morley's "On Answering Letters." In his charming essay, in which he discusses his own delinquency in his correspondence, Morley wittily draws a picture of most of us when we try to rationalize why we haven't answered a few letters recently arrived. It's fun to read humorous material that shows us how similar most people are about some things. It's not only amusing; it's downright reassuring. I really ought to answer that letter after all!

Comments

1. Each of the paragraphs above was written by a different student, yet there is one thing all have in common: *the personal touch.* Do you see how life and warmth is added to any kind of writing when the author relates the ideas to his own experiences?

2. It should be clear by now that the essence of a good answer to a power question is the extent to which the writer

has selected from the material read only those references that help him discuss the problem intelligently.

3. The final point to stress is that a good interpretation can be ruined if the writer makes no effort to insert language interest and sentence variety.

II. THE BOOK REPORT

Usually, in addition to the required literary works assigned for general study in your English class, you are periodically expected to read independently other books selected from a supplementary list or recommended directly by your teacher. Behind this program is a twofold purpose. One is to get you to develop a lifetime reading habit. The other is to continue to train you to appreciate and evaluate the books you read and to discuss them intelligently with other people. The training, of course, comes from the reports you must deliver on your outside reading assignments.

The form of these book reports varies from school to school and teacher to teacher. Both the written and oral kind are popular, but no standard report form is universally followed. Indeed, the progressive teacher of English looks for and encourages originality in a report as much as in a regular composition. The best thing we can do, therefore, is to tell you what to look for in the major literary types, indicate what is covered in most book reviews (student and professional, written and oral), and assume that you will adapt the suggestions to the particular requirements set by your own school or teacher.

A. *What to Look For*

1. *Fiction:* When an author tells a story that he has invented—whether in the form of a novel, play, long poem, or short story—he is writing fiction. The narrative material may be based upon fact, but presumably the events did not happen exactly as described to people who are clearly identifiable. Otherwise, we would have a biography of some sort. At any rate, the qualities that distinguish good stories from bad are practically the same for all the forms, with a few variations here and there. We will list first the questions that point toward the main characteristics of all fiction. Following these, you will find attention directed toward some additional qualities that refer to items peculiar to the particular form in which the fiction was presented.

a. Background

Where and when does most of the action take place?

To what extent are the buildings, dress, habits, and language markedly different from what you are familiar with?

How much does the background influence the actions or personality of any of the main characters?

Does the author seem to be thoroughly familiar with his setting? If it required research, do you think he did enough? Do the scenes ring true?

How well does the background create moods?

b. Plot

If both are present, how well are the main story line and the subplots interwoven?

What is the likelihood that the events could take place in real life?

What is the turning point of the action?

Do the incidents follow one another naturally, or do they seem to have been mechanically inserted by the author?

How well does the author create suspense, if any?

How many loose ends are left at the end of the story?

How logical or reasonable or probable or unusual is the ending?

What devices used by the author seem to indicate that he depended too much on chance to carry his story forward?

c. Characters

Who are the main characters? Are they like real people? Of whom do they remind you? Friends? Family? Prominent people? Movie or television stars?

Which are the most interesting? Why? Which remind you of yourself? How?

Do some of the characters seem to develop and change as the story progresses, or do they all remain about the same from beginning to end?

What are the strengths and weakness of the central characters? What incidents can you cite to support your conclusions?

To what extent does the personality of any character determine his or her success or failure?

What character did you like most and which did you dislike? With which ones did it make a difference to you whether they were happy or sad? Why?

Which ones helped you understand people you know a little better than before?

What minor characters are interesting? How would you describe one or two in a single sentence?

If you were the author, would you develop one or more of the characters differently? How?

How well does the author seem to know people and what "makes them tick"?

d. Theme

What do you suppose was the main reason for the author's telling this story? To amuse? Entertain? Preach? Convert? Criticize? Present a social problem?

What is he trying to prove, or what life experience is he trying to explain?

What is the main point of the story expressed in a single sentence?

If there is a problem in the story, how well does the author solve it? Or suggest a solution?

How has the book influenced your own thinking? What new ideas have you come away with?

To what extent has this story stimulated you to read others on the same theme?

If you were designing a book jacket, what illustration or symbol would you draw to point up the main idea?

e. Style

How well does the author present his scenes? Does he make you feel as if you were an eyewitness?

How do the sentences run—long, involved, sharp, varied? What difficulties did you have with the vocabulary?

How well are the emotions portrayed? What devices are used to do this? Were you moved to tears or laughter anywhere? Why?

Did you get angry at any of the characters? When?

How do the characters talk—the same as people like them would in real life, or do they seem to be talking out of the mouth of the author?

Does the author seem to invent phrases or have you heard many before? Give examples.

What is the tone of the language? Warm and friendly? Wise and fatherly? Cold and formal? Dry as dust? Rough and tough? Genteel?

If some of the language is strong, is it offensive or necessary to maintain the atmosphere and the nature of the characters? Give proof. Do you suspect that some bits were put in by the author mainly to be sensational and help the book sell? Cite examples that are really unnecessary.

Would you want to read more by this author because of the way he writes? Why?

What do you think of the choice of the title? How does it suit the story?

f. General

In what way have you changed your mind about certain beliefs you had before?

How different do you now feel about a type or group of people?

How significant is the theme in relation to world or life problems?

What is there interesting about the author's life that is reflected perhaps in the story?

How would you compare this story to another somewhat like it that you read previously?

What do you think the central characters would be like twenty or so years after the end of the story?

What chance does this story have of becoming a classic, if it hasn't already become one? Why?

Additional Questions on a Novel

How would this story turn out as a play? A movie?

How much of the book could have been eliminated if the writer had been more economical? Where should it have been expanded?

Would this book be more interesting to some people than to others? Why?

Do you recommend reading this book in one sitting, or can it be handled in sections? Why?

Additional Questions on Short Stories

What single mood is created?

Toward what single effect does the story point? Mystery? Horror? Humor? Sadness? Romance?

If there is a surprise ending, does it sound reasonable?

Do you feel let down at the end? Why?

Additional Questions on a Play

How imaginative is the scenery? To what extent would a few more sets have improved the progress of the story?

Does each act or scene end in a challenging way and set you up for what is to follow?

What well-known actors and actresses would you recommend for the various parts? Why?

Would this story have been better told in novel form? Why?

How natural does the dialogue seem? Has the dramatist made the characters say things which they normally wouldn't if they were real people? Give examples.

How consistent are the characters? Do they suddenly do things that you had been led to believe they wouldn't or couldn't?

Was there too much talk and not enough action? Where?

Additional Questions on a Long Poem

What rhythmic pattern is used? How much does it contribute to the movement of the story?

If the lines rhyme, how well does the scheme fit in with the mood and tone?

What lines or figures of speech are most likely to be remembered?

How easy was it to follow the story?

What difference would it have made if the story had been told in prose?

2. Non-fiction: There is such a great variety of books in this field that it would be impossible to cover all types—from little how-to booklets to massive encyclopedias. However, we can tell you what to look for in the types commonly recommended by teachers for outside reading.

a. Biographies

Where and when did the subject of the biography spend most of his life?

What events of historical significance were occurring at the time? Which of them did the subject help to shape?

What are some of the *human* elements in the subject's character? Refer to home life, friends, anecdotes.

How does the author feel about his subject? Is he fair? Has he an ax to grind?

How authentic is the evidence presented? Was enough research done to support character analysis? What kind of references are used? Hearsay? Personal papers? First hand acquaintance? Other writers? Friends and associates?

What unusual character qualities did the subject have? What unusual talents?

What were the most significant moments in the subject's life? What were the turning points?

To what extent was the subject the kind of person with whom you could have been friends?

How important was luck in the subject's career? Courage? Perseverance? Stubbornness? Influence of friends?

What obstacles did the subject overcome?

What were the subject's major contributions to the welfare of mankind? In what ways was the world better off because the subject lived?

Why, if at all, was the subject worthy of having been written about?

What actor or actress could best portray the subject on stage or screen? Why?

b. Autobiographies

Practically all the questions on biographies would be used, except that those designed to test point of view and authenticity would naturally be directed at the subject, since he would be responsible for his own material, having written it himself. Some questions would have to be eliminated; they wouldn't apply to a self-analysis.

c. Essay Collection

What are the chief subjects discussed? Are they one-sided or do they show varied interests?

How scholarly does the writer seem to be? What evidences are there of professional training, extensive experience, wide travel, broad acquaintance?

How careful is the writer of what he says? How sensitive is he to other people's feelings? Does he support what he says, especially if it is opinion?

How fresh and unusual are the writer's viewpoints?

What kind of person does the writer seem to be? What would be his choice in clothing, house furnishings, books, leisure activities? Is he the kind who shakes hands and pounds the back, who just smiles warmly and invitingly, or who nods distantly when introduced?

How worthwhile are the ideas? How convincing are they?

What would you say about the sentence structure, vocabulary, and phrasing?—involved? difficult to understand? informal? conversational? witty and varied? cold and impersonal? Cite examples.

What else by this writer are you planning to read?

d. General

The questions that follow would apply to books that are difficult to classify but are popularly read—those on political, social, psychological, or educational subjects; books on travel or real adventure; surveys of historical periods.

Why was this book written? What does it contribute to our culture? Was there a need for information in this area?

What is the major field of interest? How broadly is it covered?

How well does the author make his point? How satisfied are you with his conclusions?

What kind of authority does the author seem to be? What are his qualifications to write on the subject? How many of his facts are the product of personal experience?

What is the author's general point of view? Liberal? Conservative? To what extent does his point of view color his presentation? What, if any, evidences are there of propaganda? Does he show signs of bias?

To what extent does the author "doctor" his material, leaving important things out and inserting difficult-to-prove items?

How logically is the material planned and developed? How easy is it to read and understand?

What are the most noteworthy ideas or experiences?

What are the chief qualities of the style (sentences, words, phrases, tone, imagination, etc.)? What are the chief weaknesses?

What do you know now that you didn't know before?

What has been made clearer as the result of reading the book?

How much would you support the author's conclusions in a debate? How much would you attack them? Why?

To what extent have you been stimulated to do some of the things the author did or to go where he went?

What other books on the same subject have you read that you consider superior or inferior? Why?

To what kind of person would you recommend this book? Who should avoid it? Would you try another by the same author? Why?

B. *How to Prepare the Book Report*

Even though there is no standard form, you can use certain guides which will help you handle practically any type of book report requested of you, written or oral:

§ Plan your paragraphs in accordance with the number of words expected, just as you would do with any composition.

§ Select for discussion only those features of a book that were sufficiently outstanding (good or bad) to be worthy of comment. Suppose, for instance, you found nothing special about the setting or theme but were greatly amused by the author's style and the people he wrote about. All right, talk about these in a good, solid paragraph for each—and mention the other items, if at all, as briefly as you can.

§ Use the "What to Look For" questions to help you gather specific material for the paragraphs *and then prepare the usual outline!*

§ Include in your beginning paragraph enough about the type of book it is, the title, author, setting, and theme so that the reader or listener will get a quick idea of its general nature.

§ Working from your outline, which has prepared what you want to say about the items you have selected for discussion, develop each middle paragraph around the central idea—your feeling for or against a particular feature. Use *as details* references to the book to support your opinions. In this respect, handle the paragraph exactly as you would in an answer to a literature question.

§ Let your ending paragraph summarize your general reaction to the book. Tell why you did or did not like it by referring again to the points you developed in the middle paragraphs.

We will try something different in the way of examples for this section. It would be unwise to give you a few complete book reports because no two should be alike and, as we've said several times now, no standard form can be suggested. Instead, therefore, you will find sample opening, middle, and closing paragraphs from both professional and student reviews so that you can see how various items are handled and can adapt the techniques to your own reports. The professional samples will be starred thus: °.

Sample Beginning Paragraphs for Book Reports

(Most frequently mentioned: title, author, type, setting, theme)

°1.

A Guest and His Going by P. H. Newby (Reviewed by James Stern)
If the British take their pleasures seriously, they are not slow to treat serious subjects lightly. Who would have thought that the Suez crisis, which actually precipitated Britain into a war in 1956, would provide material for a comic English novel in 1959? Yet in P. H. Newby's hands it has in "A Guest and His Going."

2.

Benjamin Franklin by Carl Van Doren
What I find to be most interesting in biographies is the intimate glimpses I get into the real character of great men and women. In Carl Van Doren's "Benjamin Franklin," I was amazed to discover that this was not a

dull man who spent most of his time talking politics or
experimenting. I was fascinated by his various affairs of
the heart and learned to appreciate this great patriot
precisely because he had some weaknesses, too.

*3.

The City That Would Not Die by Richard Collier
    (Reviewed by Drew Middleton)
    This is a book about one city, London, and one night,
May 10th–11th, 1941, when Adolf Hitler's Luftwaffe
launched the heaviest attack it had ever made on London, or, indeed, upon any other city. From the events of
this night Richard Collier has fashioned an authentic,
horribly vivid story of a city enduring twelve hours of
torment and surviving—battered, burning but unbroken.
    As the war wore on, there were heavier raids. The
night described in "The City That Would Not Die"
saw 708 tons of high explosive and eighty-six tons of in-
cendiary bombs dropped on London. By midwinter of
1943–44 the British were dropping a higher tonnage
night after night in Germany.

(You will recall that it is quite acceptable to use a two-
paragraph introduction in some instances.)

Sample Middle Paragraphs for Book Reports

1.

The Hairy Ape by Eugene O'Neill
    Basically, this play is a lengthy character study. Yank
is typical of people who live in their own private little
worlds and are shocked to discover one day that they
don't fit into any other society. This huge stoker hadn't
realized, before he met Mildred, that his rough appearance and rowdy manners were repulsive when viewed
by persons who were sensitive and well-bred. When he
left the security of the hold of the ship and came out
into the pitiless glare of life in a big city, he was re-
buffed on all sides. He didn't know how to fight back
and therein lay the essential tragedy of his personality.

2.

A Bell for Adano by John Hersey

The people of the town of Adano behaved as most people would who had been pushed around for years. They were suspicious of strangers, didn't trust them. This is what made it so hard for the Major to do his job. He had to proceed slowly and gain the complete confidence first of the inhabitants. When they found him to be capable, warm, and exceptionally understanding, they cooperated completely. This is so typical of people everywhere. They respond to kindness and hope. Hersey shows great skill in getting to the core of character, whether of an individual or a group.

*3.

The Triumph of Surgery by Jurgen Thorwald (Reviewed by Francis J. Braceland)

The story is told through the medium of one Dr. Hartmann, whom we meet in London in 1881 as he attends the Third International Medical Congress. Though the narrator, named after the author's maternal grandfather, is fictitious, the events he chronicles are real, having been carefully researched and reported with scrupulous attention to detail. The excitement, the emotional tension, and the fascination the reader experiences as he visualizes the scenes of these epoch-making events are testimony to the skill of an author who has the facility of placing the reader in the operating room as the drama unfolds and who also has the ability of writing medical history as though it were a series of four-alarm fires.

4.

The Yearling by Marjorie Kinnan Rawlings

For the first time I became conscious of how much style can contribute to the enjoyment of a book. By frequently using short, simple sentences, Marjorie Rawlings is able to match the plain, bare lives of her charac-

ters and blend her descriptions into a harmonious
pattern. In a brief paragraph, with eight quick strokes
of her pen, the author achieves remarkable drama as she
presents the touching scene in which Jody discovers
that Penny has told Ma to dispose of the boy's pet:

"He went to his room and closed the door. He sat
on the side of the bed, twisting his hands. He heard
low voices. He heard a shot. He ran from the room to
the open kitchen door. His mother stood on the stoop
with the shotgun smoking in her hand. Flag lay flounder-
ing beside the fence."

I think I understand better now how to use stark,
direct language to create excitement and suspense.

5.

The Red Badge of Courage by Stephen Crane

Reading about Henry Fleming made me change my
whole attitude toward the true meaning of courage. I
had always thought that the very courageous person
never experienced fear. He just went ahead and did
heroic things without giving a thought to the conse-
quences. But as I see it now, real bravery emerges only
after fear has been conquered. One has to be either very
stupid or very mad to expose himself to danger and not
worry about his own welfare. By running away and then
returning to fight gloriously, Henry developed the maturity which enables a person to face a challenge with determination even while his heart is pounding with doubt.
"The Red Badge of Courage" teaches a lesson every
young man or woman should learn.

Sample Ending Paragraphs for Book Reports

1.

The Old Man and the Sea by Ernest Hemingway

It is a book I enjoyed reading very much and would
recommend to anyone who likes plenty of action and
suspense. The story has all the qualities one would want:
powerful, forceful writing by the author; an underdog
hero and a sea full of enemies; depth of emotion (I felt

so sorry for the old man); and a length just right for a single evening's entertainment.

*2.

May This House Be Safe From Tigers by Alexander King (Reviewed by Taylor Caldwell)

Those Europeans, and Americans, too, who can find no vivacity in America, no interest except in the passing, the new, the trivial and the mean, no passion but for petty things, and no splendor, will see America through Mr. King's eyes. They will share his wonder, his awe, his laughter, his love and his devotion for his adopted country and will discover America again, vital, aspiring and young, colorful and passionate.

3.

Jane Eyre by Charlotte Brontë

On the whole, I would say that I am not sorry I read this book. I didn't care too much for the stiff way the characters talked and acted, some of the lengthy descriptive passages which could have been shortened or eliminated, and the lack of action in spots. But it was a relief to meet a heroine who wasn't the most beautiful woman who ever lived, a hero who wasn't perfect either physically or morally, and a stress on virtue which is rare these days. It may take you a while to get interested, as it probably did if you read Hardy's "Return of the Native," but once you get into it you find yourself becoming increasingly more reluctant to put the book aside.

Do you see what makes a good report? You don't just tell the story. It is as wrong here as it is in an answer to a literature question. Of course, you don't have a built-in problem to discuss as you do when you are held to satisfying the requirements of a question. But this merely gives you greater freedom to select the points of interest that you wish to stress in order to prove that your estimate of the book is based upon solid grounds.

III. THE REVIEW

As a change from reporting on a book you have read, you are sometimes asked to see and analyze a play, motion picture, or television program. The technique involved in the *review,* as this type of composition is called, is almost identical with that of the book report. Since someone had to write the original play or script upon which the dramatic production was based, the same guide questions used to evaluate a book can be applied to the efforts of the author as presented on a stage or set or in a studio. The only difference is that you are expected to comment on some additional items when you are reporting on an actual performance.

Additional Questions on a Live Play

If a single set was used, what limitations did it impose on the flow of the action? If none, why was it adequate?

If more than one set was used, how effective were the various changes? Were they all necessary, or could some of the sets have been eliminated? What would you say about the imagination and skill of the set designer? How effective was the lighting? The background music, if any?

What was outstanding about the costumes? Were they appropriate to the time and place of the action?

How well was the acting directed? What about the pace? Did it drag? Was it too rapid and confused? Were the transitions smooth? To what extent could the delivery of some of the lines have been improved by better direction?

How well were the actors suited to their parts? How forcefully did they speak? How clear was their diction? How effectively, by voice and action, did they vary their performances? What actors did the best jobs? Why? What ones performed poorly? Why? If the latter, what actors would you have selected instead?

If this was a musical, how original and creative was the music? How many songs do you think you will remember?

Was the story just thrown in, or did it have genuine dramatic quality? What about the voices of the performers? Were they good actors with poor voices, or poor actors with good voices, or a happy combination of both? How well were the solos worked in? Did the events leading up to the songs seem artificial or were they so well developed that the interruption seemed quite logical and natural?

Additional Questions on a Motion Picture

(Use all the questions above on the live play *and* the ones that follow.)

How effective were the outdoor scenes? Were they shot in natural settings, or were they faked?

How well did the cameras assist the action by focusing on important details? What were some of the unusual camera techniques used to enhance the photography? What improvements could have been made in the shooting of the picture? If color was used, how much did it contribute to the photographic quality?

What was unusual about the screen on which the film was shown?

How effective was the sound? What special musical effects were used?

If the motion picture was based upon an original book or play, how did the telling of the story compare to the reading or acting of it? What were the advantages and disadvantages of one medium as opposed to the other?

Additional Questions on a Television Production

(Use all the questions above on sets, costumes, direction, acting, camera work, sound, *and* the ones that follow.)

To what extent, if at all, did the commercials intrude?

If the script was a cut version of a longer piece, how much did the production suffer because the story was condensed? Would an even shorter version have been better? Would another half hour or so have helped? Why?

If the script was original, how well did it take advantage of the techniques of television production?

If the production was of a non-fiction type—panel discussion, news report, on-the-spot coverage of an event—how well did the cameras contribute to avoiding monotony? How wisely were the panelists, reporters, or interviewers selected? How well did they speak? How suitable were their personalities to the program?

What over-all effect did the program have on the audience? Was it proper material for the minds of people of all ages? If not, what types were aimed at most?

A typical review of a play, motion picture, or television program would take the following form:

Beginning Paragraph: The usual title, author, setting, and theme, plus theater (play or motion picture), or time and station (television).

Middle Paragraphs: A paragraph or two based upon the highlights developed through the guide questions used for evaluating books. A few paragraphs based upon the guide questions immediately above. The number of paragraphs will, of course, depend on the required words and your selection of qualities you wish to evaluate.

Ending Paragraph: Again the general estimate with the summarized reasons for your conclusions and recommendations.

What Should You Know About Letters?

There are those who say that the art of letter writing is fast disappearing.

These mournful words are not without some truth. For one thing, there is the telephone. Years ago, if you wanted to keep in touch with someone who was far away, order some goods from a store, or raise the roof because something had gone wrong with a delivery, you wrote a letter. Now, often all you do is dial a number and talk.

Then there is the booming greeting card business. At one time, if a friend had a birthday, became ill, got married, reached an important anniversary, or became a parent, you felt obligated to send at least a brief note. Today, you go to a store, pick a card with more or less the right message, and send it off. You do the same thing if you want to invite, express thanks, or offer condolences. Your language can be witty, daring, incredibly dull—depending upon your taste and the price of the card.

There's nothing wrong in all this. It would be foolish to recommend that you go back to the letter writing habits of the eighteenth century. It makes sense to take advantage of the convenience and time-saving features of both cards and telephones.

And fortunately for those who worry about our writing habits, the situation is not desperate yet. Mountains of mail still go out of and come in to homes, offices, and stores every day, and a great many of the letters are not prefabricated messages. There are several good reasons. A long distance call is much more expensive than a stamp and a few sheets of stationery. Employers insist that you write to them before you come in to talk about a job. Then, too, you want to write a letter on other occasions simply because it is better manners to do so or because a telephone call will not get the best results. Yes, despite all the concern, one thing is certain. No matter how little writing you do after you leave school, you will continue to write letters. So let's examine the three *informal* (or social or friendly) types and the three *formal* (or business) types that you should know how to handle since you may use them frequently.

I. INFORMAL LETTERS

A. Recommended Form:

> 1182 Robertson Court
> Riverdale 63, New York
> January 23, 19——

Dear ———,
   X..
....
....

                      Sincerely,

                    ———————

NOTES

1. This is the preferred block form, open punctuation style used most frequently these days. Each line of the sender's address and the date begins directly below the preceding one, and no marks of punctuation are placed at the ends of lines.

The indented, closed heading is still used by some, although it is becoming relatively rare:

> 1182 Robertson Court,
>   Riverdale 63, New York,
>   January 23, 19——.

(Observe the indentation and punctuation of lines.)

2. You should use the same form on the envelope as you do in the letter.

3. Regardless of how close you are to the person receiving your letter, you should use the heading, unless you have printed stationery. Then the date (upper right) is sufficient. It is common courtesy not to force your reader to go searching around the house for your street or zone number when the return envelope is being addressed.

4. Note a *comma* after the salutation.

5. The first line is indented just as it would be for the beginning of any paragraph, and all subsequent paragraphs are handled the same way.

6. The complimentary closing (also *Yours, As ever, Cordially,*—almost anything warm and friendly will do) is also followed by a *comma.*

7. Don't be sloppy about your materials. Get some decent stationery and use it.

B. *Contents*

1. *The Friendly Letter:* Think of it as a long distance conversation. When you do, you will readily admit that if you were face to face with the friend or relative you have written to, you wouldn't be able to get away with something like this:

_____

_____

_____

Dear ,

   I received your letter and was very glad to hear from you. Everybody here is fine and I hope you are, too.

   How are things? Not much happening here. You know, get up, go to school, do homework, go to bed. That's about it.

   Oh yes. Went to a party last Saturday night. Met some old friends of yours. Had a pretty good time. That reminds me. Finally went skating for the first time this season.

Well, I guess it's about time for dinner. Don't forget to write and let's have all the dope. Hoping to hear from you.

Your friend,

Comments

This letter is utterly worthless. Take that mechanical opening, which is a complete waste of words. Of course you received the letter! Otherwise you wouldn't be replying to it. And of course you were glad to hear from a friend; no need to state the obvious. Nor is there any reason why you have to sound like a hypochondriac at the beginning of every letter. Sure, you are interested in your friend's health as he or she is in yours. But unless there is something special to be said about it, why make it sound like a formula? Take it for granted that all is well and go on to more newsworthy topics.

In the second paragraph you announce that you have nothing interesting to say and then you prove it. It's like telling someone that you are a dull speaker and warning him not to listen.

In the very next paragraph you contradict yourself. Nothing to say? You went to a party and met some friends. Fine. What did they say? Wasn't there something new with at least one of them? You had a good time. Why? Why didn't you give some details about that skating trip? Who was there? Anything amusing happen? And why the poor sentence structure? Must you insult your friends by using your worst English on them? Don't they deserve your best?

Paragraph four is the biggest blow of all. You think so little of your friend that you snatch a few minutes to tell him nothing and then you rush off to eat. Why not confess that it is too much trouble to keep in touch with those you like? And why bring this mess to a close with that annoying fragment used to death: "Hoping to hear from you"? If you write letters like this, with or without the fragment, you should not be too hopeful of getting a reply.

✓ *Here's what you should do:*

1. The first thing is this. You've heard it before and you will hear it again. It's the theme of this book. ANY TIME YOU WRITE A PARAGRAPH OR MORE YOU ARE WRITING A COMPOSITION. A letter is no exception.

2. Don't just ramble along. Write in paragraphs. Don't fire away in all directions. Select one or two items to talk about and then develop them into full-fledged paragraphs, with topic sentences, *details,* vivid language, and all the rest of it.

3. Start right in with an interesting opening, as you would with any well-written piece. If you must inquire about health, do so at the very end somewhere. You don't have to lead up to the beginning. Begin!

4. Tell *your* news first. If the letter you are answering has some questions in it, answer them afterward in a paragraph or two—with details.

5. If you think you have nothing to write about, take a tip from what has been learned about letter writing from ex-servicemen. Ask any one of them what he looked forward to most eagerly when he was away. He'll tell you it was a letter from home. Then ask him what he enjoyed reading about. He'll say this:

> What did Mom cook for dinner last Sunday?
> Has that leaky faucet been repaired yet?
> How's my kid brother (or sister) behaving?
> Have you had the first snowfall?
> Where are you going on your vacation?

And you? If you were writing to him, what would you want to know? You'd want questions like these answered: What are your quarters like? How's the food? What's the latest training routine you've learned? Have you made any friends? When do you expect to get a leave?

The questions summarize the main point about what to write in letters. The person absent from familiar surroundings wants to hear about the ordinary things of his former environment so that he can identify with it once more. The one who is back home is interested in that which is different from what he hears, sees, and does every day. The one who should decide what you should write about is not you but the reader of your letter! Don't think of yourself and what has happened to you as the only source of interest. What seems dull to you may be exciting to one who is away. You can work the weather into an attractive paragraph if you try, or a ride in a bus, or an incident in class, or a discussion with your parents. Imagine what you would talk about if you were in the same room with the reader. That's what you should write about.

6. Don't feel that you must give an excuse for bringing the letter to a close. When you have nothing more to say, you are finished. Offer some final greeting, if you must, sign your name, and let that be an end to it. You aren't being abrupt when you do this; you are just being sensible and avoiding being a bore.

7. Use your best English, not to show off but to make what you have written worth reading. There's no question about the truth of this bit of advice. Forceful, vivid writing creates interest in itself. Be proud of your language. You'll be pleased at the compliments your well-written letters will draw.

8. Whenever possible, try to involve the reader in the situations you describe. This establishes a point of contact and a feeling of being a part of the experience.

Here are two letters written by a couple of friends. Nothing particularly exciting has happened, and yet the intimate tone and the detailed descriptions make each the kind of letter I am sure you would enjoy receiving:

From the One Who Is Away

　　　　　　　　　　————————————
　　　　　　　　　　————————————
　　　　　　　　　　————————————

Dear ————,
　　Well, it's over, but it wasn't easy. Moving into my

dorm, I mean. Father got me up here just before noon. How the old bus ever made those snaking Pocono hills I'll never know. You know me and my stuff; it was all over the rear seat, in the trunk, and on my lap. We were sure a spring or an axle or something would break. It reminded me of the time your brother took us up to that farm in Connecticut and we had to lie on some blankets in the back because there was no place to sit. Anyway, we found my room eventually, although it would have been simpler if we had hired a couple of Swiss Alpine guides. The freshmen get put into these old mansions that have a million rooms and just as many staircases—narrow, steep, and rickety. To get to my place, we had to go through the kitchen, open a door, climb about twenty-seven steps, stagger past some wardrobes in a narrow hall, and finally fall two steps **down** into what they call **quarters for two.** First time I've ever lived in a dropped bedroom.

Now that I'm getting used to it, however, I'm growing fond of it. The ceiling has a real attic slant, and that makes everything snug and cozy. On one side somebody built all kinds of little closets and drawers, giving us loads of room to keep odds and ends neat and out of the way. A double desk in front of the one window looks out on a gorgeous back yard, with its rolling lawn framed by some fine old trees. Off to the right, at the rear, there is even a tiny fish pond. It's so restful looking through that window. The bunk beds are a bit of a problem—yes, that's what they are. They stand smack in the middle of the room, and what with one thing or another always on the floor you have to learn how to navigate around them. We've learned how, but my poor shins and lumpy forehead will never be the same.

You know what? I think I'm going to like it here. I'd be sure of it if you were around, too. I'll tell you all about my roommate next time, but get a letter back here fast!

Affectionately,

From the One Back Home

_____

_____

_____

Dear _____,

You escaped just in time. About two hours after you left, a few snowflakes started to come down. Then it became so thick it looked as if somebody was pouring white paint out of the sky. The weather man says we got sixteen inches, but it seems more like ten feet to me. At the moment the view through my window is almost as beautiful as that back yard you talked about in your letter. The houses are all gingerbread and spice, with white icing, and the clean, snowy blanket has given the outdoors that sterilized purity of appearance found in hospital rooms. But the picture will not be so pretty tomorrow morning when we try to get the car out of the garage.

I'm so glad you're settled and, judging from the description of your room, satisfied, too. Do you remember that horrible "closet" we shared the first summer in camp? Compared to that, what you have now sounds like a suite at the Waldorf. I'm sure you don't have to hang your things on a couple of nails in the wall, or keep your shoes on the window ledge, as we had to do in dear old Watonah. And I imagine your bed has a real spring in it, not that bundle of quarry stone we had to sleep on for eight weeks.

Yesterday I finally got around to returning those blue slacks we had agreed I didn't like. If you think Belstrom's was a madhouse when we went shopping just before you left, you should have seen it two weeks later. Everybody's aunt or mother was there, and for the same reason I was—to return or exchange. I realize now that some of them must have brought things back because their nieces or daughters just hadn't had any more room in bags or valises (if what you tell me about your luggage is an indication). While I was there I ran into Billy Wilder. You know, he works there Saturdays to earn money to run his "heap," as he calls it. He asked for

your address, and when he did you could have knocked
me down with a broken fender. Did you know you had
made a conquest? If you don't keep me posted on this
one, I'll never speak to you again, do you hear?

Yours,

———————

2. A "Thank You" Note: When you have visited someone's home or have received a gift from a close friend, a card
is much too impersonal as a means of expressing your appreciation. Instead, write a brief note. Be specific, original, intimate. Mention the gift and tell why it is something you can
use, or, if it was a visit, give details of that part of the experience that you enjoyed most. For example:

———————————
———————————
———————————

Dear ————,
   That was a weekend I will always treasure. The swim
in the lake and the trip to the county fair were only the
highlights of two completely wonderful days. Thank
you so much!

Gratefully,

———————

———————————
———————————
———————————

Dear ————,
   Your gift really solved a problem for me. I had been
wondering whether I would like an electric shaver. Now
I know. It's surprisingly good, and is everything you said
it is. Thanks, George.

Appreciatively,

———————

3. A Condolence Note: When someone you know very
well has suffered a great loss, you will want to express your

regret in your own words. Here again a brief, hand-written note is best. Some cautions:

Don't be "terribly shocked."	Much too standard and formal
Don't be philosophical.	Very irritating
Don't overdo your emotional reaction.	Sounds too artificial

Be simple and sincere. Say what you would if you were face to face with the mourner, perhaps like this:

_____
_____
_____

Dear _____,
I know there is little I can say at a time like this that will be any consolation to you. But I did want you to know how sorry I was to learn of your terrible loss. Can I help in any way?

Sincerely,
_____

II. FORMAL LETTERS

A. *Recommended Form*

72 Lake Shore Drive
Flemington, New Jersey
October 16, 19_____

The Philbert Novelty Company
16–23 Newbury Road
Los Angeles 5, California
Gentlemen:
    X...
....
    X...
....

Very truly yours,

Vernon C. Crowley

Vernon C. Crowley

NOTES

1. The block, open-punctuation form is preferred.

2. If the stationery has a printed letterhead, only the date is necessary, upper right. Otherwise, the full heading, as usual.

3. Write (preferably type) the full name and address of the company, including the zone number, if there is one; precede this with the name and title (if any) of an individual, if the letter is being sent to one person.

4. Note the colon after the salutation.

5. Indent normally for the beginning of each paragraph of content, unless you are using the severe block form, as is done occasionally:

Dear Sir:

....

....

....

....

In the latter style, the content is single-spaced and the paragraphs are identified by double-spacing.

6. A comma follows the complimentary closing.

7. The common practice, in typed business letters, is to skip at least four spaces after the closing so that your name can be typed in under your signature. This is to make sure that the proper spelling of your name can be verified.

8. Business letters written in longhand very often show an extra space skipped before and after the salutation and another before the complimentary closing. This practice varies, however.

B. *Contents*

1. *The Letter of Application:* One of the most difficult things to do is to try to sell yourself. And yet, this is exactly

what you must do when you apply for a job. The problem becomes even greater when the application is made by letter because you are up against rather formidable obstacles:

§ Except in rare cases, you are not going to be hired directly from your letter. The best you can hope for is an interview.

§ If your letter is in response to an advertisement, yours will not be the only one received. You will be competing with many others.

§ There will have to be something in your letter that will make it stand out sufficiently to attract the attention of the prospective employer.

Magazine articles are frequently written on how persons who adopted unusual approaches were selected for interviews immediately because of their imagination, originality, and inventiveness. For instance, letters like the following have worked for some in the past:

                  ————————————
                  ————————————
                  ————————————

————————————
————————————
————————————

Gentlemen:

Look no further. I'm your man. Just tell me when to report for work.

                  Very truly yours,

              ————————

                  ————————————
                  ————————————

————————————
————————————
————————————

Dear Sir:

You don't have to spend another dime on ads in the

"Times-Herald" for a copywriter. The best one in town
is available right now. Just call Re 8-2217.

Confidently,
——————

Although these examples make interesting reading and got
results for the people who wrote them, you can be certain
that most employers nowadays are not impressed with the
brash, almost offensive type of application. The novelty of
this kind of approach has worn off. Preferred today is the
individual who can offer solid qualifications and concrete
evidence that he will make a desirable employee, either on
the basis of his training or academic record. Your objective,
therefore, should be to present an attractive application that
will reflect your best abilities and most impressive background. You might bear these principles in mind when you
write:

1) Be realistic about yourself. As a high school student,
your experience is necessarily limited, as is your training.

2) Try, therefore, to apply for jobs for which some outstanding aspect of your school record or a proved ability of
yours makes you unusually qualified. For instance, if you
have received very high marks in physical education and do
well in athletics, you will make a desirable employee in a
summer camp or beach resort. If you have specialized in
commercial subjects—can type well or can operate various
business machines efficiently—you will fit well into an office.
Or if you are outstanding in mathematics or science, consider applying to a large company that has a laboratory or
research division. In short, pick your spots so that you can
emphasize your strengths in your letter.

3) Don't necessarily wait until a suitable advertisement
appears in a newspaper. Make your own opportunities. Investigate among your friends and relatives, business publi-
cations, even the telephone directories, and draw up a list of
places where your talents can best be used. Write with or
without an invitation, remembering to be respectful, business-
like, and sincere.

4) Be brief and forthright in your language. The letter of application, too, is a composition and subject to its rules of unity, interest, and correctness. Omit any information about yourself that does not promote your suitability for the position. Busy executives don't have time to waste on several pages of personal data, however charming these accounts may be.

5) Be sure your spelling, grammar, and punctuation are flawless. Carelessness here is certain to destroy your chances.

6) Make everything about the letter high in quality— good stationery, neat typing, a well-balanced layout with the context centered on the page. If you must write in longhand, don't let your handwriting betray you.

7) Include mention of at least the following:

> Nature and source of information about the job
> Age, educational background, training
> *Special qualifications* (either certain abilities or pertinent experience)
> References
> Request for an interview

Leave questions about salary, hours, and benefits for the interview unless specifically requested to mention these items.

You can handle the contents of the letter in either of two ways. The usual form involves covering the various topics directly in the text, like this:

Gentlemen:

I am interested in joining your staff as a general counselor during the coming season.

I shall be graduated from the Westbridge High School in June, at which time I shall be eighteen years of age. My best grades to date have been in English, biology, and health education. I have been an active member of intramurals in softball, basketball, and volleyball and have been awarded three gold medals.

For the past two summers I have worked as a counselor-in-training and junior counselor at the White Lake Day Camp in Haines Falls. In addition to my regular duties, I assisted in putting out the camp newspaper and served on the First Aid Squad.

The following people have indicated their willingness to supply references in my behalf:

James C. Wilson, Director, White Lake Day Camp, Haines Falls, New York

Arthur L. Treat, Faculty Coordinator of Intramurals, Westbridge High School, Westbridge, New York

I shall be happy to appear for an interview at your convenience.

Sincerely yours,

Thomas Bolton

Thomas Bolton
(Lu 8-7211)

Paste snapshot here.

The other method of application, very popular in recent years, is to send a brief note, supported by an index or library card on which is supplied the necessary personal information:

Dear Sir:

Enclosed you will find a card on which are listed my qualifications for the job of junior draftsman, advertised in yesterday's "Post-Sun."

I should appreciate an opportunity to discuss my application with you personally.

Very truly yours,

Roger Kranette

Roger Kranette

Front Side of Card

Roger Kranette   1127 File Street
                                  Canton, Ohio
                                  Da 8-4774

Age: 18

Education: Graduate, June, 19——
                Wilson Technical High School (Same
                    city)
                Major: Mechanical Drawing
                Minor: Blueprint Reading
                Honors: Certificate for Excellence in
                    Drafting

Experience: Summer employment (2 years)
                Jules Connor Company (Construction)
                1374 Watson Boulevard
                Canton, Ohio
                I have also assisted my father, who is
                    a mechanical engineer.
                                                (over)

Reverse Side of Card

References: Mr. Jules Conner (address above)
                Mr. Carl Tremper, Teacher of Me-
                    chanical Drawing
                Wilson Technical High School

                Rev. Winford Beame
                Christ Church (Same city)

                        Paste snapshot here
                                        Roger Kranette

2. The Letter of Complaint: Some years ago, about six
months after I had purchased a new car, I observed that
there was something wrong with the paint on the hood. In
bright sunlight, the undercoat could actually be seen beneath the final coat of colored lacquer. When I brought this
condition to the attention of the dealer, he was not too sympathetic, claiming that the car was no longer under the fac-
tory guarantee.

Thereupon I wrote a letter to the parent company in Detroit, Michigan. Within a week, a representative called me at my office, expressed interest in my description of the defective paint job, and promised to be in touch with me again. A few days later I received word from the dealer that I was to bring the car in for inspection by the representative. This I did, and the result of the examination was an offer for a re-painting of the hood at no cost to me.

Anyone who knows how anxious reputable companies are to maintain their good will with the public will not be surprised at this prompt and satisfactory adjustment of a legitimate complaint. However, more than merely illustrating a sound business policy, this little story about an automobile shows you how a letter in the right place can often accomplish much more than any amount of talk.

So, when you are dissatisfied with something you have bought and can get no satisfaction by a personal appeal, try a letter if there is a responsible organization behind the product. Not only will you often get better results by "going to the top," but you will have a dated record of the whole transaction and will be able to use it as evidence should some question arise at a future time. When you write a letter of complaint, be sure to:

§ ascertain first exactly who it is that can best handle your problem

§ give the price and the date of purchase of the item

§ mention the name of the store (if it is a branch and you are not writing to it directly), the department, the number of the sales slip, and the name of the salesman.

§ present a detailed description of your complaint (and be sure it's reasonable!)

§ suggest a remedy

§ indicate when and how you may be reached for further discussion

§ maintain a courteous and sensible tone. Most mistakes are unintentional.

Example

_____
_____

_____
_____
_____

Gentlemen:

On July 23, 19— I ordered books in the amount of $23.47 from your Madison Avenue branch (Sales slip #12785, Dept. 1B). When the shipment arrived, I discovered that "The Face of England," by W.S. Shears (Spring Books, London) had been sent instead of "The Face of London," by H.P. Clunn (same publishers), which I had ordered.

Please arrange for the exchange of these books as quickly as possible, since I need the material for a report I am preparing. Someone will be at home any weekday before noon. I assume there will be no further shipping charges. Thank you.

Very truly yours,

Niles Buhler

Niles Buhler

3. *The Letter to a Newspaper or Public Official:* A community in New Jersey, worried about the prospect of disastrous forced landings and the sleep-destroying screech of powerful jet motors, became aroused when it learned that state officials were planning a huge airport in its midst. A national audience of millions was astounded at the incredibly dramatic sight of a television comedian walking off a show, while it was in progress, as a protest against censorship of his material. Suburban teenagers were indignant over the latest slap at their status when they read about proposals to raise the minimum age for a junior operator's license from sixteen to seventeen or eighteen.

These three events occurred recently within a few weeks of one another. Now, what do you suppose the people involved did to indicate their displeasure? Most, of course, voiced immediate shock and annoyance, grumbled for a few days, then promptly forgot about the problem. Some went a step further and discussed with their friends what they could do about the situation, but never quite lifted their objections out of the talking stage. Others may have made some telephone calls and felt satisfied that they had expressed themselves vigorously. But the ones who really influenced the final decisions were those who sent letters—to officials, to newspapers, to the television station, to political leaders. At this writing, the proposed airport site has been abandoned, the comedian has been publicly invited to return, and the new licensing bill has not come out of committee.

Too few of us realize how effective a well-written letter can be in stimulating action. We tend to accept the notion that one letter more or less won't make much difference to anyone. But it is obvious that one letter multiplied by thousands can be enormously influential or, if published in a newspaper, can set off a chain of correspondence that will grow into a mighty protest.

And there are occasions when one letter all by itself will bring results. I once tried an experiment with one of my evening adult classes. I asked each student to select a situation that had been personally disturbing for some time and could be remedied by official action. We then decided who would be the logical person to be told about the matter and proceeded to express our criticisms and recommendations in writing. Altogether twenty-seven letters were sent out.

Among the things that happened in the next few weeks were these: A gang of workmen showed up on the street where one of the students lived and repaired a large hole in the pavement that had been there for eight months; the borough president had read and acted. Another young man, who had written to the Lieutenant Governor, was visited by a state bank examiner, who told him how to go about getting better interest rates on a recent disadvantageous installment purchase contract. A third student received a reply from a senator's secretary and was invited to outline his tax relief plan for parents of children attending college. The senator wanted to include the suggestions in a bill he would sponsor. At the end of the experiment, every letter had been answered, only three got form responses, and twenty-one out of twenty-seven writers were rewarded by some direct action.

The fact that you should get into the habit of writing letters when your interests or principles are involved is very well summarized in a memorandum I received only this morning from the Office of the President of New York University. An effort was being made to purchase land for faculty housing in an area where existing facilities were clearly inadequate. Some private interests were concerned lest the tax advantage to which an educational institution is entitled might create an unfavorable comparison with the rents in profit-making buildings. This explains the reason for the last paragraph of the President's message:

"In matters of this kind, there is bound to be opposition and oftentimes those opposed make known their objections by writing either to the newspapers or to city officials. May I suggest that if you believe our plan has merit, you may care to write a letter to ——————, expressing your opinion of our proposal. The ——————, as you know, is Chairman of the Board of Estimate, before whose body this question eventually will be resolved. This —————— might be of considerable help to us in our efforts to solve a difficult problem."

As usual, in writing a letter to a newspaper or a public official, you follow the rules of good composition:

§ In the beginning paragraph, briefly identify the issue at hand and express your point of view.

§ In the next paragraph, give reasons, with *specific details,* why your stand is worthy of support.

§ Then indicate how the result of following your suggestions will prove beneficial, or make recommendations for improvement if such plans have not yet been developed.

§ Finally, especially in correspondence with elected officials, give some idea of how broad a section of the population shares your opinion. It always helps your cause if you can hint that you are not without sympathizers who may make themselves felt at the polls.

As an example, we will use the letter I actually sent in support of the university housing plan mentioned above:

Dear ———,

You are doubtless aware of the efforts of New York University to purchase a parcel of land directly south of two units of Washington Square Village so that buildings providing decent faculty housing can be erected. As a member of the faculty, I consider it my duty to urge that you give this proposal favorable attention when it comes before the Board of Estimate for consideration.

For many years there has been an acute shortage of apartments where faculty members can be housed at rentals that are within their limited means. It is not unusual for instructors to pay more than a week's salary every month for a single room in a dilapidated, century-old firetrap. This situation has made it necessary for most of us to travel long distances to class, thus cutting into time that might be more profitably spent in conferences with students. Moreover, the university has been seriously hampered in its efforts to attract outstanding educators to its staff. One has to have a comfortable and reasonable place in which to live before he can decide to move his family out of established quarters.

The erection of faculty housing at the Washington Square site will help alleviate the present unsatisfactory condition. But think of this, too. The university is also planning, if it is successful in its bid, to include a laboratory elementary school on the premises. Under the circumstances, you can readily understand that the benefits to the city of the proposed project would be far more than would accrue from merely providing apartment facilities for a group that has heretofore been relatively ignored. Better teachers in our schools will mean better citizens in our town.

The welfare of more than 3,000 faculty members will be at stake when you deliberate on the question. We will naturally be keenly interested in the decision handed down by the Board of Estimate. Surely, other than objections raised by self-seeking interests, there can be no valid argument against the housing plan.

Respectfully yours,

Assistant Professor of English

How Would You Write a Term Paper?

We have been concentrating on how you should write the great majority of the compositions required of you in high school, the relatively brief ones rarely exceeding 300 words. But in some courses, especially in your senior year, you may be asked to submit much longer pieces of writing that may be loosely classified as *term papers* or *research reports*. Typical among these are studies of an author's characteristics or surveys of literary movements in honor English classes, analyses in depth of various topics in your science or social studies courses, and independent investigations encouraged by teachers of special subjects like psychology, merchandising, or home economics.

Learning how to prepare and write a term paper can be helpful to you not only for your immediate needs but for later writing activities as well. If you go on to college, you will discover that a research report is an inescapable requirement of many courses, and your instructors will assume that you know how to do this particular kind of job. Moreover, whether you eventually enter a professional or industrial occupation, with or without a college degree, you will learn that research is often the foundation upon which progress in the working world is built—and the ones who can go out, investigate a problem, and return with an intelligently written report on it are the ones who get ahead.

Let's see what some of the characteristics are of the term or research paper:

§ It's a composition—containing more paragraphs and perhaps somewhat fuller ones than those you usually write—but basically it is just a longer composition. Remember that! This means you must observe every principle of good writing we have discussed in the previous chapters.

§ Its length varies according to demand, normally from 1000–3000 words, or, if we break it down by our paragraph formula (100–150 words each), it contains somewhere between ten and twenty-five paragraphs.

§ It is different from the free-expression type of composition mainly in that background of information you are expected to have before you begin to write. The short themes might be classified as the products of unprepared writing. You get a topic like "Window Shopping," and you are not expected to do more with it than set down some personal observations in an interesting style, writing "off the cuff," so to speak. The source of information is *you* and *your experience*. You can start and finish such a composition in an hour or so.

The research paper, on the other hand, must be based upon definitely prepared material. Your own information, extensive as it may be, is not enough. It must be supported by authoritative references, statistics, and quotations that you can get only from outside sources. A report requires considerable library work, investigation of all or part of the contents of at least five books or periodicals, and incorporation in the writing of unquestionable proof of practically everything you say by direct reference to the source of your information, with footnotes and a bibliography as verification of your research. The same topic, "Window Shopping," that might be handled completely personally in one sitting as a regular composition in an English class would probably take you weeks to do as a term paper in a class in merchandising. You would have to broaden your treatment of the subject, gather and use information about such varied aspects of it as when window shopping originated, where it is most popular, what kind of people enjoy doing it, and what the average window shopper likes to see.

§ Your approach to a term paper is determined in advance. You must be thoroughly serious, analytical, scholarly, and well-organized.

To produce a good piece of research, you must proceed in the same series of orderly steps as you would with a shorter composition, but with special emphasis upon the planning stages. That's the key to the whole thing. The way you set up your material will determine the quality of your report. No amount of superior writing skill will substitute for authentic details supplied by well-documented notes.

I. PRELIMINARY SELECTION OF THE TOPIC

Ordinarily, you are permitted to choose your own topic, either from a selected list or with complete freedom provided your selection is within the subject or course area and meets with the approval of the teacher. In any case, before you consider any possibility, think about the answers to some guide questions (unless you are arbitrarily assigned only one topic).

How well is it related to my interests or needs? Don't pick a topic because you *think* you may be interested in it. If you know nothing about a limited field, have never had any experiences in it, or don't even recall ever having heard about it before, you are gambling against time when you decide it's worth a try. It may turn out all right, of course, but the odds are heavily against it. You may be led into the mistake many students make of stabbing at four or five possibilities before settling on one. Spending a little time examining your tastes or figuring out how the research you do for one subject can be useful elsewhere will save you wasteful trips up blind alleys.

Make your choice only after you can offer yourself good reasons for wanting to investigate the subject more thoroughly. Perhaps part of the research you do for a report on Charles Dickens in your English class can be of use in your social studies class when you study social conditions in nineteenth century England. You may have a hobby that ties in; for instance, coin collecting might lead you to a survey of the monetary systems of one or more countries. Or your future plans may influence you. What do you hope to become? A sales executive? All right, what about investigating the sales techniques of a Marco Polo or a Benjamin Franklin? You like reading mystery stories? Ask your English teacher whether you can be allowed to find out why Edgar Allan Poe has been called the father of the detective story.

You can see, then, that the primary source of topic selection is still you. But this time your interests and experience direct you toward an avenue of research rather than provide you with the material itself.

How interesting will it be to the reader or listener? Suppose you were working for an industrial organization and were asked to bring in a report on a highly technical subject that involved equations, formulas, and other extensive mathematical data. You would quite understandably confine yourself to these details and carry out your assignment without wondering about how entertaining your material was going to be. You would be sure of your employer's interest because he wouldn't be looking for stimulating language so much as he would be anxious to get the facts and recommendations that might enable the company to make more money.

However, for a school report that must be read by a teacher or heard by students, the matter of interest is very important. Here you are being judged on your ability to write as well as on your skill in research. And you know that a paper consisting mainly of symbols, charts, and diagrams is not going to be welcomed very cordially by people who may be neither as interested in nor as informed about the subject as you are. Avoid, therefore, topics that by their very nature are guaranteed to appeal to a limited audience and make dull reading or listening for most.

How easy will it be to find material? This is where you start working. Mind you, the actual research is not done now. Your objective is to browse through several reference sources so that you can make up your mind whether to keep your topic, revise it, or try something else. You go to the library and begin to look around. Be sensible about it. If there is very little material available or you will have to wait weeks before some of it can be secured for you, go back to your teacher and talk it over. You may have picked a topic that doesn't lend itself to research or isn't important enough to warrant having things written about it. In that case, get busy on a new choice at once. But don't start off with the idea that your report must be the last word on the subject. If you can locate about a half dozen references, you should be able to cover your topic well enough to satisfy the requirements of most high school reports.

Now, a bit of advice. It is your obligation as an intelligent student to become familiar with the frequently used sources of information in a well-equipped library. Unless you have a first hand acquaintance with these valuable aids to research, you cannot hope to do a quick and efficient job of gathering material for your report. It wouldn't make sense for you to have to give up on a topic because you didn't know where to look for the information. Test yourself on the following questions, which can serve as a self-analysis of your knowledge of library tools. If you don't know the answers to some of them, go to the nearest library and investigate personally until you do. You won't find the answers here because that would be defeating the whole purpose of this chapter.

Library Questionnaire

1. The best place to look for the latest information on a current topic is (a) an encyclopedia (b) *Readers' Guide* (c) the card catalogue.

2. Only living people are listed in (a) *Dictionary of American Biography* (b) Harper's *Dictionary of Classical Literature and Mythology* (c) *Who's Who in America.*

3. A biography of Daniel Webster may be found in (a) *American Yearbook* (b) *Dictionary of American Biography* (c) *Who's Who.*

4. A bibliography is a (a) life of a person (b) list of references (c) debate.

5. The best brief history of the American labor movement would probably be found in (a) *Encyclopaedia Britannica* (b) *World Almanac* (c) *Encyclopedia of the Social Sciences.*

6. To bring this history of the labor movement up-to-date, the best place to look would be (a) the vertical file (b) *Readers' Guide* (c) a combination of both.

7. To locate a quotation from a famous poem you would look in a book by (a) Fowler (b) Roget (c) Bartlett.

8. One of these encyclopedias has a detailed alphabetical index volume: (a) *World Book* (b) *Britannica* (c) *New International.*

9. To look up information about a play or short story, you would consult the Index by (a) Untermeyer (b) Krapp (c) Firkins.

10. The quickest way to locate a particular topic in a book is through the (a) appendix (b) table of contents (c) index.

11. To find out in which of Dickens' novels the character Uriah Heep appears you would consult (a) Bartlett's *Familiar Quotations* (b) Brewer's *Reader's Handbook* (c) Granger's *Index.*

12. The name of the Nobel Prize winner for literature last year would be found in (a) *Cambridge History of English Literature* (b) Goode's *Atlas* (c) *World Almanac.*

13. To learn how to pronounce the name of a country you would consult a book by (a) Knott (b) Lippincott (c) Rand McNally.

14. To get a brief summary of the plot of a novel you would turn to (a) Walsh's *Heroes and Heroines of Fiction* (b) *Oxford Companion to English Literature* (c) *Reader's Digest of Books.*

15. The copyright date of a book is found (a) on the title page (b) on the reverse side of the title page (c) in the appendix.

Assuming you are reasonably familiar with library reference sources, you would not abandon your topic until you had checked with each of the following:

A. *Your Textbook*

If your topic is an extension of a subject studied in class and covered in your textbook, look at the end of the chapter that dealt with the subject. The author has probably listed the names of the books he used to get his information. Or he may have supplied the titles at the end of the book in a bibliography. Get some cards or slips of paper and jot down this information for each book:

Author (last name first)
Title of the book (underlined)
Publisher
Date published or latest copyright
Number of volume (if more than one)
Pages (if supplied)

B. *Reference Works*

These are the books, in single or multiple volumes, that supply condensed accounts of any subject you can think of. The various biographical dictionaries, encyclopedias, atlases, gazetteers, yearbooks, annuals, literary histories and handbooks, indexes, and language guides summarize for you pertinent information about famous people, places, events, historical movements, scientific achievements, and literature. Perhaps more important than the facts you can get from these general reference works is the titles of additional books that are often listed at the end of articles. These, too, jot down on cards or slips in the same way you did the textbook references.

C. *The Card Catalogue*

You have probably learned in the library work that is part of every course in English how to handle the title, author, and subject cards that are found in this primary source. Start with the references suggested by your textbook and by the general works. Look up the call numbers of the books on your cards. You will find these numbers on the upper left hand side of the catalogue card. Jot them down. While you are at the cabinet, check the key words of the title of your topic against additional catalogue cards. For instance, if you have selected "Fur Trading in the West," try "Fur," "Trading," and "West." Use more cards for listing these.

D. *Readers' Guide to Periodical Literature*

If your topic is the kind about which articles appear in newspapers, magazines, or journals, you must also consult the *Readers' Guide*, which is a monthly publication later bound into volumes covering one or more years. Here again you can find information, by title, author, or subject, about articles that have been published in hundreds of periodicals. The advantage of using such a source is clear when you realize that you may have selected a topic that is so new that it has not yet found its way into books. Again, you put any suggested lead on a card or slip by:

Call number (if periodical is bound)
Name of author (last name first)
Title of article (in quotation marks)
Name of periodical (underlined)
Volume number
Pages covered by article
Date of issue (month, day, year)

E. *Vertical File*

You may have observed librarians cutting out articles from various periodicals or leafing through pamphlets and brochures that come in daily. These materials are eventually placed into large manila folders that are then labeled and filed upright in cabinets reserved for this purpose. Filing is alphabetical by subject headings or identifying names or titles. Here you have the most up-to-date information it is possible to get. Accounts or analyses of important recent events thus become available for your inspection long before they get into magazines, let alone books. Continue to use your cards to jot down reminders so that you will be able to find the information again later.

F. *The Librarian*

A slogan found posted in many stores could well apply to libraries: "If you don't see what you want, ask for it." Librarians welcome the opportunity to help visitors find information. Don't hesitate to talk over your problem with a librarian if you are having difficulty locating useful references. She is a professional at this game and can offer you invaluable assistance.

G. *The Questionnaire or Personal Experiment*

Suppose you can find very little help in the books or periodicals you examine, but you still believe that your topic would make an interesting report. You can do something about it by becoming your own authority. Get your teacher's approval first. Then decide what information you will need to support your main ideas. Let's say the topic is like one mentioned before: "Window Shopping." Construct a questionnaire in which you list those questions that will get for you the facts you need. Cut a stencil, if you know how, or ask one of your friends to help you with this typewriting job. You should have no difficulty thereafter getting permission to have your stencil run off on one of the school mimeographing machines. Distribute copies of the questionnaire among your classmates in every subject and ask them to return the completed forms by a given date. If you are successful in doing all this (and if you are persistent the project is not too hard), you will have available genuine first hand information that you can refer to in your report, information that will be very interesting to your teachers and classmates because they helped gather it.

Another original research technique that can be substituted for or added to book or periodical references is the experiment. Your topic is, for example, "Using the Right Seed to Grow a Good Lawn." You find that there is much to read about organic content of the soil and its relation to various seed strains. Wouldn't it be a good idea for you to find out how the soil around your house can be tested? You could get a testing kit, take samplings from several sections, and run the tests yourself. Your findings included in your report would give it a positive quality that is often lacking from accounts of what other people have done.

II. FINAL SELECTION OF THE TOPIC

If you did not stop before you were halfway through with your browsing among the reference sources to decide that the material available was too scanty, difficult to organize, or not likely to supply an interesting report, you will by now have completed your preliminary investigations. You may, however, at this late date wonder whether you really have chosen wisely. This is no time to change. You would lose time, certainly, and would find it difficult to get started again. The best thing to do, if doubts have been raised in your mind, is to change the direction of the topic so that you can take advantage of the material you have already located. Discuss it with your teacher. In most cases, your request to convert a listed topic like "Fur Trading in the West" into "Early Methods of Trapping Animals" (because the latter has more interesting possibilities) will be approved. Whatever you do, get your topic into its final form as quickly as possible. Don't get involved in an unrealistic search for perfection, or you will find the deadline for handing in your report upon you before you have written a word.

III. NARROWING DOWN THE TOPIC

Now you must pause to re-examine your topic in terms of the number of words you are expected to write. For a comparatively short research paper, you will not want to go too far afield. In such a limited space, it would be better to give many interesting details about a few ideas rather than little bits of information about a great many. Consider, then, whether your topic needs further refinement or limitation. While you might be able to give fair coverage to "The Development of Education in Colonial America" in 5,000 words, you would have to narrow down your topic to perhaps "Public Education in the Massachusetts Bay Colony" if the assignment called for only 1,500 words. It is essential that you think about the scope at this point, so that you don't do a lot of reading and note-taking only to discover later that you have to get rid of much material because you have far more than you need. This doesn't mean that you may not want to make more changes as you gather your notes or prepare the outline. Even if you do, however, you will at least have started your actual research with a reasonably clear idea in your mind of the approximate range of the subject.

IV. TAKING NOTES

After you have narrowed down the topic to the general limits within which you expect to pursue it, look over the cards or slips you have gathered during your preliminary search for reference material. If your topic has been revised substantially, you will have no use for some of the cards because they are no longer pertinent. Put these aside. Now take the rest, one by one, and turn to the pages you had decided earlier would give useful information. Don't start your note-taking right away. Read the section through first to get the feel of the author's ideas and to decide where they will fit into your outline. Then, if you believe that a quotation from the original can clinch a point you will want to make, good. Take it down, *word for word*, mark the page number, and leave some reminder to yourself to use quotation marks when you incorporate the passage into the body of your report. If you expect to say something later that will have to be backed up by authority, briefly summarize the main idea from the source and again list the page number.

Use additional cards for the notes and, to keep things in order, adopt some lettering or numbering system. For example, if your first source card refers to a book, place the identifying numeral in the upper right hand corner thus:

Call	Author	I
Number	Title	
	Publisher	
	Copyright date	
	Volume number	
	Pages	

Your first note card gets the numeral plus a letter:

> *(Reminder of the main idea—in a word or two)*   I-A
> A quotation *or* a good idea summarized *or* a
> series of facts *or* a chart, diagram, etc.
>   Page number

Your next note card gets the numeral plus the next letter:

> (Either a new idea or point *or* a   I-B
> continuation of the notes on the
> previous card)
>   Page number

Proceed in the same way with your next reference, numbering the cards II, II-A, II-B, II-C, etc. Be sure to include the page numbers where your material was found and could be found again if you had to check it. Besides, you will need this information for the footnotes, which we will talk about shortly.

Don't copy too much. Your teacher will expect the great majority of the words in your report to be in your own language. Moreover, frequent interruptions in the continuity of the paragraphs, in the form of long quotations, can lead to interference with the reader's progress. Let *your* style come through, not that of a half dozen other writers. To avoid the temptation to quote more than you should, make most of the entries on the note cards reminders rather than detailed copies of the original text of your references. The single word or two that you write at the top of a note card to indicate the point covered will often be enough to bring to mind an item you plan to include eventually in a paragraph, and the brevity of such a note will force you to be original in your choice of words. The two main purposes of your notes should be:

—to provide you with references to support your statements
—to help you form the outline that must precede the writing of the report.

V. PREPARING THE OUTLINE

Because of the greater number of words to be written, the outline for a research report must be more elaborate than the one for a short composition. The planning is done on four levels.

Direction of the Topic

To achieve the true purpose of research, your report must do more than merely summarize what you read in selected books and periodicals. While you are gathering your notes, decide upon a clear statement of what use you will make of your research material—what criticism you want to offer, what opinion you want to express, what comparisons you want to draw, what recommendations you want to propose, what predictions you want to make. You must go beyond your notes and do some original thinking of your own. This will give your report direction and prevent its sounding like a digest of reference works.

For instance, if you were to write on "The Helicopter in Commercial Aviation," it would be pointless to give a bare recital of the history of this aircraft. The reader could understandably say that if he wanted only this information he could have gone to the sources himself and very likely have gotten a more comprehensive coverage of the subject than is contained in your paper. On the other hand, you could organize your material so that it promotes the idea that the helicopter has only scratched the surface of its commercial possibilities, and you could make suggestions for increasing the use of this odd-shaped plane. The evaluation of the helicopter's potential and the suggestions would be your original contribution to the report. The first thing you would do in preparing your outline, therefore, would be to write directly under the title a complete sentence indicating the direction your report will take:

The Helicopter in Commercial Aviation

Much greater use can be made of the helicopter in commercial aviation.

Incidentally, your guiding statement, sometimes also referred to as your *thesis*, automatically sets up the main ideas you will want to express in the introductory and concluding paragraphs.

Once you have made up your mind how to handle your material, re-examine your note cards. Discard any that will not help you advance your ideas. Arrange the rest in accordance with the plan suggested in the next step.

Breakdown of the Topic into Major Ideas

Now you consider the total number of words to be written and divide your material into broad headings, under which related ideas can be grouped to represent the individual paragraphs. It's as if you were preparing to write a series of compositions, each dealing with a specific aspect of a general topic. A 1,000 word report might break down this way:

> Introduction (100 words)
> I. Major Idea (400 words)
> II. Major Idea (400 words)
> Conclusion (100 words)

For 2,500 words you might do it this way:

> Introduction (200 words)
> I. Major Idea (650–700 words)
> II. Major Idea (650–700 words)
> III. Major Idea (650–700 words)
> Conclusion (200 words)

Let's see how this worked out in an outline prepared for an excellent report written by a student on "The Search for Perfection," a survey of some of the early attempts in America to establish Utopias, or ideal communities. The writer chose this as the *thesis* (direction of the report):

The Search for Perfection

Ideal communities have invariably failed in this country because of weaknesses in human nature and the systems of government attempted.

Since this was going to be a 5,000 word report, the writer quite sensibly decided to break down the topic into five major ideas. An analysis of the notes suggested that the best arrangement would be a study of five typical communities that attempted the ideal and failed. Thus the preliminary outline looked like this:

Introduction (250–500 words)
(Statement of thesis)

I. Community of Rappites (700–900 words)
II. New Harmony (700–900 words)
III. Brook Farm (700–900 words)
IV. Oneida (700–900 words)
V. The Icarian Movement (700–900 words)

Conclusion (250–500 words)
(Evaluation of thesis)

Note that the Roman numerals stand for the broad headings under which the related paragraphs will later be grouped. Note also that as the total size of a report increases, the introduction, major ideas, and conclusion correspondingly increase. Compare this with the organization suggested above for a 1,000 word paper.

The breakdown of the topic now enables you to gather your notes into an appropriate number of bundles, in this

case five. Again you have the opportunity to eliminate any
that will not fit in. A good idea is to put a rubber band
around each bundle so that none of the cards get mis-
laid.

Arrangement of Paragraphs Under Major Idea Headings

Your next step is to proceed with each major idea as if
it were a composition unit in itself. You plan the actual paragraphs, and their number will depend, of course, upon the
total words. For 1,000 words you would have possibly this
arrangement:

Introduction (100 words)

I. Major Idea (400 words)

      Paragraph 1 ⎫
      Paragraph 2 ⎬ 125–150 words each
      Paragraph 3 ⎭

II. Major Idea

      Paragraph 1 ⎫
      Paragraph 2 ⎬ 125–150 words each
      Paragraph 3 ⎭

Conclusion (100 words)

For 2,500 words, this:

Introduction (200 words)

I. Major Idea

      Paragraph 1 ⎫
      Paragraph 2 ⎪
      Paragraph 3 ⎬ 125–150 words each
      Paragraph 4 ⎪
      Paragraph 5 ⎭

II. Major Idea

Paragraph 1 ⎫
Paragraph 2 ⎪
Paragraph 3 ⎬ 125–150 words each
Paragraph 4 ⎪
Paragraph 5 ⎭

III. Major Idea

Paragraph 1 ⎫
Paragraph 2 ⎪
Paragraph 3 ⎬ 125–150 words each
Paragraph 4 ⎪
Paragraph 5 ⎭

Conclusion (200 words)

You understand, I'm sure, that such an arrangement must be flexible. You may vary the number of major ideas and the paragraphs related to them to suit your purpose and the size of your paper. Always bear in mind what was said before; it is wiser to say much about a few things than to say little about a great many.

Since the writer of "The Search for Perfection" was planning for a long paper, the introduction and conclusion were broken down into paragraphs, as well as the middle. The still tentative outline now looked like this:

Introduction (250–500 words)
Thesis: *Ideal communities have invariably failed in this country because of weaknesses in human nature and the systems of government attempted.*
  A. Meaning and Significance of Utopias
  B. Background of Utopias in America
  C. Preliminary Comments on Utopias

I. Community of Rappites (750–900 words)
  A. Origin
  B. Facts about the Leader

    C. Adoption of Collective System
    D. Life in Harmony
    E. A Similar Group
    F. Decline and Downfall

II. New Harmony Community (750–900 words)
    A. Securing the Land
    B. The Leader
    C. Beginning of Non-religious Community
    D. Daily Life
    E. Constitution
    F. Decline

III. Brook Farm (750–900 words)
    A. Origin
    B. Organization
    C. Daily Life
    D. The School
    E. Decline

IV. Oneida (750–900 words)
    A. General Characteristics
    B. Leader and Religion
    C. Exodus from Putney
    D. Strange Beliefs and Practices
    E. Departure of Noyes
    F. Decline

V. The Icarian Movement (750–900 words)
    A. "A Voyage to Icaria"
    B. Early Beginnings
    C. Various Settlements
    D. Community Prosperity
    E. Failure

Conclusion (250–500 words)
    A. Decline of Utopias in America
    B. Possible Causes Reviewed
    C. Likelihood in Contemporary America
    D. The Future of Utopias Here

Note that the *Roman numerals* stand for the major ideas and the *capital letters* represent the paragraphs.

Arrangement of Details Under Paragraph Headings

When you get to this point, you have reached the final stage of the outline: the insertion, *in detail,* of the material you will include within each paragraph. You sort your notes within the bundles in accordance with your outline of major ideas and paragraphs, and mark the cards again so that you will remember where to place particular quotations, facts, diagrams, etc.—and in what order you will want to place them. This time you should use a red or blue pencil so that the new markings will stand out.

In our sample below, based on the report we have been using as a model, we will not repeat the entire outline. At the end of this chapter, you will find another example of a completed outline. For the moment, we will take two excerpts, showing the introduction and one of the middle major headings in detail. This should be enough to give you the idea of how the final breakdown is handled:

Introduction (250–500 words)
(Statement of thesis)

    A. Meaning and Significance of Utopias
        1. Search for a better world
        2. Backward glances, over-ambitious plans
        3. Reality vs. idealism
    B. Background of Utopias in America
        1. Mainly first half of nineteenth century
        2. Belief in innate goodness of man
        3. Jacksonian influence
        4. 1609—Jamestown
    C. Preliminary Comments on Utopias
        1. Search for religious, intellectual freedom
        2. Typical "joiners"
        3. Record of failure

IV. Brook Farm (750–900 words)
    A. Origin
        1. Transcendentalism
        2. Famous persons connected with it

B. Organization
   1. Really an association
   2. Shares of stock
   3. Membership rules
C. Daily Life
   1. Community dining hall
   2. Nursery group
   3. Industries
   4. Other activities
D. The School
   1. Education in all grades
   2. One hour of manual labor
   3. Teaching devices
E. Decline
   1. Internal differences
   2. Fourier
   3. New plan
   4. Austere rules
   5. Departure of noted members

In your final version of the outline, as you can see, the *Roman numerals* stand for the major ideas, the *capital letters* for the paragraph headings, and the *Arabic numbers* for the details within the paragraphs. If you wanted to break it down even further, you would use the lower case letters— *a, b, c,* etc.—under the Arabic numbers.

VI. WRITING THE REPORT

As with any composition, you write a rough draft first. In the introduction, you try, of course, to create interest, suggest the contents covered by your outline, and suit the length to the total number of words to be written. As you noted in the outline sample above, you will surely need more than one paragraph for this purpose in the longer reports. Similarly, the ending should be flexible in length and do its job of re-emphasizing your point of view and your conclusions based upon your findings. In general, you follow the suggestions made previously for creating good opening and closing paragraphs, remembering that in these two parts of the report you have your best opportunities to display the originality of your thinking.

In the middle paragraphs, you simply convert the outline into a smoothly flowing development of the major and subordinate ideas. As you write, you may want to leave out some parts of the outline, or additional ideas may occur to you that should be included. Don't hesitate to make alterations that you think are desirable, but adjust your outline later so that it corresponds with the text of your report. Take special pains to maintain good continuity within and between paragraphs. Make sure, when you go from one major idea to another, that the change is clear but not so abrupt as to be confusing. On the whole, try to give the impression that, although much of your information is based upon references, your handling of the subject matter is entirely the product of the way you have analyzed and directed the topic. Let me add one more statement here, without comment. "Plagiarize," according to the dictionary, is "to take and pass off as one's own [the ideas, writings, etc. of another]."

VII. FOOTNOTES

You should try not to refer directly to your sources more than two or three times on any one page. When you do have to identify something (a quotation, summary, idea, chart, diagram) as coming from one of the books or periodicals you read, you indicate it as a *footnote*. There are various approved techniques for handling these entries. If your teacher wishes you to use a particular style, you will be told what it is in advance, I'm sure. But, should you fail to receive specific instructions, use the method that is simplified and being widely adopted nowadays:

§ Place each footnote at the bottom of the page where the reference was made.

§ Number the footnotes consecutively. On the first page

for which you have to enter a footnote, start with 1. The next one, whether it appears on the same or a subsequent page, gets 2, and so on. If you use 25 footnotes in all, the last one will be numbered 25.

§ In the text, at the *end* of the reference, insert the number that matches the footnote slightly above the last letter and punctuation of the last word.

§ In your footnotes, list the information about your sources as follows:

Book: Full name(s) of author(s), title (underlined), and page number

Periodical: Author(s), if any, title of article (underlined), name of periodical, and page number
Handle bulletins, pamphlets, and brochures in the same way. If it is a newspaper, add the column number to the page reference.

General references: Author(s), if any, title of article, name of reference work, volume and page number.

It is assumed that in your bibliography you will give *all* the necessary information about your sources.

§ You needn't bother trying to remember the elaborate Latin reference signs formerly used with footnotes. If you have two footnotes from the same source on one page, indicate the second one by the simple "Ibid," which means "In the same as above." If your teacher permits it, mention only the last name of the author and the page number *after* you have used a reference at least once before. This assumes that your bibliography does not include two books by the same author or two different authors with the same last names.

§ Study the excerpts from a completed report at the end of this chapter for examples of how footnotes are entered in the text and at the bottom of the page.

VIII. CREATING LANGUAGE INTEREST

There is no reason why a research report has to make dull reading. Good continuity, avoidance of repetition, varied sentence structure, economical phrasing, and carefully chosen words are devices that are just as effective in a lengthy paper as in a short one. Be informative and scholarly, but be interesting, too. That's the only way to get maximum results and grades.

IX. REVISING YOUR PAPER

Here you follow the suggestions made in Chapter VII about polishing your written product before preparing the final draft. There are several additional things you should look for in a term paper or research report while you are in the revision stage. Double check your quotations to be sure they have been properly punctuated and have been recorded word for word (correctly spelled). Make certain that the footnotes appear at the bottom of the proper pages and that you have provided the required information about author, title, and page number. Go back over your outline and check it against your text to see that both agree. Get rid of any phrases or sentences that you may have unconsciously taken from your sources without marking them with footnotes. Finally, take a count of the total words used. If you think your report is a trifle short or considerably longer than expected, talk it over with your teacher before you do anything drastic.

X. THE FINAL DRAFT

—Try to type the copy you will hand in.
—Use a folder inside of which you will insert your report. Your name and class are sufficient on the outside cover. In some classes, you may get extra credit for an illustration that symbolizes your topic.
—On the first page list:
     The title of the report (centered)

Your name, class, the name of your teacher,
the school, and the date (lower right)

(The exact order and position of these entries varies.
Find out if there is a standard form for your class before
using the recommendations above.)

—Attach your outline next so that it acts as a table of contents. Some students list the page numbers next to the
major idea headings for further aid in locating points
covered.

—Now put in the report itself. Skip about four spaces between the text and the footnotes on each page. Some
writers draw a line at the bottom of each page of text
and insert the footnotes beneath it. Remember the con-
secutive numbering and the simplified listing.

—Collect all your primary source cards for your bibliography, which is the listing of the references you have
used. Arrange the cards alphabetically by the last names
of the authors. If a reference has no author's names attached to it, use the title as your alphabetical entry.
Now head a page "Bibliography," and copy the information from your cards. Take down everything except the
call numbers and the identification symbols you added
in the upper left and right hand corners. Spell carefully
and punctuate properly.

—Number your pages, but not those containing the outline
and the bibliography. When you have done this, you are
ready to hand in your report.

To summarize some of the suggestions made throughout
this chapter, herewith are excerpts from a 5,000 word report
submitted by a student in a social studies class. We will
study the introduction, several pages of middle paragraphs,
and the conclusion. Observe how the outline serves as a
table of contents; note carefully how the footnotes are
entered; examine the arrangement and punctuation of the
bibliography listings. And keep this in mind when you read
the text. It is a documented piece of research, but it is a
well-written composition, too!

The Development of Education in
Colonial America

OUTLINE

Thesis Sentence: Education in colonial America, although irregular and struggling, produced many of the guiding principles that still influence our schools today.

Introduction

A. Background
   1. Obstacles
   2. Struggle
   3. Desire for education
B. Determining Factors
   1. Problems
   2. Major influences
C. Suggested Study
   1. Differences
   2. Practices
   3. Our debt

I. New England
A. Massachusetts Bay
   1. Boston Latin School
   2. Dorchester
   3. Ordinance of 1642
   4. The laws of 1647
   5. First tax-supported school
B. Main Principles Established
   1. Public education a duty
   2. Community, not central, responsibility
   3. Separation of elementary and secondary schools
   4. Selectmen
C. Other New England Colonies
   1. Rhode Island
   2. New Hampshire, Maine, Vermont
   3. Connecticut
D. Types of Schools
   1. Dame
   2. Latin Grammar
   3. Academies, prep schools

    E. General Features of Schools
        1. Curriculum
        2. Books
        3. Teachers, discipline
        4. Policies with girls

II. **New Netherland**
    A. Comparison with New England
        1. Neither compulsory nor public
        2. West India Company
        3. Attitudes toward public education
    B. New Amsterdam
        1. First public school
        2. Poor teachers' pay, facilities
        3. Latin School—1652
        4. Dr. Curtis—1659

III. **Middle Colonies**
    A. Pennsylvania
        1. William Penn
        2. Enoch Flower—1683
        3. Problems of lack of unity
        4. Society of 1754
    B. Delaware
        1. Law of 1640
        2. Contributions by Sweden
        3. Later developments
    C. New Jersey
        1. English efforts
        2. Period after 1702

IV. **Southern Colonies**
    A. Influence of England
        1. Absence of Puritan, Dutch influence
        2. Private schools favored
        3. Orphan schools
    B. Maryland
        1. Law of 1696—county schools
        2. Similarity to Latin grammar schools
        3. Low teacher salaries, poor facilities
    C. The Carolinas
        1. Charleston grammar school
        2. Laws of 1710 and 1712

V. The Colonial Colleges
A. Harvard
  1. Bequest of 1636
  2. Admission requirements in 1643
  3. Courses of study
  4. Headmasters: Eaton, Dunster, Mather, Leverett
B. Yale
  1. Act of 1702
  2. New Haven, Elihu Yale, 1718
  3. Bishop Berkeley
C. Other Colleges
  1. Princeton
  2. Rutgers
  3. Pennsylvania

Conclusion
A. Influence of Church
  1. Religious leaders
  2. Dual role of church
B. Early Policies Still Prevalent
  1. Community responsibility
  2. Need for education
C. Forecast
  1. Present importance
  2. Space age
  3. Desire to learn

The excerpts that follow illustrate the complete introduction (3 paragraphs), the development of the first major idea (*New England*—4 paragraphs), and the complete conclusion (3 paragraphs).

The Development of Education in Colonial America

All Americans take great pride in recalling the perseverance and courage of the early settlers of this country. To establish a foothold, the refugees from European religious and social persecution had to fight against a strange environment, frequently hostile natives, and rather indifferent and grasping rulers overseas. We know how they struggled with crude tools to build homes and houses of worship, bent their backs over the soil to make it yield crops, and kept their flintlocks oiled and ready for sudden attacks. But some of us do not know that in the midst of their grim fight against man and nature these dedicated pioneers also found time to do something about the education of their young.

With loosely organized governments and public funds not readily available, the task of building schools was not an easy one. But somehow these valiant people managed to sow the seeds that grew into the handsome schools and well-trained teaching staffs that we know today. Many factors influenced the development of education at this time. Among the most important that determined the eventual pattern "were the compactness of community life, the aggressive singularity of Puritanism, a well educated leadership, many of whom were college graduates, the combination of church and state, and an alliance with commercial enterprise." [1]

Although these influences existed among the colonies as a whole, they by no means produced the same kind of results everywhere. A study of the individual systems shows how greatly they differed from one section of the country to another. Despite these differences, certain practices emerged that are still in existence today. Certainly it can be said that public education as we know it can be traced to colonial days, and, as we think about it, we realize how greatly we are indebted to the vision and courage of our forefathers.

Our survey must start with the Massachusetts Bay Colony, which was the first to make its schools a public charge. It was strong and prosperous almost from the beginning and had settlers who saw the need for teaching the children. Moreover, they were eager to supply the means. In 1635, at a Boston town meeting, the people voted to hire a schoolmaster and thus founded the Boston Latin School, which was largely supported by the wealthier citizens. However, a few years later a school was established at Dorchester maintained wholly by a public tax. This started the way for the development of other Latin schools, in the more prosperous townships, and in 1642 an ordinance of the colony made education compulsory. [2] This law made it a must for parents to

---

[1] William Drake, *The American School in Transition*, p. 69
[2] Edwin E. Slosson, *The American Spirit in Education*, pp. 1–21

give an account of the instruction received by their
children. If the officials felt that a child's education
had been persistently neglected, they had the right to
apprentice him to an occupation. The law would have
been a very good thing if not for the fact that it required
education but could not provide it.[3] By 1647, the colony
realized the need for more adequate education and made
it obligatory upon every township of fifty householders
to employ one person who was competent in the field of
teaching reading and writing. Failure to do so meant a
fine. In addition, every township of 100 families had to
establish a college preparatory grammar school. This was
the foundation for the first American tax-supported public school, and set a tradition that is followed today.[4]

These ideas would have worked well were it not for
the fact that some towns found it cheaper to pay a fine
than support a schoolmaster. Another obstacle was the
Indian raids, which made parents afraid to let their
youngsters leave the house unprotected. Despite these
problems and the fact that fees were sometimes charged
in the schools and children were not compelled to attend
if parents preferred to give them private instruction,
some main principles were established. In fact, it is
surprising to learn how many of our basic educational
statutes can be traced to this colonial source. The first
is that no community, regardless of how small it is, may
evade the duty of supplying public instruction. The second is that it is the responsibility of the community, and
not the central government, to provide education. The
third is that elementary schools must be organized and
handled separately from those on the secondary level.
Finally, the idea of having a committee of selectmen
run each school is directly comparable to our own local
school boards, and the reason for their existence is the
same. Parents want to have control over the education of
their children.

Elsewhere in the New England area, all of the colonies
except Rhode Island had made provision for education
within a few years of the first settlement. Newport and
Providence gave donations of land for schools, but before
1800 there was no general law authorizing the towns to

[3] *Ibid.*, pp. 10–12
[4] Harvey Wish, *Society and Thought in Early America*, p. 55

maintain schools. It may have been because there was no
union here between church and state, and the government did not concern itself with sustaining an educated
ministry. But in New Hampshire and Maine progress was
as extensive and as rapid as in Massachusetts. Vermont,
too, got started early and by 1777 it had passed a law
putting upon the legislature the duty of establishing a
school or schools in each town "for the convenient instruction of youth." As for Connecticut, its record for
schools was to be envied. Before 1650, education was
compulsory; in 1672, 600 acres of land were given to
each city in the state to be used for erecting a grammar
school. Generally speaking, New England was an excellent example of how the churches and the various governments worked together to encourage instructional
programs.

Among the types of schools developed in this active
area were the Dame School, which taught its pupils to
read and write, and the Latin Grammar School, which
did not function too well because of frontier conditions.
An idea of the quality of the instruction can be derived
from a statement by Reverend John Barnard, of Marble-
head, Massachusetts, who wrote: "By that time I had
a little past my sixth year. I had left my reading school,
in the latter part of which my mistress had made me a
sort of teacher, appointing me to teach some children
that were older than myself as well as smaller ones."[5]
The grammar schools, which prospered most in Massachusetts because of their proximity to Harvard, were
soon replaced by the private academy or prep school.

What went on inside these schools is worth mention-
ing here. In the Latin schools, boys were given intensive
training in the complexities of Latin grammar and were
often made to speak the language in class. The curricu-
lum of the common schools included reading, writing,
arithmetic, and religion. Reading and spelling were
taught from books containing the alphabet and the
Lord's Prayer.[6] The advanced children of the day used the
New England Primer, which lasted until the end of the
colonial period, or the American Primer Book. The for-

---

[5] Alice Morse Earl, *Child Life in Colonial Days*, pp. 97–99
[6] Stuart G. Noble, *A History of American Education*, pp. 25–29

mer contained spelling words, short sentences for reading, and a series of theological couplets, such as this:

> "In Adam's fall
> We sinned all."[7]

As for the teachers, they enjoyed high social prestige, especially if they had been imported from England. Their major requirement was to be sound in faith. Discipline in the ungraded classes was harsh. As a rule, the more conscientious the teacher, the worse time his pupils had. As the frontier was pushed farther west, it became inconvenient for children to go long distances to a single school, and so the custom grew of having the teacher come to the town. In 1789 a Massachusetts law made it a requirement for all teachers to have a college education.[8] Before leaving this section, a word should be said about the policies toward girl students. They were hardly ever admitted to the grammar schools, but did receive instruction in the Dame Schools, including training in sewing through the use of samples. An examination of the practices outlined above shows that there was not much uniformity, but unmistakable progress toward a regular school system was evident.

(Now that you have had the opportunity to study the introduction and some of the middle paragraphs, here are the ending paragraphs of this paper.)

Our analysis of the growth of educational policies and facilities in colonial America shows clearly that the need for providing instruction for the young was strongly stimulated by the religious leaders of the day. They knew how important it was to keep the flame of learning alive, and with it the spread of the faith. That's why they often stepped in, as was shown, when the community itself made no effort to organize classes. This was a fine example of how the churches fulfilled their purpose of serving God by ministering to the needs of man. Although our present system is founded on the principle of separation of church and state, made necessary I'm sure by the many different religions among us, we should not forget what

---

[7] Wish, p. 55
[8] Slosson, p. 20

we owe the brave men of the cloth who would not let their people forget that at times a book is as powerful as a gun.

We must also pay tribute to the intelligence of the frontier planners of education because they recognized the worth of the philosophy of community responsibility for education. Many of the lawmakers came of the wealthier classes and could well have afforded private tutoring, but they saw in public schools the best means available to promote progress within their communities. This attitude has become so well accepted through the years that its merit is not even debatable. Our parents may complain about rising taxes, but they wouldn't dream of arguing against the necessity of providing public funds for schools. Even childless couples understand that they have a stake in the education of other people's children. They know how rapidly a state or a nation can deteriorate if the citizens do not keep pace with scientific and cultural progress. It is unquestionably true that this nation grew stronger and assumed its position of leadership in the world faster because its first settlers worried about schools almost as much as they did about food and shelter.

They left us a rich heritage. Proper education has become more important than ever to the growth of our country. In this space age, as the rocket race grows hotter and hotter among nations, the answer to the charges that we have been falling behind must be found in the schools. The demand in recent years that science courses be increased and standards generally raised is proof of the fact that only by turning out more and better-educated young men and women will we be able to catch up or forge ahead. Our problems may have occurred lately because everything has been made too easy perhaps for us, with our beautiful buildings and well-equipped classrooms. Our public schools still operate under the broad principles established hundreds of years ago, but we need a return of some of that colonial desire and courage. Then nobody would surpass us because the United States would have the best-trained minds in the world. We are not missing the means nor the facilities; we don't have to seek instruction in log cabins by barely literate schoolmasters. All we need now is the will to do it.

The Development of Colonial Education in America

BIBLIOGRAPHY

Butts, Freeman, and Cremin, Lawrence A., **A History of Education in American Culture,** Henry Holt & Co., New York, 1958

Canby, Henry Seidel, **American Memoir,** Houghton Mifflin Co., New York, 1947

Cubberly, Ellwood P., **The History of Education,** Houghton Mifflin Co., New York, 1948

————, **Public Education in the United States,** Houghton Mifflin Co., New York, 1947

Drake, William, **The American School in Transition,** Prentice-Hall, Inc., New York, 1955

Earl, Alice Morse, **Child Life in Colonial Days,** Macmillan Co., New York, 1957

————, **Home Life in Colonial Days,** Macmillan Co., New York, 1954

Feininger, Andreas, "Citizen Ben Franklin and His Beloved Philadelphia," **Life,** Time, Inc., New York, 1959

Langdon, William C., **Everyday Things in American Life—1607–1776,** Charles Scribner's Sons, New York, 1937

Meyer, Adolphe E., **An Educational History of the American People,** McGraw Hill Book Co., New York, 1957

Noble, Stuart G., **A History of American Education,** Rinehart & Co., New York, 1954

Slosson, Edwin E., **The American Spirit in Education,** Yale University Press, New Haven, 1921

Wish, Harvey, **Society and Thought in Early America,** Longmans, Green & Co., New York, 1950

How Should You Handle Compositions on Examinations?

If you could take as long as you liked to complete it, there would be nothing special about writing a composition for a mid- or end-term test in school, a state examination in English, or a college entrance essay question. Admittedly, under these conditions, you miss some of the advantages of doing an assignment at home, such as having a dictionary handy for checking spelling and vocabulary or drafting friends and relatives to act as consultants. But when you find that, in order to answer all the questions on an examination, you must start and finish a composition in an hour or so, your biggest obstacle is not the lack of help. It is the time limit.

To overcome this handicap, you must train yourself to write under pressure. You don't eliminate any of the steps recommended before; you streamline them. Let's see how this works in a typical situation:

QUESTION

Write a composition of 250 to 300 words on one of the topics below:

The family doctor	Why I like ballet
The hunting season	Earning and learning
Judging farm land	A celebrity I've met
My first formal	The bells in my life
The Chinese puzzle today	Commercialized athletics
Students from other lands	Experiments I'd like to try
The value of mathematics	Effects of science upon our
Careers for the handi-	amusements
capped	(30)

286

This question happened to be one of six on a three hour examination. How much time would you have allowed yourself? To avoid being caught short, you should learn to apportion your time in accordance with a standard procedure:

Steps	In this case
Convert the number of credits assigned into a percentage of the total.	30 out of 100 or 30%
Now apply the percentage figure to the number of *minutes* allowed.	30% of 180 (3 hrs.) = 54 minutes
To be on the safe side, add about 10% for an essay question, if there are also some short answer types that can be worked faster.	1 hour for the composition, from rough draft to final copy

The number of words required and the time allowed will vary, of course, since not all schools follow the same practices in examinations. However, once you have learned how to handle a composition of 300 words in an hour, you should have little trouble adjusting your schedule to slight differences up or down.

All right, then, we go back to the question. You have one hour to write a composition of 250 to 300 words on any one of 15 topics. This is how you should divide your time.

The First Fifteen Minutes

(The following plan is based on the assumption that you have been permitted to *choose* a topic. Naturally, if only one has been assigned, you skip the first item below.)

1. *Selecting the Topic (3 minutes)* You can't afford to waste time making up your mind or bemoaning the fact that not a single topic looks inviting. You have to pick one; so get started immediately. Use the elimination process. Take a

pencil and, in the first minute, cross out every title that deals
with a subject about which you have very little information.
This might reduce the original list to these:

The family doctor
My first formal
Earning and learning
The bells in my life
The value of mathematics
Commercialized athletics
Experiments I'd like to try
Effects of science upon our amusements

Now, if you are not very strong in mathematics and science,
and you've learned that writing about sports is very difficult,
you cross out four more titles, leaving:

The family doctor
My first formal
Earning and learning
The bells in my life

You have one more minute. Ask yourself some questions.
Have you ever gone to a formal dance or party? Do you
work after school or during the summer vacations? A girl
might be interested in the first, a boy in the second. But suppose you must say "No" to both. Then you are down to the
last two:

The family doctor
The bells in my life

You can see that by elimination you have arrived at the topics
that can be handled by anyone. We all get visited by doctors and the lives of students especially are controlled greatly
by bells. Which do you pick? *You pick the one that is closer
to a recent experience.* If you haven't seen a doctor for a
long time, you may have trouble recalling details and emotions. *Cross it out.* You practically live by bells. Your experience here is as recent as yesterday.

Before going on, let me say this: The reasoning thus far

has been sheer guesswork. No elimination process can be the same for any two students. Undoubtedly, we crossed out three or four topics that might have suited you better than the one selected. Suppose you did know a lot about and enjoyed hunting or the ballet or mathematics. Good. Then you would have included one or more of these in your final pair. The main thing you must do, in the first three minutes, is to get your choices down to no more than two, and then make the final decision. A very strong interest or preference will make your job of selecting a topic easier. But when they all look alike to you, limit yourself to the titles that can be developed without special information.

2. *Narrowing Down the Topic (4 minutes)* Now, as usual, you take stock of the number of words required. For 300 words, you know that the best arrangement is two middle paragraphs. With this in mind, you re-examine the title you have chosen. You must narrow it down quickly so that you can develop it by featuring two main ideas.

Settle for the first ones you can think of. They are probably just as good as any others that might occur to you if you had more time. And to help yourself think, ask yourself what generally happens in connection with the topic. For instance, your reaction to "The Family Doctor" might be that you get sick and he comes. As for "The Bells in My Life," you hear them in school usually and there must be at least one you enjoy hearing and one you do not. There you are. Focus your attention on the familiar aspects of the topic and you will be able to narrow it down without any loss of time.

3. *Preparing the Outline (8 minutes)* Here is where the streamlining begins. You forget about trying an unusual approach if one does not occur to you in 60 seconds. On an examination, unless something comes in a flash, you will lose time by stopping too long in an effort to be strikingly original. If you get an inspiration, by all means go ahead with it. But don't press. Time is the ruling factor.

In most cases, you will go directly to your outline. *Don't leave it out!* We went over this point before. The few minutes you spend now will save you many more later and unquestionably bring about better results. Get busy. Draw the two lines:

_____   _____

Insert the paragraph headings:

The family doctor

The need for a doctor   *The visit*

OR

The bells in my life

Lunch hour   *Before a test*

Put your details in:

The family doctor

The need for a doctor	*The visit*
sore throat	his cheerfulness
mother's concern	gentle poking
stalling tactics	reassuring words
telephone call	prescription
dread	relief

OR

The bells in my life

Lunch hour	*Before a test*
third period	the night before
struggle with geometry	lack of study
hunger pangs	one more period
clock watching	clock watching
desperation	desperation
bell of joy	bell of doom

The Next Twenty-five Minutes

You are ready for the rough draft. You must practice until you can write at the speed of 12–15 words a minute. This is not difficult to do if you have prepared an outline. You know what's coming and you can pour out the words, knowing that you will have time later to get your material into its best final form. For this purpose, skip spaces between lines.

If you can't think of a good narrative beginning paragraph, use the standard type: a sentence or so introducing the topic as a whole, a few sentences suggesting each of your main ideas and indicating what point of view you will take, and a final sentence leading into the body of the composition. Then, following the outline closely, write the middle paragraphs. Avoid introducing new details as you proceed because they may throw you off the track. Just concentrate on two things. Keep your sentences complete and as varied in structure as you can manage. Use words that are concrete and colorful.

Finally, write the last paragraph, again remembering that any extended effort to introduce a special effect may cost you valuable time. Before you get to the test, review some of the suggestions made in the earlier chapters about writing good ending paragraphs. This will enable you to choose quickly the type that is best suited to your composition.

The Last Twenty Minutes

It would be quite accurate to say that your ultimate success with your composition on an examination depends upon what you do before and after you actually write the final copy. You must use an outline if you want good organization and proper development. And you must *revise* if you want a minimum of errors and a maximum of interest.

Spend a few minutes doing a thorough job of checking your paragraph and sentence structure. Make sure you have good continuity, clearly defined topic sentences, and no fragments or run-ons.

On an examination, you won't have time to do any extensive polishing, but you can use another three or four minutes inserting some words that change vague concepts into concrete images. Check your spelling carefully. Follow this rule faithfully. *When in doubt, use a substitute.* Don't take chances. If a construction sounds grammatically incorrect or awkward, change it to a simpler one.

After you have completed your major revisions, you should have just enough time left to write a clean final draft. When you are copying, it is possible to write neatly at a speed of more than 25 words a minute. You are familiar with the material and have worked on it three or four times. Try it. Take any composition you have previously written and copy it. You will see that the suggested speed is not too much for you.

A word in summary! Your first reaction to the plan just presented for writing compositions on examinations is likely to be: "It's impossible." If you have never done it this way before, your doubts may be justified. For a while you may have difficulty completing the steps within the time limits. But you must work on this system to master it.

An examination is like a race against competition. You are expected to put forth your best effort because you will not get a second chance in the same contest. But you know that you can't even come close to your top abilities unless you practice. Not long ago, a college high jumper began to clear seven feet consistently. What do you suppose he was able to jump when he started? Six feet? Six feet four inches? Whatever it was, it surely took him months, perhaps years, to reach his peak.

Therefore, don't give up before you make a real try. If you go at it with determination, it won't take years for you to develop the proper techniques. One thing is certain. A good composition of about 300 words *can* be written on an examination in an hour or less. Thousands of students before you have learned to do it. You can, too, if you are willing to accept the self-discipline required in any training schedule. Good luck to you in your future writing endeavors.

APPENDIX

A Selected List of 100 Composition Topics

A Teenager Looks at Himself

Advice to the Lovelorn

The Art of Wood Carving

You Can't Buy Peace

Reaching for the Moon

The Law Is on Your Side

Now, You Take This Teacher

It Was Fun But _____

They Couldn't Put It Over on Me

That Was the Key Play

Fighting the Steering Wheel

New Hair Styles

Why I'm a Rebel

The Man (Woman) Has It Best

Parents as Matchmakers

You *Can* Trust People

The Best Students Are Girls (Boys)

Snow Means Money to Me

My Parent's Favorite Child

_____ Is the Best Day

The Experiment Worked!

Those Exercises in Gym

We Dress to Please

The Family Conference

On My Best Behavior

Moving Into a New Home

How to Avoid Household Chores

I Had a Feeling It Would Happen

Manners in the Lunchroom

Test Tube Miracle

I Have My Rights, Too!

The Editor's Lament

An Architect's Dream

What's New in Clothes?

Keeping Calm at Exams

An Evening on the Telephone

Inside Information

Charity Begins Inside

Chemicals on the Farm

Gliding Down Hill

Were the Old Days Better?

If I Were Only Like _____

Definition of a Cheap Skate

My Favorite Animal

Talk Is Cheap

I'd Love to Visit _____

Never Again!

Alibis for Coming Late

Saved by Quick Thinking

Troubles of a Stenographer

Strange People I've Known

Are We Getting Soft?

Shopping Spree

Can Animals Think?

Are Imported Products
   Better?

If I Were a Baby Again

Losing a Friend

Getting "the Breaks"

Act Your Age

Why Bother About Politics?

They Had Me Cornered

It Wasn't as Bad as I
   Thought

I Lie Awake and Think

Television Is Growing Up

The Last Court of Appeal

Another New Gadget

Who Are the Best Drivers?

Grandstand Managers

Send Your Contributions

Swing Your Partner

It Was the Best I Could Do

I Learn About Taxes

Democracy in Action

Borrowing Dad's Car

I Like Cats

I Believe

The Radio Is Still Popular

Does She Have a Friend?

See Your Country First

I Didn't Deserve It

It Made Me Feel Proud

I Bake My First _____

How to Earn Extra Cash

A Stereo Fanatic

My Pen Pal

Two Cures for Accidents

Time to Start Digging

What Are Good Commer-
   cials?

Another Disease Conquered

Souping Up a Jalopy

Public Enemies

Chemicals in Drinking Water

Bowling Night

Swapping Clothes

Learning to Skate

Report to the Dean

Faster Than Sound

Candidate for Teachers' Hall
   of Fame